THE BARS OF

ATLANTIS

Translated from the German by John Crutchfield,

Michael Hofmann, and Andrew Shields

Edited and with an introduction by Michael Eskin

FARRAR, STRAUS AND GIROUX

NEW YORK

THE BARS OF

ATLANTIS

SELECTED ESSAYS

Durs Grünbein

Farrar, Straus and Giroux
18 West 18th Street, New York 10011

Some of these essays originally appeared, in slightly different form, in *Little Star* ("Three Miniatures," "To Lord Chandos: A Fax from the Future," and "The Stroke of Apollo"), *Poetry* ("Why Live Without Writing"), and *Chicago Review* ("The Thinker's Voice").

Library of Congress Cataloging-in-Publication Data
Grünbein, Durs.
    [Essays. English Selections]
    The bars of Atlantis : selected essays / Durs Grünbein ; translated
from the German by John Crutchfield, Michael Hofmann, and Andrew
Shields ; edited and with an introduction by Michael Eskin. — 1st ed.
        p. cm.
    ISBN 978-0-374-26062-0 (alk. paper)
    I. Eskin, Michael.   II. Title.

PT2667.R842A2 2010
834'.914—dc22

                                                    2009043066

Designed by Jonathan D. Lippincott

www.fsgbooks.com

1   3   5   7   9   10   8   6   4   2

CONTENTS

THE DIVING BELL AND THE BRISTLEMOUTH
The Art of Grünbein's Prose

In two of his less well-known dialogues—*Timaios* and *Critias*—Plato tells the story of an ancient civilization that lived, once upon a time, on an island "bigger than Asia and Libya put together," located "far beyond the Pillars of Hercules"—that is, somewhere, past the Strait of Gibraltar, in the Atlantic ocean. "Nine thousand is the sum of years," according to Plato, since a major earthquake hit the island and it was "swallowed up by the sea and vanished." The island in question—as you may have guessed—is, of course, none other than Atlantis, the "riddle of a culture," as Durs Grünbein muses in this collection's titular essay, that, although it only "exists in a couple of textual references," has given us "[t]he Atlantic ocean, the Atlantic Alliance, transatlantic flights, et cetera," and whose mystery and allure continue to haunt our imagination to this very day. As a result of the natural disaster that led to the sinking of Atlantis, furthermore, Plato tells us, an impassable barrier of sandbars was presumably formed that would prevent "those who are sailing out" of the Mediterranean into the Atlantic Ocean from "proceeding any farther." These mythical "bars of Atlantis," then, can be said to have represented the outer perimeters of the known world, the frontiers of the knowable and imaginable: simultaneously bespeaking and shielding, beckoning toward and cordoning off, allowing glimpses into and barring the unknown, both the uncharted spaces beyond them *and* the very mystery of the sunken island itself—the consummate image of the "abyss of the imagination," as Grünbein suggests—whose material vestiges they metaphorically embody.

It is on a journey to such frontiers of the imagination—personal, historical, and literary—that Durs Grünbein invites you in his essays. As one reader recently told me, summing up his experience of reading Grünbein's prose: "Durs Grünbein takes you to a place you've never been before . . ."

As you clear the atmosphere of the humdrum and everyday and dive headlong into the oceanic depths, the windswept wastes, the densely populated metropolises and crammed cultural archives of Grünbein's cosmos, where past and present, East and West, the sciences and the arts, the high and the low, the living and the dead, the pneumatic and the aquatic mingle and meld to create a panoramic, eerily defamiliarized *tableau vivant* of the world as we know it, you are bound to lose your bearings at first. As you get acclimated to the ambient conditions of Grünbein's world, however—the world of one who depicts himself both as a mere "little man in Germany" *and* a seasoned, globe-trotting "cosmopolite"—as you learn to see, hear, breathe, and orient yourself in the labyrinthine scatter plot of Grünbein's motley universe, you find yourself in the company of the most surprisingly diverse personages and in the most unexpected locales: Look!—there's Peter Ustinov, unforgettable, in the role of Emperor Nero, weeping for Petronius, his *arbiter of elegance*, in Melvyn LeRoy's 1951 sword-and-sandal blockbuster *Quo Vadis*; and next to him—over there—are Kafka, Büchner, Nietzsche, Darwin, and Hölderlin cavorting on a garbage heap somewhere in the former East Germany and overlooking, through the eyes of a little boy growing up in the shadow of the Berlin Wall and dreaming of those faraway places "where the wild things are," the wastes of the former Soviet empire and the heat-hazed African deserts; and over there are Seneca and

Rilke meditating on the brevity and futility of human existence, while Raphael and Titian argue about sexuality and decorum and reminisce about their last conversation with Stalin's antipode, Osip Mandelstam, in Moscow's Red Square, all the while watching the Palio delle Contrade on the Piazza del Campo in Siena; and there, out of nowhere, a school of deep-sea fish fly by, making all heads turn—fish like you've never seen before: armorhead, hatchetfish, snaggletooth, gulper eel, spiderfish, and bristlemouth . . . and over there, all of a sudden, a fax machine starts rattling and a missive addressed to one Lord Chandos arrives from the future . . .

•

Durs Grünbein, born and raised in Dresden, the capital of the German Free State of Saxony, has been called the most significant and successful poet to have emerged from the former East Germany. While certainly true in a strictly biographical sense, this characterization of Grünbein as a former GDR poet is liable to make us forget that the then twenty-five-year-old's first volume of poetry—*Grauzone, morgens* (Gray zone, morning)—appeared not in the German Democratic Republic but in then West Germany in 1988, that is, virtually at the point of the former East Germany's disintegration; that Grünbein "came of age as a poet"—to use Helen Vendler's felicitous phrase—and rose to prominence and world renown only *after* the end of the Cold War and German reunification in 1990; and that, consequently—if we choose to peg him geopolitically at all—far from being a former GDR poet, Grünbein can be said, above all, to be a poet of the New Germany and the New Europe.

It is precisely because he has managed to transcend his GDR origins and wholeheartedly to embrace, in his life and art, the freedoms, possibilities, and responsibilities brought about by the fall of the Berlin Wall in 1989, followed by the sinking of the GDR to the ocean floor of history (yet another "Atlantis") and the subsequent founding of the Berlin republic as part of a New Europe in a globalized world, that commentators on Grünbein's ever-expanding oeuvre have aptly hailed him as the first German poet to overcome the divide between East and West and to explode the cultural logic of the Cold War in the name of an inclusive notion of culture beyond nationality, monolingualism, and ethnocentrism. And while Durs Grünbein can certainly be and has, indeed, been touted—from a squarely national-political perspective—as the most significant, prolific, highly acclaimed, decorated, and widely translated living *German* poet, it would be far more true to his cosmopolitanism in life and art, most pointedly articulated in his own avowal that he tends to view himself as a poet writing *in German* rather than as a *German* poet, to think of him as a European and a world poet, above all: indeed, as one of the world's greatest living poets, who cannot help writing from a specific place and in a specific language, which happens to be German. Like Heinrich Heine, T. S. Eliot, Rainer Maria Rilke, Paul Celan, and Joseph Brodsky, to name only a few of modernity's poetic giants, Grünbein, too, doesn't fit any squarely national straitjacket.

•

The English-speaking reader will most likely be familiar with Grünbein as the author of *Ashes for Breakfast*, his acclaimed 2005 book of selected poems in English (the only one to date), featuring texts from such landmark collections as the already-mentioned *Grauzone, morgens* (1988), *Schädelbasislektion* (Skull base lesson, 1991), *Falten und Fallen* (Folds and traps, 1994), *Nach den Satiren* (After the satires, 1999), and the 2002 volume *Erklärte Nacht* (Night explained). Nothing testifies as palpably to the power of Grünbein's art—which is as much a medium of cultural memory and historical and aesthetic exploration as a continuous log of the poet's many travels and sojourns in various places and countries, as well as a sustained reflection on poetry's very possibility and necessity at the present time—as Helen Vendler's confession, in her review of *Ashes for Breakfast* for *The New Republic*, that even "with no formal knowledge of German" she "couldn't help but stay awake all night reading Grünbein's severe work—an absolutely unignorable body of verse."

What may be less well known to Grünbein's non-German-speaking audiences is that aside from his prolificness as a poet—since 2002, Grünbein has published several more collections in German, including the poetic novel *Vom Schnee oder Descartes in Deutschland* (On snow, or, Descartes in Germany, 2003), *Porzellan: Poem vom Untergang meiner Stadt* (Porcelain: A poem on the downfall of my city, 2005), among other things, an elegiac homage to his native Dresden, and the compendious *Strophen für Übermorgen* (Poems for the day after tomorrow, 2007)—Grünbein is also a prolific and, as the present volume amply attests, consummate essayist. In fact, in terms of sheer volume, Grünbein's essays have virtually outstripped his poetic output. Such essay collections as *Galilei vermißt Dantes Hölle und bleibt an den Maßen hängen* (Galilei measures Dante's Hell and gets stuck on the measurements, 1996), *Das erste Jahr: Berliner Aufzeichnungen* (The first year: A Berlin diary, 2001), *Warum schriftlos leben* (Why live without writing, 2003), *Antike Dispositionen* (Antique dispositions, 2005), and *Das Gedicht und sein Geheimnis* (The poem and its secret, 2007)—selections from all of which are gathered in the present volume—have firmly established Grünbein as one of the world's great literary essayists and cultural thinkers.

As in his poetry, in his essays, too, Grünbein succeeds in artfully interweaving autobiography and memoir with a host of broader concerns ranging from questions of history, science, and medicine, to questions of ethics, aesthetics, and politics, with special attention to the continued relevance of the past—Greek and Roman antiquity in particular—in and to the contemporary world, as well as the inevitable interpretive malleability of the past in light of our ever-evolving present. Indeed, the hallmark of Grünbein's very project as a poet and thinker can be said to consist of, as he himself avers, the ever-widening exploration and "putting to the test," as it were, of his inveterate "sensibility for the contemporaneity of the non-contemporaneous," of his indelible intuition that the dead and the living—to quote W. G. Sebald—unceasingly "move back and forth as they like" across time and space "according to the rules of a higher form of stereometry."

Thus, when in "Brother Juvenal" he accompanies the satirist through the din and commotion of first-century Rome, Grünbein simultaneously walks the streets of present-day New York, Berlin, or Tokyo in the Roman's company. And when, in "In the Name of Extremes," he zooms back to the dying Seneca, Grünbein simultaneously invites the Stoic to join him here and now in meditating on the "brevity of life," whose precariousness and unpredictability continue to re-mind us of our powerlessness in view of disasters such as the one that presumably led to the sinking of Atlantis some twelve thousand years ago, or, more recently, the crashing of Air France flight 447 over the Atlantic Ocean, into whose depths, as Grünbein has noted with doleful resignation, "yet again—alas—human beings have vanished." Plunging from the soaring heights of modern aviation to the depths of evo-lutionary time, Grünbein follows those swallowed up by Chronos' ever-receding streams into the prehistoric darkness of the "Age of Deep-Sea Fish" in the hope of shedding some light on who we are by understanding where we came from . . . On one such, particularly memorable, excursion into our aquatic past, Grünbein witnesses, as he recounts in "The Bars of Atlantis," a "natural wonder":

About a dozen prawns, tiny, glassy, soft, resembling pieces of tubing in a chemistry lab, are assembled in a silent, somehow Asiatic ceremony. Like us . . . they have formed a semicircle and are just in the process of feeling one another out with their antennae . . . a parodic version of ourselves, an anticipation by some millions of years, performed by these frail, dignified beings in their serious conclave. What was in session there, ancient and dawn-of-creation-like, was the council of prawns.

•

The essays collected in the present volume are grouped into six sections that foreground key aspects of Durs Grünbein's art. And although all the essays intersect and overlap thematically, Durs Grünbein and I have thought it best, for the reader's convenience and so as to make the reading experience more cohesive and rewarding, to cluster the texts around major, recurring themes.

The first section comprises memoiristic and autobiographical pieces introducing Grünbein, the man and author, and telling the story of the making of a poet and thinker toward the end of a century marked by global political strife, unprecedented human suffering, long decades of totalitarian rule, and, in its final quarter, the dawn of a new, post–Cold War world order; the second section is devoted to the exploration of one of Grünbein's major interests, namely, the intersection of art and science, literature and biology, aesthetics and evolution; the essays grouped in the third section pointedly articulate what may well be called Grünbein's "aesthetic credo," his views on the import—existential, cultural, political, and ethical—of the poet's craft; the fourth section features three pieces that document Grünbein's fascination with the visual arts—Renaissance and Dutch painting, in particular—

taking us on a tour through Dresden, Holland, and Italy; the three essays making up the fifth section are devoted to a detailed exploration of Grünbein's relationship to literary and philosophical tradition, focusing specifically on such predecessors as Rilke, Nietzsche, and Hölderlin; the sixth section, finally, is entirely dedicated to Grünbein's most conspicuous cultural passion: the living presence of classical antiquity as bespoken by the contemporaneity of such historical figures as Seneca, Petronius, and Juvenal.

Grünbein's texts articulate his sustained attempt to orient himself and make sense of his singular emplacement in time and space. What does it mean to be a human being straddling the old and the new millennia in the heart of Europe? What responsibilities accrue to the thinking, reflecting, writing individual today? What is the role of art in general and of the most subtle and inconspicuous of its forms—poetry—in a postmodern world in which the soteriological promises of the grand narratives of the past have been systematically subjected to a hermeneutics of suspicion? What is the significance of one man's voice within the "tangle of voices of many ages," as he writes in "My Babylonish Brain," and what can he hope to achieve in and through his art? These are some of the fundamental, existential concerns and questions that drive Grünbein's project.

In one of his most explicitly programmatic essays, "Why Live Without Writing," Grünbein offers a threefold, deeply personal explanation as to why he needs to write:

> In the first place . . . you write to escape your dread of the sheer present . . . [T]he second reason is a dilemma that concerns each individual psyche. You write, I believe, because you can't quite shake the suspicion that as a mere contemporary and biological cell mate, hopelessly trammeled up in your own limited

lifespan, you would always remain incomplete, half a man, so to speak. Someone must have put you onto the idea that only your most individual expression gives you the least chance of one day being seen in any way other than in your mortal sheath—say, as a kind of ghost. Ever since that tormenting voice (whoever it may be) first challenged you in the name of metaphysics, you've been trying by all the laws of glass-blowing, a.k.a. poetry, to fix a little window in your own diminishing time, in the hope that tomorrow or whenever you may be seen through that little peephole. If you happen to succeed in making your sweetheart, or one or two of your friends, or yourself in your peculiarity visible—the way Vermeer, say, showed his pregnant letter-reader—then it will have been worth the effort. Writing, the voice whispers to you, is the least circumstantial method of breaking out of the given and the immediate ... From which it follows, third and last: you write because the brain is an endless wilderness, whose roughest terrain can be traveled only with a pencil. As soon as we are in the innermost dreamy connections, all other art forms are dependent on verbal synthesis. The dream, as you discover when you write, is the fully authentic self. You will never have amounted to more. The world will not appear any more variegated. Which means the notion of what really exists, can, with writing, be comfortably extended by a dimension or two.

It is precisely these "dreamy connections"—also known simply as "metaphors"—that allow Grünbein to cast the familiar in the most unfamiliar light, thereby enjoining his readers to reframe and reassess acquired habits of perception and thought in the name of what he advocates, throughout his writings, as individual and political freedom, self-expression and actualization, and the courage to think "differently."

Thus, in taking you back in time to the landfills, slag heaps, and garbage dumps of the GDR—a stark reminder of the political and ecological disasters of Soviet-style *Realsozialismus*—Grünbein, unexpectedly, also takes you back to the ash-covered ruins of Herculaneum and Pompeii, famously destroyed in A.D. 79 as a result of a massive eruption of Mount Vesuvius. "I was seventeen," Grünbein reminisces in "Volcano and Poem," "when I scaled for the last time the dump that by now, even in my unconscious, had become a synonym for filth, vermin, disease, and death. Under the layers of waste piled up over decades . . . was the old Dresden destroyed in World War II, a baroque version of Pompeii . . ." Only—and this is where Grünbein's conceit becomes subtly and eerily instructive—because the destruction of Dresden, unlike the eruption of Mount Vesuvius, had nothing "natural" or "geologically inevitable" about it, it forces the seemingly trivial, yet ever-pressing, question as to the ostensible inevitability— or necessity?—of man-made suffering.

Similarly, in taking you back, in "Breaking the Body," to the nineteenth-century renegade poet and playwright Georg Büchner, who studied to become a doctor and wrote a dissertation on the nervous system in the heads of barbels, Grünbein also takes you on an exploration of the indelible connections between art and physiology, poetry and the human body, which literally resounds and resonates in every phonic articulation of human speech *and* cannot but be wholly engaged in receiving and responding to it. And in the process, Grünbein palpably succeeds, without in any way "reduc[ing] . . . humanity to a handful of zoological assumptions," in making the signal, unprecedented point that a truly humane ethics and politics cannot but be based on the recognition that "the nerve [must be put] in first place" and "the body [declared] the highest authority"—that "life is sufficient unto itself and not subject to the strictures of external or higher purposes"—a poignant lesson, indeed, offered by someone writing with the benefit of hindsight of one who has certainly had sufficient firsthand experience with a totalitarian ethics and politics predicated on the Pavlovian principle of a "collective reflexology," whereby each member of the body politic had to be disciplined into conformity, physiologically subdued to act and react in response to the stimuli of the "higher goals" of totalitarian dogma . . .

•

In his lectures on poetry, Aristotle long ago remarked that the one thing a poet cannot possibly learn is the ability to make truly novel metaphors—to perceive connections and affinities where there seemingly are none, or, at least, where the normal person wouldn't even think of suspecting any. This ability, according to Aristotle, is a gift—a gift that Grünbein, for one, not unlike the Metaphysical Poets he so admires, has abundantly received. Interestingly, Grünbein himself reflects on this gift of the imagination in one of his most memorable conceits, from the 2002 poem "Night Explained," in which metaphor is cast as a "diver" that

> . . . pulls you below, searching for treasures
> On the ocean floor—out there, in the brain. It
>   conspires with the stars.
> Metaphors: Those flat rocks you hurl into the open
> Sea from the shore, that skip on the water,
> Three, four, five times, if you're lucky, then crashing
>   the mirror,
> Lead-heavy, plumb-like. Rifts that go through the
>   ages.
> Philosophy, metered—music, joyfully bounding from
>   word to object.
> Gifts, say some—others say, skillfully crafted . . .

Tour guides—bar none, the best—on our exodus
from existence's night.

Like his poems, which Grünbein views as organically inter-
twined with his prose—"I wrote . . . essays as studies for
poems, and I also wrote poems from which essays emerged . . .
if you ask me about my essays, you are simultaneously asking
me about my poems," Grünbein recently observed in an interview with Silvia Ruzzenenti—his essays take you to times
and places you haven't been before: historic-oceanic depths or
astral-futuristic heights, or both, depending on any given
text's itinerary.

Take a seat, then, for the duration of this journey, in the
diving bell of Grünbein's prose and marvel at the exotica
floating by your moon pool . . . on your way to the bars of
Atlantis—that "meeting place for gamblers and writers,"
where, among others, as Grünbein reports, "on barstools, looking strangely stiff, celebrities from literature [sit] . . . easily
recognizable," and above which there is "a sign with the scriptural quotation 'Man is a stranger on this earth' " . . . And as
you begin surfacing again—paradoxically, as Grünbein wist-
fully intimates, metaphor, the "poetic image," is also "a surfacing," and whoever experiences it "undergoes the curative
experience" of coming up for air—and cast a last glance back
in search of a lost Eurydice, a lost Persephone, perhaps,
chances are that the only thing you'll see will be a bristlemouth winking at you, as if saying, cryptically, with Dante in
mind: "Travel is a foretaste of Hell"—or is it?

—Michael Eskin

PREFACE

If someone came along and told you, "I want to be a philosopher," the way they might once have said—old-style—to a grieving mother and weeping bride, "I'm going for a soldier," what would you think about that? Is the expression of intent enough? Or wouldn't he first have to complete a degree in philosophy to be taken seriously? What would you say if he claimed on the basis of certain inborn intuitions and extravisions to be in a position to challenge the postulates and theorems of the most significant thinkers of every age—indeed, that given the chance he would soon clear away a few of the crudest misconceptions concerning such knotty problems as time and space, existence and consciousness, matter and memory, that had bedeviled our thinking from the pre-Socratics to the postmodernists? What makes somebody in our day a philosopher? Is it a question of cast of mind, or is it just certain technical qualifications? It would appear that the license to philosophize is only very grudgingly given these days. It requires not just the ability to think with utmost consistency but also a degree of brazenness. And in general the green light to proceed can be given only by an academic institution.

With poets, things are different: they continue to fall from the sky. They don't come when called for, and they can neither be predicted nor made in universities. Then, once they are there, no one will ask them for their qualifications. Legitimation comes to them in a flash, through their cheekily or hesitantly issued poems. No one asked for their books, they just appeared—*Les Fleurs du Mal*, *Leaves of Grass*, *The Stone*—those myriad articulate solitudes that suddenly emerge on the wayside and take their stand.

—Durs Grünbein

I

BRIEF REPORT TO AN ACADEMY

How do you introduce someone you know only in passing? It has never made sense to me why this person should be familiar to me just because I kept running into him. All I can tell you is that I was born on October 9, 1962, in Dresden, where I grew up as the only child of youthful parents.

My father and mother were twenty-two when I appeared on the scene one afternoon with the usual caterwauling. Like everyone else, I was traumatized by birth. Decades later I came across a poem by the French poet Pierre Jean Jouve that brought the shock to mind:

I saw a puddle of green oil
That had leaked out of a machine and for a long time
I stood thinking on the hot pavement of the seedy
    quarter
Thinking and thinking of my mother's blood.

What happened then was a cheerful childhood spent in the provinces, where the emphasis soon came to fall on *spent*; in other words, the thing was pretty soon over. To this day, I have been unable to shake the conviction that when you throw open your arms to clasp life, you are caught up in the wind and are blown backward into the future, and each successive period is less magnificent than the one before, so that the feeling of loss is pretty soon immeasurable. Nor is the end any consolation, it's just a limit set to this infinitesimal quotient of happiness.

The name of the province was Saxony, an old cultural landscape turned ash gray, comprising a conflagration site the size of a city or whatever was left of this city after the war, called Dresden. All the learning I received in its walls—years at school and years in libraries and long wanderings—finally culminated in one single, slightly vengeful conclusion. In a farewell poem to the city, I described it as what it was, a baroque ruin on the Elbe.

My early desire to be an American Indian persisted in the form of a susceptibility to nomadism that has also driven so many of my fellow Saxons, and the propensity for con tricks that allowed me to go on dreaming into my early adulthood. When the dreams came to nothing (it's fairly standard for people from my part of the world to get their centuries mixed up), I wanted to become a vet, with Africa as the setting of choice. But the reality of veterinarian life, drastically described to me in the course of a career interview, alarmed me so much that I took my hat in disappointment; the Serengeti would have to die without me.

Things took their inevitable course; I remained ensconced in the shadow of a Chinese wall, cooped up in a space that was only a little larger, and to visitors hardly less fearsome, than Albania. Then one day, suddenly and unannounced, in the manner of someone coming into his own after noticing that all those things that preoccupy others have no need of him, I started to write poems. Novalis and Hölderlin were my first ancestors: the former's *Pollen* together with the disturbing appeal of his *Hymns to the Night*; the latter's "Prayer for the Incurable," his ravaged playground of the gods. "Like rushing streams, the end of something takes me with it, that once extended as far as Asia"—lines like these from Hölderlin's "In Lovely Blue" swept me off my feet well before my understanding was able to cope with them. At seventeen, a friend lent me a tattered paperback copy of Ezra Pound's *Cantos*, and that accelerated the catastrophe. Since that time, I have written with an alertness that goes backward as well as forward, and this impossible condition, the duration of a few breaths between antiquity and *X*, can only be endured if slowly and line by line I check my voice, the body, and what was caught in the inner ear.

One day, and this wasn't in a dream, I pictured my situation as that of a swimmer caught in a current coming out of the future.

No wonder, then, that many a thing was mere occasion for me, fleeting sensation and personal chronogram. I thought less and less about raising objections to the politics of the day, since understanding and interpreting cost me more than any thinking and doing. I experienced—and I say this with a degree of shame—I experienced the collapse of the dictatorships in the East as just that, a collapse, in which I was passive, an unpolitical dreamer, albeit an occasionally amused participant in critique and demo. However overwhelming the experience of the end of the Soviet empire was, it became fertile for me only five years later, in Italy, when I was visiting the sites of Pompeii and Herculaneum. Only there did I see the effect of that massive explosion called time, the delayed rain of shards of civilization, and, in the famous calamity, under the volcano, evidence of a kind of memoryless memory—*deus absconditus*, or whatever you want to call it. Poetry, as I always knew it would, would get on the case—what else was it there for? In the house of charred furniture I paused, for hours all historical agitation was suspended, calmed by the murals in the mystery villa. In those small rooms—no bigger than a pigsty, some of them—with their scribbled lines of poems, obscenities, and decorative drawings, I felt myself better understood than in all the classrooms, barracks, and attics that had ever held me. Then, at the sight of the anonymous fresco representing dream and birth, the entanglements of sex and knowledge, ages and seasons, I had an illumination of what writing, above and beyond anything current, might be all about. The fact that the subjects were all foregathered before Calliope's throne in the mystery frieze at Pompeii, I found incredibly encouraging.

Ever since that pivotal year, 1989, I've been on the road. Berlin, the city where I've lived these past ten years, is like a transit lounge from where I've struck out for my various destinations; it might just as well have been New York, its opposite number and for me from early on the embodiment of the metropolis. I've dropped out of university and spent several years working in the theater, before, by chance as much as anything else, publishing my first book. Even now it makes me nervous to think of the particular sequence of events that's governed everything in my life subsequently.

One more thing before I finish, a sort of official clarification, if you will. My name, however unexampled in its strangeness it may seem to you, is not an artistic invention. It is merely the name that the law and my parents' obstinacy did not want to spare me. The fact that it occurred to you to include it in the list of names of the members of this academy encourages me like an exhortation from an unexpected quarter. Thank you.

VOLCANO AND POEM

The date doesn't matter, or how the catastrophe came about, but one day it happened, and the volcano erupted over those living in its shade, innocents in the homely confines of their markets and workshops, their brothels and gardens, bustling city-dwellers on the Bay of Naples. Whole conurbations were buried in the twinkling of an eye; from city gate to city gate entire networks of streets went under in the lava rain, thousands of human beings were suddenly killed, turned into carbonized dolls. A civilized world was completely preserved in the mire: Pompeii, Stabiae, Herculaneum. It wasn't for another seventeen hundred years that the first coin was unearthed, and with it history and symbolism . . . or a little flask of ointment, a cheekbone on a marble plate, and hence life and beauty. There, rib to rib inextricably, a copulating pair of skeletons was brought to light, and with it love and desire. Here, in a villa on the highway out of town, beside the cemetery, a library was unearthed, and so those too came back: religion, mythology, philosophy, literature. Each individual item had been sealed up in lava and debris by the volcano, and now they all were returned to the present, the portraits of the gods and the pornographic doodles, the frieze of the mysteries and the latest slogans, the board game and the papyrus scroll, and that fragment from the book of one Philodemus of Gadara, *On Poems*—the apex of Classical poetics. In it, unaffected by the catastrophe or by natural decay, are several paragraphs from the old debate on content (hypothesis) and literary form (lexis), on harmony and coherence in a poem, and on the author as a separate factor, beyond content and technique: "The poet in search of completeness must bend his mind not only to move his listeners, but to be useful to them, and offer them good advice."

Under Herculaneum's ashes, as fresh as on the first day, is the poet's notebook, in its Greco-Roman version. Not enough that he be psychopomp, therapist, and faith healer; what he does is also required to entertain, to give pleasure. It should be both pedagogic and psychogogic. A few words disclose the oldest secret of the trade, namely, that the only poet to win every reader's vote is the one who manages to combine *dulce* and *utile*. The sweet and the useful, both at once, that was the formulation of the most renowned Roman *ars poetica*, in a letter from an aging writer of odes and satires. It's a long and stony road back to Horace.

This was where it all started: a volcano visible for miles around, the focus of a landscape; Vesuvius was the name. For centuries it was silent, and for centuries smoke clung to its summit, a branching cloud in the shape of a conifer. At its feet stretches the plain with its towns and villages, once inhabited, once buried, the field of farmers and diggers, the patient earth. Prey to rain of ashes and seismic quakes, wars and Spartacist risings, and always the inhabitant's eye returns to the eerie mountain around which the myths group themselves like shadowy superstitions. Ever since the end of Pompeii, since its geological birth, the likeness of this volcano has appeared in thousands of vistas, it has been repeatedly described and sketched, it has entered a kind of global subconscious, while its cone over the years and the centuries has gradually flattened.

I had the idea of being one of the inhabitants of Campania, living with the mountain always within view, and I recall how as a child one day near Dresden, I saw a different mountain, around which my thoughts have revolved ever since. I saw it for the first time out the window of a streetcar going into the city, past allotment gardens and scruffy woodland, a massive brown mound. The thing that lay there in the distance, under dense clouds like a volcano, conical, with a broad flat top, was a gigantic garbage heap, the final accumulation of all the indigestible trash that the city excreted each day. For a long time, I merely observed it, asked people and heard their warnings, tales to frighten me off, and then, with friends, I went on my first expedition to the place. No wire fence, no yelling guard could prevent us from making it up to the very top, where there was a hundred-foot cliff of trash, overlooking a sandy plain where the Russians conducted some of their military exercises. From up there, we could see the city and make out the approach roads taken by the garbage up from the valleys in a sort of reverse of the streams of lava. This was my childhood dream, a forbidden territory where we swarmed like scouts in search of adventure and happiness, or just useful bits of trash. There was a sign beside the approach: NO ENTRY—PARENTS WILL BE HELD ACCOUNTABLE FOR THEIR CHILDREN. But our curiosity was stronger, everything lured us on, the burning car tires, the promising bulk of decayed furniture, things vomited forth from households, and, above all, the sweetish smell of rot. Our place of pilgrimage was a garbage mound that had no name, our instincts hovered around a place that grown-ups avoided, a repressed or suppressed or forgotten zone, extruded from the places where we lived, where the city's refuse was piled in a mountain, an artificial Vesuvius we could see from miles away. At first, we just scrambled aimlessly around its fringes and slithered about swearing on the slimy top leveled by bulldozers, but before long we started picking things up. A stack of seamy magazines first; a couple of intact green bottles in a pile of broken glass, odorless; a charred photograph album, and suddenly photos slid out of it, pictures of dead people; a leather folder with, on investigation, old coins hidden in the lining, or Iron Crosses. Rolls of bandage turned up, an artificial leg, a pack of condoms, and our subsequent question *What are they for?* Which remained unanswered. Beauty, love, desire—we hadn't been made aware of any of that yet. Poetry and philosophy . . . if I happened across books, then they were bound to be schoolbooks, it was never mythology or anything like that. A couple of monthly magazines from the period between the wars, that was a treasure; a sheaf of poetry in a gray wartime edition, who knows if it was Horace or Hölderlin, that was little more than an oddity. Half a motorcycle meant more than any edition of the classics. A rat skewered on a bicycle spoke was more precious than a still life in a mangled frame. Adrift between pubescent desire and a sensitivity we didn't know we had, we were always bored. Was that a way in, a sign for a "poetics of the first glimpse"? It was such a long way from there to poetry.

Today, I know that almost every city has its own Vesuvius. Our modern-day volcanoes are the large slag heaps beside open workings, the garbage heaps and dumps of all kinds, the mighty soaring scrap heaps on the edges of our cities. From time to time, they like to remind us of their existence, and then they send a rain of ashes back on our settlements, they spew out poison and filth, the groundwater is discolored, and pollutants come to rest on people's roofs. In terms of the history of the planet, it's as though there had been a transfer of volcanic activity, as though it were in the process of reversing itself in the degree to which civilization has been built up. Pompeii, or any other city that's to be inundated, is slowly ringed with garbage: what counts after hundreds of years are the waves of detritus and retrieval, sedimentation and archaeological discovery. It is in such cycles, arrhythmically, that art history runs and poetics shows as confused recognition. Actuality, says Machado, is the wind in Homer's eyes. And life, adds Ungaretti, is nothing but a process of decay decorating itself with illusions.

I was seventeen when I scaled for the last time the dump that by now, even in my unconscious, had become a synonym for filth, vermin, disease, and death. Under the layers of waste piled up over decades, thus went the rumor, was the old Dresden destroyed in World War II, a baroque version of Pompeii. Here, on the northern edge of the city, its ruins had been piled up to form a massive table mountain, crumbled church portals were stacked on top of defunct balconies, the galleries of bombed theaters on the torsos of fire-blackened statues. And, as if this sublime trash had drawn all sorts of common-or-garden refuse in its wake, everything else had merely followed, the domestic waste from apartment blocks left on the ruined site of an abolished city.

It was at that time I began to keep a notebook, little exaltations that looked like poems and could be shown only to a very few intimates. If there was a subsequent attempt at any sort of poetics, that could only draw on the finds of my early years. And then Horace's decorum would be both the discharge of civilization and that lava in which "first glimpses," objects and gestures, scenes and thoughts, are preserved like living things surprised by death. For the law of the preservation of form, which long had a volcanic underground, in the modern period changes under pressure from the gush of mass-produced objects. Something becomes separated from the stream of goods, cools down, and is wrapped under a vacuum seal. Rendered obsolete and functionless, it starts to accumulate that very time so continually absent from the present from which it was taken. If you break the seal, vowels turn into artifacts, lines of verse prove to be little capsules loaded with emblems. Whatever is subsequently encountered by the pickax, the archaeologist's brush, the digger's shovel— all that is the stuff of poetry.

BREAKING THE BODY

Speech delivered on the occasion of being awarded the Georg Büchner Prize in 1995

What do the cranial nerves of vertebrates have to do with poetry? What is comparative anatomy doing in the monologue of the dramatic hero? What path leads from the gill chambers of fish to the human comedy, from rhythmicized prose to the brain's outpouching into the facial nerve? Peculiar questions—they alone suggest what was bound to happen if literature engaged with the real, if the study of nature shaped style, if zoological fact and the medical report found their way into the novella and the drama . . . until the genre lay in pieces, with fragments as the result, delirious notations, somatic poetry. One of the few who could have answered these questions is dead. He died young of typhus, which he contracted, it is believed, while dissecting fish specimens—a poet, unique, his name: Georg Büchner. I admit I was shaking at the knees at the idea of having to talk about him on this occasion. Now the time has come, and I am trying to keep my cool.

For there is more at stake here, at least as I see it, than the annual visit of an unclassical classic. Thinking Büchner's project through to its logical conclusion, we are dealing here with a turning point in literature, a shifting of perspective at the very moment when a German philosopher conjured the specter of the death of art.

If the verdict is correct, then Büchner was one of the first at the grave, and his oeuvre is the earliest commentary on the reading of the will. Büchner—and although this could be demonstrated, I merely want to state it here—braved a sortie, an act of liberation under the most severe duress. With a *salto mortale*, he freed literature from the imposition of having to remain playfully oblivious both to the misery of the real and to real misery. What he managed to achieve was nothing less than a complete transformation: physiology absorbed into literature. And this was no *Sonderweg*, as it turned out; it was the beginning of a series of experiments that have continued to this day. If poetry is understood as one language among others, then this meant the modification of the majority of its forms of inflection. What emerged was a harder grammar, a colder tone: the appropriate tool for an intelligence amputated from the heart.

·

The road there was long, and he went down that road with giant steps, growing stronger under the force of circumstance, parrying each blow ever more rapidly with every piece, pushing the limits with every new draft. *Danton's Death*—that great song of farewell—spread out across several voices, speech punctured by groans, the hunger for life and the longing for death embodied in a handful of immortal characters. Or *Lenz*—that breathless report on self-dissolution, a self that evaporates in the mountains like steam. *Woyzeck*—the criminal case as medical record, with a symptom as large as all of small-state Germany of Büchner's day. How humiliating for later ages is the speed with which he rushed through the forms, as if he wanted to leave all literary genres behind as quickly as possible so as to be able to devote himself wholly to the study of nature . . . as if only here he would be able to find the key to understanding the real driving forces, the energies inside the body: the affects, the stuff history is made of. Everyone knows the famous lines, as well as their echo. "We'd have to smash our skulls open and tear the thoughts from the very fibers of each other's brains," says Danton in the first act, only to cut himself short in the second act: "A mistake crept in when we were made, there's something missing, I don't have a name for it, we'll never discover it by groping around in each other's guts, so why smash open each other's bodies to try to find it?" Between the first and the second statements an abyss opens. It is the abyss bodies vanish into. In the new, gruesome light shining up from down there, history appears as that intermediate age in which the Last Animal meets the First Man: he himself *is* that Last Animal. In the darkness of enlightenment, deep in the sleep of reason, in the night of conscience that keeps falling again and again, Büchner saw that creature appear. And sometimes his shock tipped over into laughter, into monological ire.

•

Caravaggio captured the scene. One of his fleeting sketches depicts a nighttime dissection: two half-cloaked persons settling down to work on a lifeless body by the light of a candle sticking out of the cut-open belly. It is a drawing in the manner of the horror stories man tells himself about his end. In its feverishness, it resembles the terse events in Büchner's fragments.

•

Here I would like to pause briefly . . . in order to highlight one of the central moments at the heart of an oeuvre replete with pivotal passages (German Studies can tell you a thing or two about it). The scene is a study in Strasbourg, and in it sits a young man with a very high forehead, bent over books, magnifying glasses, and dead fish. For three long months, he doesn't leave his study. Dissecting and drawing, he spends the next-to-last winter, the next-to-last spring of his life writing his dissertation, half-dead from exhaustion, driven by the promise of a professorship, which meant the safety of Swiss exile for the political refugee. The short text he writes during these weeks—a study of the nervous system in the heads of barbels—will later become his job talk at the University of Zurich, bearing the simple title "On Cranial Nerves." I have always read this text as the fragment of a confession, as a kind of literary manifesto. Putting aside all period-related and soon-to-be-dated hypotheses, what is immediately striking about this text is Büchner's meticulousness in isolating and studying each individual nerve. Isn't this—given Büchner's caliber as a poet—more than merely a coincidence? An important lead, perhaps? Without wanting to gloss over the rift between literature and natural history in Büchner, or to reduce his view of humanity to a handful of zoological assumptions—doesn't Büchner's very subject suggest that he was looking for answers here, of all places, about something that gave direction to all creaturely existence? His insistence on the importance of the sensory apparatus can hardly be understood any other way. Büchner pursues by way of biology what had long been subterraneously growing "sensitive roots" in him by way of literature.

What is a nerve? he wonders. Where does it lead, and where does it come together? What is its evolutionary purpose? Are there basic forms of nerves that always reappear from one animal species to another, in different arrangements but with the same origin? What does this structure mean for physical sensation, pain, and the fear of death . . . which he once writes about as follows: "They say it lasts only a moment, but pain has the subtlest sense of time: a fraction of a second can last an eternity." And, finally: What is the body, considered in terms of the nervous system? What is history considered in terms of the body thus scrutinized? These are questions to which that autopsy may have led him. And these are also the questions that, even today, provide the basis for raising objections to every kind of social contract, social reform, revolution, or utopia. In their light, Büchner's perhaps most desperate question reveals its radical thrust: "But are we not in a perpetual state of violence?"

Make no mistake about it: what is significant here is not that his research engages the natural philosophy of his age so much as that he puts the nerve in first place, declaring the body the highest authority. Here we have a poet who derives his principles from physiology as others before him did from religion or ethics. From pure zootomy, he extracts the insight that life is sufficient unto itself and not subject to the strictures of external or higher purposes.

"Everything that exists, exists for its own sake."

In the dissected body, the skull (violently) pried open, he discovers the principles of a viable and free coexistence . . . as well as its ever-threatening negation: radical failure, from within the guts. For autopsy is the surest path to the loss of faith, or, for those for whom this is not enough, to the fortification of faithlessness. Dissecting the body is the royal road to the absurd as much as to utmost pragmatic humility. Where else if not inside the moribund body may we hold equality— the blueprint we all share in common—in our very hands? And doesn't such gut-gazing ultimately entail something as unheard-of and cogent as the invention and proclamation of universal human rights? Büchner, a doctor's son, tried to right society from this physiological vantage point. Could it be that his passion for politics was nothing but resuscitated fatalism and self-motivation, comparable to the experiments of Galvani, who applied electric shocks to torn-off frog legs? His signal question—Are our senses too crude, or are they sufficiently fine-tuned?—remains open. Whether only the flaws in the fabric of creation stand out or its organic beauties as well, whether freedom of spirit among individuals prevails over inscrutable desire, violence, and thick-skinned loneliness will depend on how we answer it. A century later, coming from a different direction, the painter Francis Bacon reached the same insight. In words not unlike Büchner's, he summed it up as follows in the course of an interview: "One's basic nature is totally without hope, and yet one's nervous system is made out of optimistic stuff."

Georg Büchner examined this stuff; again and again, he turned this lining of nerves inside out and made it flash forth in the spoken word, in the frozen moment of shock. The new, dramatic driving forces appear in the light of medical microscopy, they are exploratory forays into the vegetative realm, case studies performed on the living object, *en détail.* Beneath the writing, the nerve is at work; behind the play of facial expressions, the affects reign supreme; and only there, in the bodies of the pushed-around and pushing-around protagonists can be localized the driving forces that make histories and stories seem plausible. Büchner registered early on, and not at all coldly, the cracks that run through each of us. He was the first to observe this lying, stealing, murdering individual with diagnostic curiosity, one hundred years before the great bourgeois catastrophes and long before Kafka's futile attempt to retire it, operetta-style: "Who can fathom human nature!"

•

As a high school student, Büchner had already watched his father dissect at the hospital. At eighteen, he is a student of comparative anatomy and psychopathology in Giessen, used to working with cadavers on a daily basis. He quickly begins letting off steam in sarcastic witticisms. Among friends and in letters, he sends greetings from cadaver to cadaver. *Danton's*

Death, written fifty years after the French Revolution, scraped together from historical documents, emerges amid zoology books and anatomical atlases. It is the final report on a sickness unto death. Original quotations from standard works on the revolution are incorporated like transplants into Büchner's own dramatic text. The blood does not want to clot at the tissue's edges. Like chopped-off limbs, the dead heroes' words continue to twitch on the dust-covered stage. This is how he creates his own style—modeled on Shakespeare, branded by medicine, treacling with juvenile vanitas. According to the Young German Karl Gutzkow, he suffered from a ubiquitous "autopsy compulsion."

The active, collecting spirit of order had run aground, the acceleration had begun. What Goethe referred to as the "appropriate euphemism" is completely absent in Büchner. His language does not gloss over anything; it's just as torn and full of nervous tension as the situation it stumbles up from. Psychomotor activity now determines the plot: the show booth as moral institution is closed; opened in its place is the theater of anatomy.

Although Goethe, the humanist, still collected bones while walking across a battlefield as material for his osteological studies, his travel report *The French Campaign* is conspicuously silent about it. Decades later, he held Schiller's skull in his hands; thus end the humanist's dreams—as a cannibalistic swan song in terza rima on viewing the remains of a friend. Büchner listened to all these dreams, including the involuntary ambient noise, the scratching and scraping of regular versification. Jacques-Louis David, the history painter, is said to have studied the twitching of the dying in the interest of graphic realism. In his diary, the executioner Sanson describes how the cart going to the guillotine went past a café where Citizen David, sitting on a windowsill, was drawing the condemned. Büchner holds on to the individual nerve, and not just for research purposes. One senses how a jolt has gone through the metaphors. Once and for all, they have been released from their artificial supports: the end of shadow boxing, of the clanging of automatons. Büchner opposes his anthropological realism to the "tremendous work of idealization" that Schiller still thought he had to perform. From now on, all that counts is what takes place in the "world of the body"—a world that, according to St. Just, must be ruled by brute force, by terror and mass murder. In this world, Büchner sees the new sufferings piling up and, hidden behind its forces, the future laws of nature. From the beginning, his landscapes are those "graveyards of the spirit" that Hegel talked about from the bird's-eye view of the philosopher. Even where, in good Hegelian fashion, Büchner takes up the idea of a world spirit wending its way through society, he first stops to look at the mounds of dead bodies left by the wayside. There is no democracy without its barbaric episodes; a constitution without dismembered bodies can no longer be imagined. "Just follow your slogans through," says Mercier, "to the point where they turn into flesh and blood." And Danton agrees with him: "These days, everything is fashioned out of human flesh. It's the curse of our age. And now my body's to be used as well." History and revolution cut deeply into the flesh, they leave crushed bodies in their wake—this is what creates such a distance between them and redemption. And this is why every social model is worthless that doesn't take into account the fragility of these pitiful bodies. It may be that utopias are sought with the soul, but they are carried out on the bones of mangled bodies, paid for with the biographies of those who are dragged along into each successive ugly paradise.

In *Demise of the Egoist Fatzer*, Bertolt Brecht has captured the temporary conclusion to this historical sequence, just in time for standardized killing to make it to the factory floor:

the reduction of the body to mere waste material. In the First World War, while the Woyzecks were croaking by the millions in the trenches, a deserter in Mülheim scribbles his new equation on the wall. What is a dead body? ". . . 170 lbs. of cold meat, 4 buckets of water, 1 packet of salt."

•

Back in the present, I will close quickly and simply, with one final scene. In Berlin, on the evening of October 7, 1989, when I woke up from the initial euphoria of the first day of a wave of demonstrations that washed away the other Germany, I found myself astonished by the sight of a monstrous machine. On the median of one of the typical colossal thoroughfares in the city center (which, like the Parisian boulevards or the Muscovite prospects, followed the model of postrevolutionary city planning and were laid out as pure marching zones for the military or the police) stood a Russian tank that had emerged from nowhere or from one of the bunkers that served as underground garages. Its turret, painted with the emblems of the GDR's National People's Army, was screwed down, the cannon pointed across the roadway toward Alexanderplatz. I no longer know if it was the tremendous tonnage of its appearance or the (Asiatic) distance it seemed to rule so easily: a loiterer heading home from the battles, straggling far behind the others, I was suddenly overcome by a desire to lie down, right there, in the shadow of the tank and lean against its steel chains and wheels for minutes on end with my eyes closed. The threatening vehicle, the machine of the civil wars, had awoken a primeval need for sleep in me. The body had come this far, now it sought rest, a break from history. It had had enough of all that, enough of the streets as wide as runways, of Peace Squares and death strips, of morning roll call and skewed prefab high-rises, of urban monotony and delusions of security, of conditioned stir-

rings and simple-minded languages, and, finally, of the long
socialist twilight, the lethargy of an entire landscape which
that body had blundered into by accident as if into a giant
trap. I wanted to rest, to cut myself off from East *and* West,
from the disastrous clamping together of the divided sides
of all relationships and brains, to lie down and sleep in the
middle of the minefield, to forget the powerlessness, the
physiological dictatorship, and all the years of collective humiliation . . . to fall asleep, to forget the insults to the intellect,
to find a moment's peace, leaning against this heavy, tracked
vehicle that stood there as if unmanned. Here it was the body
that, on a sudden and childlike whim and *prior* to all words,
desired to yield to its own exhaustion: after all, it had had to
endure longer, having been more oppressively stifled than my
ever-ready-to-defect thoughts. It was as if with the tank
behind me I wanted to oversleep history, just this once, for
minutes on end, before everything gathered momentum
again, to forget the body in a dreamless sleep.

•

I thank the Darmstadt Academy for a prize that I could hardly
refuse and that (so much still lies ahead of me) I would have
nevertheless preferred to see in other hands, awarded for an
entire oeuvre, a life's work. Büchner's age at his death can
hardly be a source of comfort to me, much less an alibi.
Thinking of him, I don't see any of my other ancestors, I see
this unique, meteorlike image: the young poet as sphinx.

CHILDHOOD IN THE DIORAMA

Strange, already as a child he was drawn to the inert.
In museums he would long pause before the diorama
With the animals at a standstill, grouped naturally
Against painted scapes, dense forest scenes, and Himalayas.
Fairy-tale-like, enchanted, the deer would prick up their ears
As soon as he stepped closer in the neon light, eyes aglow.
Next door, he saw the hole in the caveman's skull
And forgot about the rival's club blow,
Their battle over the fire site.
The Egyptian mummy had withstood millennia
With its brain removed. Only with the melting
Of perpetual ice had this mammoth come to light.
The most beautiful butterflies, palm-size,
He saw skewered with pins. Once, it was
As if their wings were still quivering—in memory
Of all those felled trees and tropical winds.
A draft, perhaps, had blown through the displays.

Among the great coups of the nineteenth century was the harnessing of the spirit of technology in the production of illusion. Invention, or progress, in and of itself, would never have been enough of a motive; no, it took the love of illusion that had perhaps never expressed itself so directly and forcefully. Competition for novelty and strangeness, the intensification of the product world via trade and industry, a passion for collecting and scientific method awakened in the public the need to behold and have before it, in effigy, if nothing else, all these new treasures. Enraptured curiosity led to the institution of designated sites for the projection of desires. Palaces of collective dreams threw open their gates. Institutes generously borrowing from nature's visual cornucopia drew startled crowds. Exhibition halls that resembled great greenhouses with their vegetable promises became the wonders of two worlds, the inorganic and organic, all heaped up into one single mélange parted only by glass, dammed only by mirrors. In the space of a few decades a market was established whose one and only stock in trade, albeit refined by every conceivable technological twist, was the quid pro quo: something that mimicked something else. Subtle or blatant, exotically implausible or deceptively realistic, it was the fleeting appearance that in those years went on sale. What was on offer in all its aspects, in every form but always payable in hard cash, was illusion as such, evoked in wax and in flesh-colored sheen, projected onto silver gelatin and later on film, in naturalistic painting, as cast from a living model, and as complete preparation. And the effect was a mass conversion. From that time on, there was no life without the spirituality of illusion, no consciousness independent of phantasmagorias. This is where may be found the beginning of consent to a virtual reality that straightaway extended its influence into all areas of life and was able to blur its boundaries like a dream that it was in the process of collectivizing. Walter Benjamin marked this first act of an age of technical reproduction in the notes for his *Arcades Project*: "There were panoramas, dioramas, cosmoramas, diaphanoramas, naveloramas, pleoramas (from *pleo*, I sail), fantoscopes, fantasma-parastasias, *expériences fantasmagoriques et fantasmaparastatiques*, indoor scenic voyages, georamas, optical picturesques, cineoramas, phanoramas, stereoramas, cycloramas, *panoramas dramatiques*."

One of the oddest of these illusion machines was the animal diorama. Like all machines of this type, it's out of date now, its thrill value long gone. For some it may never have ceased to work, but to the viewer pampered by animal film and wildlife zoo it now appears as a boring holdout from museum-worthy miracle chambers. A few perplexed-looking animals put there to look lifelike; any child will see that they're stuffed. Perhaps the extraordinary laboriousness, the precision of the reconstruction will win some respect, but the theatrical pathos of this "nature" won't add to it. Unlike the rare panorama picture, the diorama can be found quite frequently in museums of natural history, rarely in prominent spots, usually halfway to the stockroom, reduced to the status of backstage shop window. Devoid of commentary, merely relying on the overwhelming impact of a look, it is bound to disappoint the modern appetite for the didactic. It can as little illustrate the latest biological discoveries as a model of Watt's steam engine can show quantum physics. The mere appearance, a construction of the nineteenth century, is not enough either; the Darwinian drama of some life-and-death struggle in a little peep-show booth is simply too unspectacular. Unlike the dinosaur park, which is as old as crystal palaces and world's fairs and which is going through a renaissance today, the animal diorama is not likely to be revived any time soon. But one can still predict that its great age is bound to come . . . when the necessity arises to document successively each dying species in its typical environment. Species death is the future of the diorama—the last archive, which will give testimony of the vanished biotope and the animal displaced by the human.

When I was little, there was a time when I nagged my grandfather almost every day to take me to the museum. In the years before I started going to school I spent the summers with my grandparents in Gotha. I was soon so fed up with the usual walks through the town parks and the famous orangery that I preferred knocking around on my own. There was only one thing I needed adult accompaniment for, and that was the natural history museum. Six years old, innocent of letters, interested only in swans, cars, trains, and dogs, I found myself, for the first time, in the grip of a little mania. My grandfather got the picture as soon as I charged ahead of him on my leash, up the wide staircase and into the museum, before he had finished counting his change at the register. To find me, he had to dive into a suite of little *séparées* on the ground floor, all curtained off from the corridor. I would be standing behind one of the curtains, silent and holding my breath, as if playing hide-and-seek, all sense of time gone, because in front of me was the heat-hazed African savanna. Or I might be leaning against the glass, shivering, with floes of ice stacked up in front of the gelid blue horizon. When my grandfather came along, I would point mutely into the bamboo thicket at a marauding tiger, or warn him with a glance of the wild boar in the underbrush. In front of me, close enough to touch, was an endless distance with which I was heartily familiar already from stories, dreams, and memories. To my remembering eye it was every bit as real as the corporate park outside, or the Thuringian woods beyond. What to my grandfather was at best a copy, a piece of jungle nicely imitated and about as interesting as the window display in a fur shop, was to me identical with the nature outside. This was exactly how I'd always imagined the Arctic wastes, where polar bears live. Wasn't this the view you had standing on the deck of an ice-breaker bound for the North Pole? And this vegetation, typical of Amazonian regions, wasn't this the actual rain forest in whose tangles you lost your way choked by lianas, punctured by poisonous vipers? Was it just my will to imagination? Every detail had to fit, any breach would straightaway have been noticed by my childish expertise. And yet I knew precious lit-

tle about tropical plants, some of the animals' names I heard
for the first time, thanks to my grandfather's encyclopedia-
drawn information. The difference between him and me
wasn't in the attention to detail, in more or less romantic joy;
it was in our appreciation of the whole that we differed. What
was defined for him by being irretrievably on the other side of
the glass, as illusory as Dürer's patch of grass, was for me continuous with this side: it was only a chance pane of glass that
prevented me from setting foot on it. It was just as much part
of my world as a suite of rooms in some stranger's house, or
the natural coexistence of landscapes we had visited at one
time or another. There was the moor next to the limestone
cavern, the coastal dune next to the mountain stream under
pines. No understanding of geography had separated the
places for me, scattering them on different maps like the constellations. In my field-and-meadow topography, there were
flexible frontiers, and what I stood staring in front of had previously submitted to the rules of archetypal memory. I had
somehow already seen the armadillo when I first saw it in the
familiar sandy steppe. At a glance, I took in what plants flourished on the Siberian tundra and what animals lived in the
Australian desert. The various settings behind glass, concentrated tableaux of the typical nature on each of the five continents, accorded precisely with my child's sense of probability
as I set about conquering the world. No sooner was I past the
curtain than I stared in fascination at scenes that were equally
familiar and exotic. It was the world of picture books and
adventure stories that I had known for ages: a stretch of Mexican *llano*, a slab of Antarctica, deer in a dappled forest clearing, somewhere in Europe . . . As though hypnotized, I took in
every single blade of grass, the tint of the leaves, the anatomy
of the animals in their respective postures: sniffing, resting,
eating. Were they standing so still because they'd spotted me?
Would they still be there when the museum was closed? You

had to hold your breath so as not to alarm them. When you watched them for a long time, you started to feel dizzy. The animals, secretly observed from behind bent twigs, frozen in an eternal clearing—long before I knew what an epiphany was, they put me into little states of ecstasy and followed me into my dreams.

Today it seems to me that at such moments my whole childhood was received into the diorama. Like the Chinese master draftsman who in the end crosses over into one of his painted landscapes, the imago of the child slipped into those interstitial spaces, part-near, part-distant, the ideal place for it. As if under a spell, the exotic things encountered there mingled with fragments of experience from the early years. All those fresh instants, formed by surprise, the first descent into a disused mineshaft, the lamp-lit procession through the forest at night, the peek over the rim of a chalk cliff by the sea: here in the museum they were inventoried as archetypal dream images, and it had to be possible to summon them at will, when their time was come. The diorama was open sesame, where memories were stored as geographical primal motifs.

•

Viewed phenomenologically, the diorama is a veritable pasture for the grazing eye, melding diagram and slice of life in one long shot. In its imaginary space, the illusion of nature finds its apotheosis as a perfect recollection of nature. Because montage, through the means employed, remains invisible, it helps you to speculate with probability. Naturalism is the product of the seamless arrangement of details: every centimeter is copy, and the whole thing looks lifelike. In the diorama, the biotope recurs as a genre scene, external space is a frozen stage on which plants and animals stop dead for a split second. Only after looking for a long time do you begin to sense that this instant will go on forever. In the arrangements, there is a state of mimetic stiffness, corresponding to the dead and discarded in nature itself: the bleached skeleton, an ossified piece of hide, a midge set in amber. This is perceived as a discreet shock, the abruptness of the encounter coinciding with the recognition of frozen life. The fact that both nature scene and moment of recognition only exist as pried out of their respective dimensions casts a shadow of doubt over the whole thing. Quotations from the animal and vegetable kingdom resonate in an artificial hollow space in the museum where the indirect lighting is designed to suggest time of day and climate. The curved back wall creates an illusion of depth. The three-dimensional foreground and painted backdrop split apart optically; that and the space-bending trompe l'oeil painting create the subliminally hypnotic effect that made the child slightly giddy. Perhaps that's one of the reasons for the long-range psychological effect of the diorama?

The eye yo-yos restlessly from the vanishing point of the painted horizon lines at the back of the foregrounded scene, the conspiratorial connection of stuffed animal, inanimate objects, and arranged vegetation. The eternal hunting grounds are cast as an interior. The tight space of a cell (no bigger in its dimensions than tomb, raree-show, cabinet) furnished with trees and bushes robs consciousness of the brief illusion of wide scenery. The eye goes back to the salient particulars whose sheer wealth recalls the notion of "nature's abundance." The sublime in the form of beauty, by a subtle twist it winds up in the panopticum where you catch your breath. The silence is arresting; no natural sound disturbs the contemplation of anesthetized nature. The spell rehearses the terrifying second of the onset of the catastrophe. Something behind the back of the onlooker, perhaps the world behind him, which has furnished the elements of the diorama, signals danger. At any rate, the animals in their three walls are compelled by something that we are unable to see. The situation is suggestive of Noah's Ark, when, with eyes widened with terror, they escaped the rising flood. Were it not for the certainty that, like wax figures, they have long since become part of a dusty object-world, one might take these dumb actors in their still life for revenants, flesh-and-blood creatures on their way back to the open spaces. It is the lack of such, all the more apparent in the excerpted, curtailed scenes that makes for the melancholy atmosphere of the diorama. What is conveyed is not so much the feeling of arrested time as of time long since elapsed. Here, as in the darkest fairy tale, there is only one thing still going the rounds: the ghost of lifelessness. In the glitter of the glass eyes, in the stillness (no wind to stir the smallest leaf) lies the menace of utterly lifeless nature, mocking any subjective experience. The diorama offers the study of what was once alive, glorifying the ossified forms just as the insect case holds out the beauty of its pinned butterflies. Everything incompatible with it, the animals' nerves and range of movements, the luminescent color of the plants, is gone. That they can no longer fade or die is the basis for their place in the glass box. Beyond death, their appeal is indistinguishable from that of wax flowers and bronze animal statues. What this *nature morte* illustrates is the fantasy of uncontaminated nature—the obverse of all efforts at world conquest in the industrial age. In the end, isn't it precisely its unrealizability that we witness in these enchanted scenes as the secret of a lost utopia?

If, as Nietzsche did, one takes the animal as proof of the eternal present, as totemic guide out of the nightmare of history, then its apotheosis may be found in the diorama. Because an animal always makes the same impression, whether to the child in the zoo, or to Herodotus' wandering gaze, it is so easy to lift it for a moment out of the fog of time. You don't have to move, everything is stationary, you listen

and look at the animal and with it at the earliest day of creation. The eagle grown onto the precipice, the endlessly grazing pair of antelope, the ever-and-ever-alert lion: in such
figures we see the transhistoric, as in the pharaoh's frescoes
and the child's memory.

The diorama could come into being only once nature
itself had been seen to be subject to history. Only after Darwin had expounded his theory of evolution in *On the Origin of
Species* could natural history turn to the task of reconstruction
using all available models. One can imagine the early dioramas naïvely, a little slavishly showing the struggle for survival.
The step from chambers of horrors and bestiaries to a depic-
tion of nature that, without mannerism, dealt with the epic of
zoology was barely less than that from the early panoramas of
travel and optical phantasmagorias to the precise reproductions of film and photography. With improved processes of
taxidermy, accuracy of detail became an obsession. Landscap-
ing, anatomical study, natural props, all were combined in a
maximally faithful way. The composition was a *Gesamtkunstwerk*: the illusion of ideal wildlife in a small space.

Perhaps it has taken until today, with the perspective of
vast devastations to the planet, to reveal the sorrow behind
the magic of the diorama. Its silent celebration of the moment
is a memento mori to prehuman nature. Only that which has
its own end in sight can appear in a diorama. Neanderthal
man in his hunting groups preceded modern urban man. The
artificial worlds of the diorama take their beauty from the
vision of the extinction of their actual models; it appears when
history has passed those points, and looking back we see them
finished in a panorama. The glorious evening light bathing
such moments is rarely seen as imposingly as in the rooms of
the American Museum of Natural History in New York City.
Its epic dioramas perform a sort of final obeisance to the
deposed animal families. Here they all are in their never-

witnessed splendor and accoutrement, dropped into the heart of the city. Like the great men of a nation in a pantheon, they stare out of their well-lit funeral chambers into the onetime continental expanses. The museum is the hall of fame where they live mummified in all their grandeur: bison and grizzly bears in the Hall of North American Mammals, whole groups of hippopotamuses and elephants in the Hall of African Mammals. The visitor, come in off the New York streets, is welcomed by the cool air of a mausoleum, the silent music of a planetary requiem. In front of the cases he becomes an analytical dreamer for hours, hallucinating a prehuman past in the archives of the animal world. One more time, fragments of a lost paradise come his way, as a parade of well-prepared bodies. The nature theater is open when, out of the endless corridors of artificial foliage and the panoramas of painted blue, scenes of a shared infancy arise before him and he finds himself again, as on the day of his first field trip, a child surrounded by plants and animals.

Was this what Baudelaire meant when, after visiting a Parisian salon, tired of always seeing the same paintings, he observed: "I would like to return to the dioramas, whose rough but powerful magic is able to provide me with a salutary illusion. I prefer viewing certain theater backdrops in which I can see my most cherished dreams in artistic form and tragic concentration. Because these things are false, they are infinitely closer to reality . . ."

THREE MINIATURES

THE SARCASTIC CHILD

We are all wolves in the virgin forest of eternity.

—Marina Tsvetayeva

You're like the sarcastic child out of some grim German fairy tale. Industry lured you out of the forest into the endless cities, and there you are, keeping your eyes peeled for some clearing. You came here to learn about fear, now you are forced to see that terror has lost its bracing effect and there's nothing left but cold, uninterrupted bustle. Life in the jungle was dangerous, the bush was one ambush. There were witches in it and animals fitted with teeth and claws, while at night the owls screeched their ghoulish secrets to one another. Sinister dwarves with piercing eyes danced around campfires, pitch-black fir trees keeled over, struck by lightning, crashing on the hibernant, the wanderer, who got lost in the forest picking blueberries. But while the tracks through the dense brush may have been dangerous, they were harmless in comparison with these city streets. The thing that holds you in suspension has something to do with the way these stories end, with the onset of a flood of moralities wrapped in trick endings. The sarcastic child of course knows this, but it can't suspend its wonderment . . .

ON THE ROAD AND EARLY SLUMBER

When I was a baby, I would often fall asleep on the road. My early childhood was like a sort of peripatetic hibernation. I was forever being taken somewhere. Irresistible hands bundled me out of one conveyance and into the next. From my mother's womb I was put on a wheeled trolley, then in a baby carriage, some car or other, then a steamship or airplane. If I didn't puke—as sometimes happened—I was usually off in no time, jiggled to sleep by the mechanism of wheels, engines, or turbines. Waking up was always the worst. Suddenly your body was expected to give up its uniquely comfortable position. After months, you were roughly picked up, tipped out, and put on your feet. The same people who purported to porter you everywhere like marsupials abandoned you, no longer fed, to gravity, and to the most dramatic struggles for balance and direction. No kangaroo would defenestrate its sleepy offspring like that. No anteater mother would jettison its baby like that, after a few hours of hunting lessons.

But that's the way it always was, first you were lulled to sleep in the belly of some machine or other, then an emergency stop and you dropped onto the cool earth. Even when you were utterly habituated to being driven around. Everything else—crawling on all fours, bum-shuffling, staggering, or taking steps—was torture, at least initially. It was only as a passenger that you had the feeling of being properly looked after, skimming over the ground like a nomad infant on horseback, like a prince in a sealed litter. As long as the movement didn't stop, you felt soothed, satisfied, and then came the shock. Once handed over to the earth, what were you to do but crawl mechanically hither and thither, up to the edge of the carpet, into the waves, into puddles of mud or deep grass.

Was your shrinking from your father's legs and your mother's arms not a reflexive response to the hurt you had suffered? You wanted to get away from the people who had set you out. Rather sit in the corner and wait for the earth itself, spinning through space, to give you an impulse—tortoise-slow, yes, but dependable. The body, on its trajectory through the seasons, sought sleep everywhere.

AWAY FROM HOME

One night, I hopped out of bed, tiptoed barefoot through my parents' bedroom, down into the cellar, past the dark bulks of coal and coke behind their retaining boards, and out through the back door into the garden. It wasn't the moon, the starry summer night over the fruit trees, the strange murmur, inland echo of tides and seas, that had lured me, a kid in blue pajamas, out onto the street. So what was it? I stopped under the first arc light, yawning. Sleepy, propped against a privet hedge, with the eye of a model train enthusiast I stopped to survey the long S shape of the street of single-story houses, and lo: there was a world of miniature toy villas.

But in the distance, very wide and gray, was the autobahn, and there, as I rubbed my eyes, was a heavy goods transporter towing my parents' house away. Was it not the same house I'd just sleepwalked out of? I turned around and found an empty plot behind me, a black lawn with a rectilinear hole with weeds hanging down over its edges. The place where my bed had stood was now uninhabited. A strong odor of mushrooms wafted toward me. Through the fence I could make out only shrubs, a few tree stumps close at hand, flat heathland vegetation, a swampy clearing in the forest.

For a long time, I held on to the initials in the garden gate. Just then it seemed as wildly implausible to me that I belonged here as that I should lay claim to a childhood in the jungles of Amazonia under the tutelage of blowpipe hunters, an agile companion to apes and primeval lizards. My tiredness felt like the jungle boy's. Stunned with plant smells, giddy with humid air full of insect swarms, he lived in an uninterrupted dizziness in wild chlorophyll. So I thought. Waking and dreaming would be indistinguishable there, only one thing was not in doubt because the body with all its nerves confirmed it: this was the place I belonged. Neighbors, finding me there later, told me I had never gone so far from home.

II

THE AGE OF DEEP-SEA FISH

Again and again, in the early autumn twilight of the cities, on subterranean excursions into mines and stalactite caves, in the vast no-man's-lands of dreams, deep-sea images unexpectedly surface, never seen before, known only from diving films. Less vivid than any lunar landscape, quarried from the darkness like underground galleries thanks to the technological possibilities of remote-controlled cameras, they are visions of the unapproachable and alien. Thousands of meters deep, these lightless zones at the bottom of the sea have been untouched by the great voyages of discovery, by history and myth. Unlike the polar wastes and even the moon's surface, these abyssal regions are still almost completely unexplored. No Captain Nemo has dreamily surveyed their expanses from his panoramic window. The reach of our imagination does not extend beyond the threatening blues and greens of the movie screen in any given second-rate U-boat epic. Thus, their expanses, far removed from our documented and charted world, correspond to the human unconscious, and like the latter, they are crisscrossed only by the beams of weak searchlights, flashing similes, and instruments. And yet there are creatures there that encyclopedias know about.

Hic sunt leones was written on the old maps wherever the wastelands began, the patches of inaccessible land, shunned by colonization and cartography. In Marco Polo's day, they were still thought to be great natural arenas—these swamps

and jungles—populated by wild animals, dragons, and primeval beasts. Phantasms according to later geographers,
superstitions according to psychologists—these terrestrial
nightmares have since given way to more sober inventories.
However, just as the space out there, the earth, conquered
and surveyed from end to end, returns in the anamorphoses of
the unconscious, so it has long been impossible to dismiss the
naive zoologies of the earth's circumnavigators. Every catch
from the nets of marine biologists dashes the hope that our
world may be inhabited by familiar creatures. These unwel-
come surprises, dredged up from depths of two thousand
meters and more, immediately trigger memories of all that
was frightful and marvelous in the ancient stories. Minuscule
as they may be, almost blind, squishy as gelatin, camouflaged
to a degree of being virtually unrecognizable—they remain
beings from another planet, another geological era.

Don't these oldest designs on the theme of "fish," so
heavily armed, look as if they were designed on a sinister
demiurge's drawing board?

These monstrous prototypes resemble
the first pressing irons, the earliest sewing machines, phonographs,
water picks, or safety razors. They
are reminiscent of gruesome toi-
letry tools, accessories for sadistic,
flesh-tearing games, or kitchen ap-
pliances with their metallic gleam.
Here, the worst fears about evolution's early military experiments come true. The sight of deep-sea fish immediately
brings the horror stories of the last centuries to mind—the
arcades and panicky wanderings through a material world
that had gone mad and in which instruments of hygiene
and surgery were thrown together with the paraphernalia of
fashion and armament in one and the same window display.

Hingelike cartilage, fins notched as if by rasps and graters, rows of stiletto-sharp teeth in mouths with corsetlike braces—all these rival the most absurd mechanical inventions of the *Gründerzeit*. Clearly, they are early versions—what with their primitive and yet so perfidious sense organs and hunting methods. Many of them have eyes that are either highly regressed or telescope-like, along with light organs and occasional, antenna-like appendages. Some squat almost motionless on the ocean floor, in the zones of scattered light, searching the water for plankton, their stalk eyes reaching upward. Others are so fragile that, like mummies, they disintegrate when they come into contact with air. When they are brought up by fishing nets, many of them, used to the pressures of the deep sea, have air bladders that swell up like balloons, their entrails then bubbling out of their huge mouths.

Reproduction runs through all the varieties of the polymorphous and the perverse. In every way their behavior is determined by darkness. Purple cells on the heads and tails of some species help sexual partners to find each other. Often, the tiny males have withered to the size of dwarves, without teeth or intestines, completely parasitical creatures at times, firmly attached to the females' bodies, their sole function to produce semen.

•

To the reader of encyclopedias, the fauna of deep-sea fish seems like a gallery of botched constructions, as terrifying as excrescences of mutated protoplasm. Taken together, they are like ancient, discarded technology, floating junk. The sea is their storehouse, the deeper the murkier, a dark landfill for all prototypes and rejects.

Here's an armorhead, its facial bones exposed, the skull nothing but mouth, as if it were made of cast-iron braces. Such a gluttonous hermit can hardly be imagined in large schools. Nor does the hatchetfish look any friendlier, this unwieldy chunk of jagged shrapnel, adorned with a silvery glittering plate—a fitting breastplate for a samurai's armor. Here is the sawtoothed, large-mouthed anglerfish with its shining eyes sitting on long, thin stalks and serving as bait. A grimace from the tunnel of horror, the leftvent (a subspecies of anglerfish) lures its prey into its maw with harmless algae, fake plants that sprout from its upper lip and chin. The bait of its shining eye, insidiously buffeted by the current, always sits right next to the murder weapon, the ravenous mouth with its simple snapping mechanism. With a sharp serrated ridge running from its jaw all the way down to its gills, the snaggletooth, like an old machine gun on wheels, enveloped in cartridge belts, is literally armed to the teeth. Hardly less anxiety-provoking is the black swallower, with its stomach like a swollen throat pouch: when it is full, the fish looks twice its size, its own mirror image along the axis of its belly. As with jellyfish and snakes, these fish swallow and digest their prey whole. The gulper eel also swallows its prey whole, as do the bristlemouth and the sabertooth fish. Only the many spiderfish roam the sea floor like blind drill heads. Standing on the tips of their fins as if on stilts, they fan across the bottom in search of the remains of plants.

Kilometers deep underwater, it seems, time has no sway over them. Having first appeared in time immemorial, long before the beginnings of continental time, they have always already been contemporaries: of the first horsetails and the Roman Empire, of the breakup of the continents and the killing machines of the twentieth century. Oceanic trenches that no plummet ever reaches are their habitat; the floors of deep seas, penetrated only by traces of light, a few lost photons, are their home. These astonishing veterans of evolution live there, in the darkness of enormous, undeveloped spaces, among clumps of manganese and suspended matter, in regions where humans are definitively absent and compared to which even lunar landscapes look familiar and cozy. No camera team has ever gone so deep as to create memories of panoramic images of submarine Serengetis, and even if a huge effort were to succeed in accomplishing this feat, the visibility would be too poor. The plankton fog would make every landscape virtually unrecognizable.

What is it that makes us think of the unconscious when we think of these regions? Is it their inaccessibility? Their immemorial topography? Or is it their geological age, unwitnessed and untainted by evolution, preserved purely in our imagination, in prebiblical darkness? Unexpected as the appearance of ammonites may be in rocky regions that in the distant past lay far beneath the surface of the sea: by daylight, they immediately lose their ancestral aura and become part of the array of familiar, soon forgotten things—sprockets, worn-out bevel gears. When separated from the water, solidified organisms—whether in petrified form or as hollow casts— enter a state of conservation that removes them from the realm of the organic unconscious. The resulting shapes are the products of dehydration. Conversely, it is the primordial fish, appearing in sudden, momentary, protean flashes, that enjoin us to think of the deep sea as a geographical reservoir analogous to the realm of the unconscious. This equation implies that the creatures encountered there are, at bottom, something like archetypes, morphological first editions playing the role of originals in the lives of our collective symbolisms, blueprints for the first rocking phantasmagoria in the amniotic fluid. Their characteristics and body shapes would then be exemplary of much that has since passed through the phylogenetic tunnel. A backward glance, then, reveals them to be as familiar as the distorted images in communicating tubes, like the first and last grimaces met on the way through the birth canal or on a ride on a ghost train. In them, the archaic is combined with yesterday's modernity, the gruesome wildness of fetish masks with the futuristic metal designs of industrial production.

What is striking is their martial physiognomy, a combination of a knight's armor with a face distorted in anger. Their mirror images are easy to find throughout history. They can be detected in old paintings in the guise of Roman legionnaires on the Mount of Olives, as well as in the Dutch school's paintings of brutal drinking bouts. As might be expected, among them we find the physiognomies of deceivers, of braggarts and poseurs, of devourers with gaping jaws, as well as the grimaces of goggle-eyed basilisks. The prototype for all those who are constantly on the lookout—from the chameleon to the operagoer armed with binoculars—is the barreleye, with its telescope eyes that point straight up. From its perspective, everything good must indeed come from above. Its look—eternally expectant and eternally lurking—is simultaneously stoic and ecstatic in the religious sense.

Along with their flashy mimicry, special organs are also often prominent. Thus, the anglerfish is a sea creature that anticipates a hunting method subsequently adopted by humans. In a sense, this fish has a rod of its own to catch its prey. The array of fins on its back is transformed into striking bait; any fish thus lured is sucked into the gaping mouth cavity within seconds. The lanternfish, by contrast, moves around like a swimming searchlight. Its specimens radiate in different colors, some blue, others orange. Some emit flashes of light to

escape pursuers by blinding them: thus, in the
pitch-black water of the sea's deepest
regions, they must seem like
mere afterimages, chimeras, like
those submarines with antiradar
paint that reveal their positions for mere split
seconds before vanishing, never to be seen again. While such
fish bring light to the darkness through their very bodies, others, passively equipped, are all eye. The extremely well-
adapted tripod fish has an extrapowerful visual organ with
which it follows the light scattered by even the tiniest creatures, the LEDs of the deep sea.

What makes their physiognomy so horrific is the lowest-
level specialization of their organs. They are all too clearly
characterized by their armaments, their bodies hardened
into masks of horror. As if designed in monster labs, their
few instinctual impulses have found their most direct and
most articulate expressions, like race cars outfitted with external motors, broad tires, and small airfoils, stripped-down
machines, naked in their almost greedy functionality. By daylight, nature only rarely, if at all, subsequently reveals itself
so unambiguously, and then only in camouflage—in ironic
decorative shapes, as in the case of certain reptiles, or the
original inhabitants of Madagascar, who are active only at
night, prosimians with eyes as large as faces and the transparent fingers of newts. Otherwise, everything lemurlike seems
banished into a phylogenetic dawn that only the unconscious
may still know something about. But still, even the trawls of
the deep-sea fishing boats glide past all this; and when, during the dissection of larger fish, in the stomach of the gluttonous lancetfish, for example, some undigested old-timers are
found, they are mostly as unrecognizable as old wallets and
gloves. They look fanciful only down there where no one
sees them, in the deep sea's dark arcades and endless rows of

shopping windows. Only there, in their own *Gründerzeit*, are they at home, these little cast-iron articles, pursuing, without haste or waste, the original plan of survival: disguise, cunning, pillage.

DARWIN'S EYES

"I remember well the time when the thought of the eye made me cold all over," Charles Darwin once wrote. The statement has all the impact of something thought for the first time. It speaks with the sudden insight into evolution's abyss. For do we really know what led to that great evolutionary leap that introduced such a complex structure as the eye into the grand cosmic order? Does our astonishment die out as soon as the first light-sensitive cell is understood as the primeval building block that even the architecture of the human visual apparatus ultimately rests upon? But perhaps Darwin meant something else. He had taken, as he so often did in his thoughts, a few million-year steps back and grasped the miraculous at a glance. With the eye, nature gains distance from and learns to observe itself. Only with the liberation of this organ from the constraints of pure biological purposiveness does the modern era in natural history begin, the chapter of disinterested self-exploration. Only with the formation of the human eye does self-determination emerge in the midst of the biosphere. It functions as much more than an early-warning system or a mere tool in the struggle for survival. Centrally positioned in the head of *Homo erectus*, it has irrevocably evolved into a comprehensive visual outfit. Until then, it had been almost exclusively a mere sense organ tailored to hunting prey, recognizing friends and enemies, and monitoring habitat. Primitive in the case of the deep-sea fish, a photocell for registering light traces at the bottom of the sea; of crystalline beauty in the house fly, a compound eye as large as the insect's whole head; grotesque in the goggle-eyed flounder, even if already concentrated into a pupil; a true precision instrument in the buzzard's cockpit; and, finally, the range finder the cheetah uses to zoom in on its prey: yet all across creation it remained a mere sensor in the service of the organism.

Not so with humans. Here, the eye has finally been emancipated from the rest of the body. Vision is now merely an auxiliary function in a much more subtle game. Who would want to claim that the human genitalia serve reproduction alone? In just the same way, the eye is also destined for more sublime ends at this provisional high point in the development of the species. Only the eye enables *aisthesis*, as philosophers have been calling perception since time immemorial, and with it the fine arts and reflective thinking. If the eye is understood as a medium of affective display, then it is, prior to all gesture and language, the foundation of expression. It is not just one among other body parts but the highest-ranking interface after the brain: it is *the* membrane in which the internal and external worlds, impression and expression get reflected—a physiological watershed, and not just due to tears.

In his book *The Expression of the Emotions in Man and Animals*, Darwin devoted several sections to the expressive function of the eyes—to what makes people raise their eyebrows, for example, to the secretion of tears when they laugh very hard, and to the crying of newborns, whose reflex in response to pain is to close their eyelids tightly, supposedly in order to protect the eyeball from excessive blood flow. Even if by Darwin's time the eye had long since become a "profane" organ, an object of physiology and no longer of theology, its reputation as the window to the soul was still widespread, and not only among the incorrigible poets for whom it continued to be the sesame that opened in a blink, as if at a magic word, ever receptive to the miracles from a thousand and one nights: those out there—the immeasurable universe in all its variety; and those in here, where such variety generated a second universe—a universe that Plotinus, blind with age, claimed was always already contained within us as the heaven of metaphysics.

On this note, a digression: it is well known that metaphysics came down to proving that in order to perceive essences, the physical eye—iris, retina and all—is not at all required. If anything, sensory perception actually obscures the truth. No optical tools are necessary to look into the realm of ideas. A visionary like Plato or Plotinus, even if 100 percent blind, is capable of penetrating to the very core of things precisely because he disregards all imperfect appearances with their accidental properties as mere blurry likenesses. For him, the error-prone eye has been replaced by the soul as the instrument of contemplation. He will not be deceived by the dirty effects of the empirical. Thanks to mathematics and conceptual intuition, he penetrates to the truth directly. Though basically mere sleight of hand, as a shift in perspective such idealism was both momentous and disastrous. Since then, *aisthesis* and *alétheia* have been at odds with each other, running through the history of philosophy in continual metamorphoses, obstructing, distorting, and eclipsing each other, depending on which side happens to have had the theoretical advantage—matter-bound vision or innate idea. The conflict, never to be settled, has become a firmly entrenched antagonism even though the natural sciences today, in their dependence on *mathesis* and abstraction, are closer to Platonism than to all previous forms of empirical knowledge. Once introduced by quantum physics, the postulate of an "observer-produced reality" gradually spread to all fields in which experiments manipulate objects, even biology.

Darwinian thought moves at the other end of the spectrum: its court of appeal is the eye. It remains beholden to matter, to its confusing variety and variability. But Plotinus' central idea is by no means foreign to it. The very same monism that, in Plotinus, created a comprehensive order of ideas according to the principle of the "world soul" and its hierarchy of hypostases first ignited the spark of the idea of evolution in Darwin, that strict observer of nature. *The one in the many and in the many the one*: for Plotinus, this was a concept born from the spirit of theology; for Darwin, it was a dynamic formula of biology, a precept for the explanation of phylogenesis from the lowest single-celled organism all the way to humans, whose "sunlike" eye so fascinated Goethe. But Darwin, throughout his speculations, kept both feet firmly on the ground—on the carpet of algae, if you will. The man who wrote whole books on coral reefs or the soil in the fields (more precisely, on the role of earthworms in its formation) never lost the ground of empiricism beneath his feet.

In his notebooks, the poet Mandelstam pointed out how much modern literature owes to the style of the natural scientist. With Darwin in mind, he spoke of the "autobiographical character" of the theory of evolution, and he came up with the image of the "ebb and flow of substantiation" in an attempt to capture the rhythms of exposition in Darwin's magnum opus, *On the Origin of Species*. No blind either/or, no claim left unchecked—instead: ifs and buts galore, amply illustrated, piles of evidence. Mind you, even for Darwin the main point was the theoretical surplus value, a synthesis of thousands of separate facts, a *philosophy of zoology*, as he himself declared. Yet, even while contemplating the general, he never loses sight of the particular, the variant form of a fern leaf, say, the insular milieu of an endemic species of finch, or the specificity of any given masterpiece of nature, be it as tiny as a thumbnail or as big and awe-inspiring as the Indian elephant. The goal of this school of seeing was to be able to read the history of its styles off nature itself, with as much respect for an early Minoan spiral form as for the colorful plumage of the belle époque, and as much enthusiasm for the domesticated as for the undomesticated species. Of course, this could be done only on the basis of an enormous collection of facts and by painstakingly processing thousands of index cards; even the eye first had to be equipped with telescope and microscope. Visual inspection, however, always remained key, it had the last word. Ever since Aristotle and Pliny's natural history, the study of the forms of animal life, zoology, had developed through observation. The Greek *zoon* signifies both at once: creature and image, animal and painting.

A striking example of Darwin's vivid style is the treatment of crabs in chapter five of *On the Origin of Species*, where it functions as evidence for the ways in which the laws of modification are expressed in natural selection and in the principle of the degeneration of organs as a result of disuse. "In some of the crabs the foot-stalk for the eye remains, though the eye is gone; the stand for the telescope is there, though the telescope with its glasses has been lost. As it is difficult to imagine that eyes, though useless, could be in any way injurious to animals living in darkness, I attribute their loss wholly to disuse." Everyone is familiar with the chitinous rudiments left over at the edge of the plate after a rich seafood dinner. Here, however, in the name of the theory of evolution, they are introduced as evidence: clues to the astonishing variability within a species. They confirm the thesis of evolution's politics of thrift. The crabs went through the same process as the bus that, robbed of its wheels and propped on a foundation of bricks, was turned into a comfortable dwelling in a Third World slum.

Only after comparing numerous individual observations, after the steady, patient work of learning by looking, did Darwin dare to leap to the boldest of his hypotheses. Without the force of biological iconography, he would hardly have been able to draw the far-reaching conclusions that still engage us today. The famous theory of evolution stands on a solid footing of manifest evidence from anatomy, geography, paleontology, and comparative physiology. Without such evidence, the genetic revolution could hardly have gotten off the ground. That is, if the thought of the eye had not made the scientist cold all over, the search for the genome would never have begun. Rarely has a scientific theory been of such consequence. As authoritative as it was popular, it provided the perfect ideology for an age defined by its faith in progress. And it soon led even further. Thanks to such groundwork, it is now possible to invest in nature. Biology has become a lucrative branch of industry, an incentive for researchers in the service of entrepreneurs. In Darwin's notebooks, there is a remark that still sounded ingenuous back then. Today, it can only be read ironically: "Hope is the expectant eye looking to distant object, brightened & moistened by emotion."

Certainly Darwin would never have gotten so far through observation alone. What was crucial was his criminalistic combinatorics, his synoptic gaze, which enabled his far-reaching interpretations. And yet the gift of observation is the prerequisite for productive comparisons. Only by fixating on the isolated, perhaps even invisible object can the hidden series be detected in the flurry of characteristics. The gaze delves into the exemplary, but it stops there only for as long as it takes to go on to the next, no, to the most distant example. Among so many local connections, the intentional approach stumbles onto the law of the series. In this respect, Darwin's eye functions precisely like the eye of the art connoisseur drawing conclusions about the style of an epoch from a handful of shards by seeing how the fragment reveals the image of the whole. Blind abstraction and a precipitate drive toward synthesis will never stumble onto the overall plan because they miss the lines of intersection in the tangle of branchings. What with all the trees, they always see only the forest.

Why should all this be brought up again? In order to gain some distance from the current state of the natural or *life* sciences, for those who prefer that term. It is important to highlight the difference, which is truly profound. The frequent talk of paradigm shifts implies that only the manner of presentation has changed, the narrative technique of the novel of *historia naturalis*. But what if presentation itself has been left by the wayside? What if the scientific spirit had at some point dispensed with the vexing task of visualization? In the processing of facts for teaching and for conference papers, what has been lost is the paradigmatic itself, in exchange for a mind-set that turns organisms into neutral material. Presentation and representation have been replaced by formalization. Mathematics and chemistry have infiltrated the essentially phenomenological field of biology. Increasingly complex models are needed to cope with the ineffable quality of the latest results. Ever since the biological sciences began to be armed with technology, intervention has replaced the study of matter. The organic is sequenced and quantified precisely as the anorganic has been for a long time, with familiar consequences for man and matter. Research *ad oculos* has become a prosthetic processing, a relentless illumination of mother nature's most intimate areas that no longer works without manipulation. Electronic probes, incubators, and cobalt guns have turned the microcosm into a combat zone. Reconnoitering was followed by a war of aggression, the experimental smashing of matter in the laboratory. Molecular biology and genetics now make clear what is meant by modern warfare. Largely invisible, witnessed only by a few specialists in protective gear, the battle of material has become a battle over matter. It is pointless to recall the natural scientist's shining eye. In the museum, one wanders through the peaceful exhibits and observes a minute of silence before going back out into today's scientific world war. At such times, it does one good to lose oneself one last time in Darwin's incorruptible eyes.

There, perfect plasticity and a mimetic gaze at nature are connected with a transparent style of exposition never again achieved. And here, today, the most extreme abstractions. Never-ending rows of formulas on billboards for experts where once upon a time the motley circus of species invited the entire family to attend the performance. A cartoon of molecules, tables, and op art instead of real flesh. Number curves where living beings once fascinated the eye with their I-am-what-I-am. Never before in the history of the natural sciences has the eye of the observer, at least that of the layman, been offered so little. Never before has there been such a range of creativity in the illustration of what can no longer be represented. Herein lies the paradox of the contemporary scientific establishment. The high cost of the expansion of knowledge, of advancing deep into the smallest cellular structures, goes hand in hand with the crisis of representation. The eye goes hungry at the feast of facts. The interested onlooker finds himself bored by the daily presentation of new insights into the blueprint of man and nature. It is better if he forgets what he saw in old atlases and full-color handbooks. The point is not that elegance has disappeared from the description of nature. Darwin himself was already far removed from the backwoods baroque of Linnaeus, that diligent biographer and registrar of nature, and was already looking back indulgently on Buffon's classical systematics born of feudal sensationalism. It was Darwin's methodological advantage that banished the epic zoology of the great Lamarck into the archives, reducing it to a bildungsroman born from the spirit of Encyclopedism. Darwin's theory of descent got the ball rolling. After him—the deluge he could hardly have predicted; after him—the march into the innermost parts of the cell, the expedition into the ghost world of chromosomes and genes.

There is a portrait of him painted in the next-to-last year of his life. This late date leaves no room for doubt: this picture is a farewell. Against a dark background, unbent, stands an old man, ready to turn around in the next moment, as if he were on the threshold to the underworld. He is wearing a brown cloak, as a pilgrim would, and holds a bowler hat in his left hand. The mighty patriarchal head with the snow-white beard makes it easy to recognize the typical nineteenth-century theory lion. It is such striking figures as this man whom the world has to thank for its greatest transformations. One sees the face of *sapientia*, a primordial landscape—the arched brow, furrowed by erudition, a countenance in which the farmer is crossed with the sea dog. Embedded in a bushel of wrinkles, the eyes: two lumps of coal in an opened mine. And it makes one cold all over to ponder all the things those eyes have seen. Most of those things will remain forever hidden to observers, whether because, unlike him, they were too indolent to try to circumnavigate the world themselves, or because most of the miracles he had the chance to see have vanished and many of the species he studied have long since died out. And not only on the Galápagos Islands.

MY BABYLONISH BRAIN

1

Poems? No, you are not presented with a subject, a style, a figurative language; as the voice tunnels its way, the first thing you are aware of is a brightness of the brain, the beaming idiosyncrasy of someone who can see things only one way, whom things look at only in a certain configuration. You encounter a severe, Socratic personal daemon—always monitory, never consoling, its presence only indicated by the stability (like breath) for which a voice struggled. Any act of writing can be traced back to the susceptibility of a stray individual, his symptoms always bursting forth, never mind how much they seek company in philosophy, political views, technical rules. Hardly ever as clearly as in a poem, the reader finds himself unexpectedly confronting the idiotic, the solitary prejudice (consequence often of defensive reflexes) with which a poet dives into his imaginary world. Irreducible, it is a picture puzzle of physiological origin, similar to nervous system, anatomy, and bone structure. Within it, speech is taken to its limits. Anecdotal moments from the life of the species as well as the individual are made palpably visible. The word is of physical origin. The only defense against the mindless language of day to day is the fully conscious word; it alone maintains the connection to the unrepeatable, to the ideography of primal perception. In a poem, the dread of an isolated being comes to the fore, trying with all its persuasiveness to make its way out.

There's a bass drum pulsing within that clothing store

Its beauty is derived from confusion, inadequacy, narrowness, sometimes rage, almost always nervously expressed sensual feeling, and culminates in a maximum of personality, wit, feeling, preference, and eccentricity—and all in the smallest possible space. Its emblem was once Baudelaire's green wig with the feather of ennui. Its ideal today—of which it must not know—is a memory machine, exact as an insect's eye, a machine for regaining time lived.

Writing begins as a sifting of initially unfocused states of consciousness through which the individual, slouching or on tiptoe, makes his way, without regard to causality or chronology. Writing doesn't care where its jumps take it, as long as it happily clutches the few crumbs its unknown consciousness leaves it. There are cracks in the illusion, the unreconciled, the irreconcilable, pushed into abrupt montage, but the meters, whatever they are, take time with them, postponed time, time for a Dantesque inspection of Hell, dialectically offered time, time in which palimpsests unroll, transhistorically running time.

I over π—that might be the first part of a formula that spits out lines of verse, with π as an arbitrary constant (temperament, behavior, inheritance, objects of desire . . .) and a biographical self that has lost all majesty, constantly questioning its own experiences. The overall effect was described some two thousand years ago by one Quintus Horatius Flaccus: "A poem is like a painting: there are some that fascinate you more as you approach them and some as you stand farther away; this one loves the dark, this other prefers to be examined by day and is not afraid of the judge's verdict; this one pleases once, but this one will still please when looked at ten times."

The poet, with his *none-to-all*, follows only his own will-o'-the-wisp, a strangeness in his own body that surprises and embarrasses him. Like a sudden physical tiredness at the sight of a clock, he is helpless to its promptings. At a random moment, when semantic ties are loosened, he begins to observe himself with interest. It's as though he were watching his own brain at work. His secret is the lesson that arrives in a split second at the base of his skull. Its deep effect cuts him off from all other speech, which is just a tide of banality, instantly forgettable. Its way of speaking to him is like a suggestion under anesthetic, the providential idea in a tight spot, the insistent murmur of a nurse trying to keep a shock victim from losing consciousness and throwing in his life.

Gaining access to the deeper areas of the brain, notation in the form of unique engrams—these are his goals; and this is why the poetics of the future is contained in neurology. In his quest for memory traces, the poet subordinates all other concerns to the obsessive notion that the whole purpose of his existence consists in joining the continuum of condensed images—herein lies the incurable mania of his pursuit. A line of Callimachus of Cyrene is as present to him as the postman's ring at the door. His girlfriend's words are audible as literary echoes, though he has learned to be careful not to say as much. He listens to the tangle of voices of many ages, the quotations and speech bits of the present, until the most striking of them are caught up in the deepest whorls of his hearing . . . until a line, a code word finally comes along and beckons: OK, follow me.

2

Shall I speak of the great quivering diaphragm, of the elusive, presumably physiological power that keeps writing together over time? It's astonishing how scenes, phrases, lines reconfigure themselves—as if their nerve endings were still alive. Perhaps the best poems, the most enigmatic compositions are written against overstimulation, as a way for memory to draw breath under the barrage of sense impressions. In its effort to oppose the mere passage of time, to pause in the wastes of information, in the "temporal fire" of which Dante spoke, memory's best ally is the red thread of the disject line, metrically scanned. From the very beginning, poetry was a function of memory, and it is its prosodic character that creates the link between the individual voice coming out of a mortal body and the narratives of the species standing over the waters and moving through cities and landscapes. In the pacing of thought and recollection, lyrical speech generates a present beyond death and this side of chronological time. It would appear that in terms of mnemonics no other mode of utterance is so adapted to human eccentricity and the associative breadth of experience. This is poetry in its anthropological dimension, which it has perhaps taken us until now to see—at the point of synthesis of various forms of thought and after the departure of metaphysics. The poetic word (which had its roots in song) is host to the oldest feeling and the newest idea, the primordial instinct and the latest subject—all fused together in an act of lightning-like imagination. Its magical secret is the immediacy, the physical presence of a speaker ever on the move, or long dead. In the variety of rhythms, in the shuffle of images, the imagination of one individual is synchronized with the world perception of all—as long as such things are handed on. Whatever guise the words adopt, from hexameter epic to chatty free verse, the decisive factor is the energetic relation between poetry and memory. Beyond the details of a given human life, and transcending all styles and ideals, the poetic word keeps intact a connection to the floor of memory, to civilizations gone under, to the all-present dead. Where else do moments of déjà vu come from, those innate or inherent symbols and tropes that make any sort of anthropological view possible in the first place? The same heart hears the love lament of ancient Egypt, the farewell song of the troubadour, and the teeth-gritted sonnet of the flaneur out at night in the big city. It took the emphasis of poetry to salvage something memorable from the wash of noise, the life-accompanying singsong of feeling and insight, and to condense it to gravel . . . a handful of words, rinsed in the waters of time.

Or was it by chance that (according to a legend that Cicero repeats in his essay on oratory) a poet is cited as the inventor of the art of memory? His name is Simonides of Ceos. At a party in the house of the Thessalian nobleman Skopas, he is supposed to have been the only survivor, when, following a recital of poetry, the ceiling of the room caved in and killed everyone. Divine providence or the call of nature (a full bladder, one assumes) had prompted him to go outside for a moment. When he returned, all the other guests were buried in the rubble, their bodies disfigured beyond recognition. No one could identify the victims, no one but the poet. By remembering the exact seating plan, he helped the relatives to find their dead. Surprised by his own gift, of which he had been unaware, he is then said to have invented a method capable of ordering memory at any time. His trick, an early consciousness technique, consisted in putting each remembered impression in a particular place, arranging a plethora of impressions in space, in a pattern that might easily serve as a blueprint for all subsequent poetry. The parable could hardly be better chosen: the surviving witness, he had shown the mourners the way; the epigrammatist and elegist had found the key to memory, indispensable basis of any obituary. He was one of the earliest named characters in antiquity, suggestive and practical, a wanderer between the inner and outer worlds. If the anecdote is true, his mnemonics was owed to an accident, a shock. Poetry was for him, as Plutarch wrote, a speaking picture, painting was silent poetry.

And once again we hear Horace murmur at the end of his life as a poet . . . *ut pictura poesis.*

But what were the pictures that etched themselves most

deeply, what scenes were forceful enough to gain access to the unconscious? Because this much is clear: that that's the place where they have clung on for hundreds of years—since fragments of poetry have become part and parcel of the symbolic imaginations of generations. Were they not always the boldest, the most unlikely, in terms of comedy or grandeur, ugliness or menace: pictures of sudden beauty and devastation, whose abruptness stirred the collective unconscious the most? Were they not the only ones to penetrate so deeply, where fear reigns, where insight emerges from thickets of murky sensation, where dream and consolation meet in a clearing? Of course, there are other things than condensed verbal pictures that reach their destination quickly, jokes, for example, or the forcefulness of slang. But the thing about these is that they reach their goal so quickly that they curtail the curiosity, the desire that an image in a line of poetry can stir. This desire can grow with each subsequent line, for the poem, which doesn't yet know its own subject, will imitate the way poetry took the very first time, not until the end will it become apparent where it was going . . . and even then it can remain unclear through which landscape it was passing, and whom its hypnotic speech had in mind. Hence, perhaps, the greatest of the many fears associated with poetry: that randomness and chaos will become song, triumph over day-to-day logic and causality, and reach the hearing uncontaminated by will or design, as pure imagination. Rejection—from the illiterate reflexes of the majority to the intellectual peevishness of the specialist—is reserved for the sirenlike qualities of poetry, its synesthetic appetites that will never satisfy the hunger for bulk reality. It is taken amiss because its radio signals are decoded only in the listener; because in an ideal case, they reach several receptor zones at once, because its appeal is to all the senses, and yet, seen from outside, remains no more than that: an appeal, less than a finger pointing, barely a gesture. Because the word, this most shopworn of all ingredients of art, is just a pretext: behind it stands the psychic act, calling with all semantic cunning for transformation. It's as in prayer: no one holds the message in his hands, no one has ever seen the addressee of his most fervent prayers, nor does he know for sure that he even exists. But, unlike prayer, which may bring momentary relief, in the poem the word falls back to the speaker and leaves him alone with his doubtful exaltation. First and foremost, wherever it's been, poetry is always where you meet yourself. As in front of a mirror, the word unleashes its magic—and the hope that it might be blind causes it to tremble slightly in all its connections. What summons it to life is the voice—the voice awakens the word from its sleep in the dictionary, paradoxically, by enchanting it. Here it provokes thought, there it passes as a whir of sonority, a moment ago it was fleeting, and now it stops dreamily and looks about itself in a world opposed to multiple meanings. "The word is Psyche" was Mandelstam's universal account of poetic language, and one can add that the great divide is between those who love language for its own sake and those who use it only as a tool. The source of the poet's shame is that he, too, is often compelled to *use* it: in fact, it's only envy that drives him to explain himself, the fear of the troubadour that he won't be listened to that makes the doubter a pedant.

Images, words, tone, and meter—these, as far as possibly reduced and isolated, are the elements. With their help the poem penetrates the nethermost spaces of memory, becomes a chunk of embodied time, visible, almost palpable, almost a thing itself, able to enter into combinations with other things in various ages. Isn't it strange that so many ancient fragments of poetry, for instance the few surviving lines of Sappho, exist in the form of shards of pottery, the so-called Ostraka? For this is basically what each poem is: shards, fragments of an earlier memory. However comprehensive it appears to be, it always needs to be supplemented. It is fatuity itself in action, the impossible clarion call for all-around communication. In front of us lies a splinter of concrete consciousness from a life we will never live—someone else has already lived it—unrepeatable, light-years away in its uniqueness, and probably even the window we peer through to see it now is a deception. Doesn't the whole thing resemble the absurd and yet diligently professional attempt to get in touch with extraterrestrial life-forms in some other solar system?

But even that is too picayune a notion and says too little about the true dilemma of a poem: (a) to strike words from the innermost labyrinths that will look like something even when seen by the light of day, (b) to make a maximum expression with a minimum of signage, (c) to convert thought into sensual contemplation and vice versa. For all of that the poem can offer only one movement: the rotation on its own axis.

What comes to its aid is time, provided, that is, that its meandering course encounters sufficient resistance on its way to oblivion. Such aids include structural elements, the back-and-forth of syllables, para-rhyme, syncopations, all sorts of pauses and caesuras, but also verbal relations, like the one that sorts cat and mouse together, or dog and moon, but never cat and moon. By its way of imposing hindrances in its chronological unspooling, whether through metrical barriers or semantic distances, the poem safeguards its own duration as much in the memory of those born later as in the unique experience stock of its contemporary reader. A poem's resistance to time is determined by how resolutely it opposes conventional reality (of physics, logic, the phenomenal world). It can have many strategies, from the imperfect analogy to the confusion of linguistic hierarchies, from the slight giddiness of arrhythmia and the mutual contamination of images to the violent yoking together of dissimilar things, to a temperature drop (in feeling or mood), or, as language is inseparable from the governing ethics, to the violation of a taboo. Isn't it true that the greater part of poetry lives from impossible correspondences anyhow? To the Metaphysical poets, no metaphor was too far-fetched, anything could be compared to anything else, even one's own self was likened to the sun. For Shakespeare, the greatest political poet of all time, the juxtaposition of diadem and dead dog was the poetic hook for his blank verse. For a poet like Mandelstam, a lyric evolutionist, it was the backward jump from propeller to tapir bone; poetry was a zoological singsong that helped keep a man warm in the cosmic chill. For Rilke it was sheen, rhyme, and surface music: death could discreetly be reflected in a shako, a gleam of war. For others, idiosyncratic avant-gardists, it was the encounter of sewing machine and umbrella on the dissecting table, a rebus as redundant as the whole of surrealism. Only a few—stylish swordsmen like Dante—saw the simile as an *image juste* emerging spontaneously, and as if on its own, from the dynamic of events; only a few caught the thought as it emerged, preserved the image *in statu nascendi*.

At the outset, nothing in us knows what the poem has in store. Not until the appearance of the poetic subject can the balance be reckoned between Alpha and Omega, between the *here* of the specific impulse and the *everywhere* of understanding communion. Arising out of the murmuring, it creates the connection to that unlocalizable, infinitely extended memory beyond biography and geography.

As long as it's on its way to you, for the duration of a quatrain, or an elegy, or ode, or satire . . . it crosses all other languages, which is what makes it cosmopolitan and gives it a position in historical space. Whatever it produces, a sigh, a physical agitation, an epiphany, or an abrupt projection of a scene, a concentrate of the physical world—until the very end there is a sense of the how incorporating the why. It lulls you, then, even as it concentrates thought and returns to each word its semantic primogeniture. It hushes the outside world, the domination of the present, by sensitizing you to another, kaleidoscopic present, as if in earnest of a profounder sense of life (from birth trauma to fear of dying), so that only the intense is actual and reality becomes a somatic category.

The poem can as well capture the instant when you pee all over your shoe as some abrupt consciousness of loss or delight on arriving in some Arcadia. The actual subject hardly matters, what matters is the expression of a certain insight, the penetration to a dimension where thinking and feeling happen, a *salto mortale* into the unsaid. It can happen casually, with the facility of a musical child, still unclouded by age and death, or with grim deliberateness, like a gambler reckoning up his failure in one last handful of verbal tokens.

The most important thing about the poetic process seems to me never under any circumstances to allow the word to slip out of its basic tension, its existential and intelligible bipolarity. Too soon attention moves on, too great the danger that poetry goes the way of all intellectual artifacts, via decadence, the vocal residue, into oblivion. Its current locus is the periphery, kept warm for it by its predecessors, rhetoric and theology. Throughout the Middle Ages, rumors and messengers did duty for journalism; today it's the press that makes the news. Once, centuries revolved around an epic, and whole dynasties assembled for an aubade, while modern wars are more and more frequently started at the behest of an illiterate for the sake of a few paper principles. That a line can manage to escape from Siberian detention, or a hermetic cycle from barbarism and the decline and disappearance of whole nations, is as good as the news can ever get. But it's been quite some time since a poem on the twilight of city life could become a guide to civilization.

Now, at the end of the twentieth century, it's perhaps time to adapt Baudelaire's phrase, the "Babylonish heart": the new

passionless arena, a place of chillier pleasures, is the Babylonish brain. As in an archive, collapsing under the weight of
its murderous protocols, its documents of criminal inhuman-
ity, it is full of old lines . . . elegy and psalm and diatribe, a
heap of loose leaves blown up by a wind. The basement of an
auction house full of precious manuscripts, it's threatened by
a catastrophic flood. No image is in its rightful place: laconism,
black humor, or the averted gaze of melancholy can still find
those scraps that once made up the stock of worldly wisdom.
But already there are signs of a new chemistry, a new tonality
that places the fragments (tradition) and fractals (the recently
absorbed) in a new conversation. Doesn't the effect of poetry
in large part depend on gaps in our memory? The bigger they
are, whether in a society of censored speech or one of information overload, the more work there is for each individual
poem—without its author, of course, needing to know. On the
one hand, as in the case of Simonides, poetry is a process of
reconstruction, on the other it's a less morbid form of confab-
ulation. Its technique is always that of bridging speech, a form
of false memory . . . albeit with the intention of piercing each
false continuum in its wandering through collective memory.
Under certain circumstances—why not?—a single word can
stand in for half a life, or the ejaculation of a Greek poet can
find itself centuries later in the form of an open question. Of
course, poetry is a form of unsolicited intimacy, not entirely
dissimilar to a schizophrenic patient picking up the thread—
as himself or as someone else—where he lost it the day before
yesterday, or else in 1207. Quite possibly this is one reason for
the suspicion of poetry on the part of the so-called healthy
majority that looks askance at abnormality and keeps a close
watch on the preservation of the more external connections.

The fact is that it never completely broke off its conversation with the world, not even in its most hermetic and idealistic periods. The fact is that the poem owes its existence to the

particular conformation of the human brain, which specializes in manufacturing the most connections in a tiny space. Perhaps its inclination to silence following the recent crimes was nothing but a reaction to the semantic freight become unendurable—at a moment of barbaric simplification, read: the dereliction of politics and economy. It has never gotten over the damage of the last world war and those breaches in civilization that were perpetrated in its shadow. And yet the poem, like the injured brain, is capable of regeneration, replacing lost expressive particles with others, crossing different functions (language, say), sloughing or sealing off dead areas.

It is true in general that poetry is one of the most cerebral of the arts. But it also reacts most sensitively to each climatic change in the thought-furrowed world. The measurements that it applies to each phenomenon are more subtle, the synesthesias of its rainbows more sensitive—perhaps they are in fact the only rainbows. It is more immediately associated with all landscape: through air roots reaching into the contrails of all flora and fauna, all speech, views, and taxonomies of the living and the dead. The different disciplines approach one another more nearly in poetry: the retina touches the speech centers, the acoustic nerve grazes the centers for movement and rhythm, and everything together roots as over a limbic weave in precognitive animal zones, closer to fear, pleasure, and aggression. And every so often it looks out *mit grossem Tierblick*—with a grand animal gaze . . . Its wealth of gesture is extraordinary, the choreography of its figures endless. Long before the invention of the computer and "neuro-romance" it was at home in the virtual—only that from the breadths of its lexical spaces, every fish scale, every hair, every grain of sand is always returned to its store untouched.

The Babylonish brain, the basic equipment of the poet today, prowls through the vistas of the city as through an art gallery. Telescopically it takes in the stars or a bit of wall in ancient Rome. As the beehive lives from the humming of its flight attendants, so it lives from the rustling of hyperbole, takes refuge behind the discretion of metaphors and allusions, ferries its phantasms like a dream of logophilia.

The poetic text is the protocol of an inner gazing.

Its method is determined by the body. Behind the semantic organization there is always an anatomical one; under the layers that hermeneutics churns, the living cells come to the surface, the substance that has made up lines since the first poetical gropings. A poem trots out thought in a sequence of physiological short circuits. Always en route through time (that of its own body, but just as much history, or the species), thought finds in a poem a place to rest, an abode among the windy speeches and pathetic views, a site for the signs and images that make up life.

TO LORD CHANDOS:
A FAX FROM THE FUTURE

This incomprehensible interior, the domain of the poets,
That physics chose to ignore until yesterday—
It has finally revealed itself, under the barrage of photons.
The soul, what is that? A state of oscillation, nothing more.
A neuronal storm, Leonardo saw it coming.
A maelstrom devouring all that is seen and all that is thought.
Alone with all the hostile words, empty to the core,
The poet stands, like a speechless child before his class.
Goethe is dead, Hölderlin. We should be writing essays
On the killing of forests in the name of printed paper.
The libraries grow, the metastases, all the registers
Of viruses, particles of matter, of stocks and humankind's
        falls,
While shade is gradually disappearing. Soon the sun will beat
        down
Unobstructed from its zenith, God's annihilating eye.

No wonder someone broke down one day
Under the weight of the search for expression.
                        "The self and its brain"—
Two authorities wrestling for the upper hand, this was too
        much
For a single human being, that self-estranged animal.
"For me everything disintegrated into parts, those parts into
        further parts,

And no longer would anything let itself be encompassed by
    one idea."

My dear Chandos, I will tell you what has since come to
    pass.
Much more than words, crumbling in the mouth like moldy
    fungi—
Entre nous, mycologists, mythologists, my friend:
It's not about Plato, Cicero, Seneca, or Crassus.
The busts long since in ruins, shards all that's left.
It's not about rats, poisoned, squealing in agony.
It's about humans, surrounded by their own kind.
In every hole in the wall, history is smoldering. Highly
    contagious,
Contaminated by ideas, by interests, the air we breathe.
The black spot beneath the nail is teeming with bacteria.

As for fungi—we are being constricted by rhizomes,
Down to our very roots, the innermost parts of our cells, the
    recesses of the brain.
And no mother there to welcome him, the prodigal son.
Fortunate Chandos, you don't know how much you have
    been spared,
What will to destruction and organized ignominy.
The cold poisoners of wells, the murderers in a storm of
    flashbulbs,
The hysteria of entire peoples, the evil in a handful of dust.
And all the leaps of the hearts, of chords out into space.
Mozart's arias, Kant's *Judgment*, the visions of Rousseau.

Let's keep our cool, Milord. Today, everyone's body is made
    up
Of ciphers that connect everything with everything. The new
    flesh

Lives, freed from nature, a life encoded through and through.
　　Your letter
Is sweet rhetoric to us, a dialogue among the dead, a
　　consolation.
Our descendants, extraterrestrials, will read it differently
　　from us.

Q AS IN *QUOTATION*

Every writer knows the moment: one day, he feels as though his solitary existence is a predicament he can escape only by leaping headfirst into quotation. Hardly any writer will be able to remember when this first happened. What's left is but the sensation of the moment itself, the stubborn fretting and hesitation preceding the decision to open one's writing, the text dictated by one's self-determination, to something foreign that insisted on being admitted by way of quotation. The sense of liberation that went hand in hand with this experience was accompanied by the certainty of great danger—the suspicion of self-surrender, the fear of semantic capitulation. A warning voice whispered: the rift you are admitting will always keep you riven. Once the first quotation has penetrated, you are no longer your own master. From now on, another voice, a thinking significantly different from yours, will cast a shadow, making everything you've written so far as well as everything you will have to say in the future appear in a different light. Quotations are caesuras in monologue, visible to all. Like cutting one's own flesh, they mark an intrusion into what is most sacred, into the closed world of subjective expression. As soon as they appear, the reader will see you only as surrounded by alien prompters, as a riven individual trapped in perilous coexistence. *Anxiety of influence* is the term used by a psychoanalytically schooled literary theory to characterize the problem. A tacit presupposition in the natural sciences and the humanities, it is considered a flaw in the arts. He who quotes capitulates. In the infinite language game, he takes the part of the beloved who submits to the lover to be penetrated. This is even true if the quotation serves as an argument in one's own defense, if its purpose is self-affirmation or even just a demonstration of civility in communication. Never can the impression of borrowed authority be shaken. Someone with a strong character will be most likely to quote the words of an unknown. He enriches himself by tacitly drawing on the intimate details of the private sphere. Everything that has ever been published is taboo to him.

Paradoxically, every quotation marks a gap in the universe of one's own expressivity, which it fills, nestling into it by way of a difference from the rest of the text. Techniques of quotation may be as diverse as motives for it are varied, but this rift in the consciousness of the one quoting always remains. The reader will never forget how the author performed a kowtow here. Whether it was motivated by lack of evidence, plain honesty, or the sense of an elective affinity with another poet, or whether it was dictated by the constraints of logical consistency—what is always striking is the very fact of submission itself.

But what is quotation? The dictionary defines it as a passage rendered word-for-word for the purposes of confirmation or evidence, and—it should be added—clearly distinguished from the rest of the text. Thus, quotation is an enclosed foreign body, akin to the mosquito or the fern leaf in amber. In everyday speech, quotation takes the form of winged words, proverbs, and witticisms by famous personalities. They are the daily bread of the scholar, for whom the meaning of the Latin *citatio* is most fully preserved: it originated in jurisprudence as a technical term for being summoned to court. Like ancient Roman judges, who would summon witnesses and defendants, scholars across the disciplines are still wont to summon words today. The prophets, the Christian authors of the Bible beat them to it: together with their subsequent interpreters, the church fathers and theologians, they have been credited with the initial attempt to create a meta-text entirely from quotation, a canon that humanity would be able to rely on by way of tradition. In every culture, the gold reserve of all quotation is constituted by what we typically refer to in the sublime terms of religion as revelation, which is supposed to guarantee the value of any other semantic currency that may be in circulation. Religions, then, are treasuries of quotations. Their holy books record, across the generations, the defining features of the languages spoken and written by all those who became literate in their names. As a rule, mother tongue and religious tradition are so interwoven that most quotations can no longer be recognized as quotations. Again and again, they are smuggled, as it were, into every individual consciousness. They creep into what you say before you even think of them. You can no more avoid them than jump out of your own skin.

But does quotation really merely testify to coercion, to an authority ruling over the speaker's unconscious? Not only would it be absurd to view quotation merely as proof of failure on the part of the person using it, but it would also be completely undialectical to read it exclusively as the work of the author's Other, and not also as a sign of his sense of filiation and capacity for empathy. A free spirit can never be blackmailed. Rather, he reaffirms his sovereignty by conjuring other free spirits—read: peers—in quoting them. He summons them to attend a meeting, or hearing, at which he happens to be the stenographer. As long as he remains in control, quotation doesn't impoverish him; on the contrary, it only enriches him—wholly in keeping with the Communist credo of a Karl Marx, who measured a person's wealth by the variety of his relationships with other people. Thus, quotation can be considered the measure of an individual's willingness to open his internal universe of meaning to dialogue. All the footnotes in a book are the marks of an author's ability to participate in dialogue. Quotation opens up an in-between space for encounters. It signifies the barter underlying all thinking. Freedom is conceivable only as the result of a movement from *I* to *you*. In terms of physics, it is the distance between two bodies that respect each other's positions; in terms of metaphysics, however, it is the mutual rapprochement of two psyches, joined through the vibrational field of the space that separates *and* unites them as their common ground. Given the double-edged character of logic and given that every truth is born of opposition, a shared sphere of circulation is requisite—in philosophy as much as in art and poetry—without which thinking would come to a standstill. In the infinite realm of ideas, autarchy is not only the lie that everyone sees through but also the illusion that exposes itself. Nowhere can the in-between space that allows identities to circulate in dialogue be seen as clearly as in quotation.

All of the above could hardly be more vividly demonstrated than through quotation. Let us call the poet Osip Mandelstam to the witness stand. To him we owe the insight that erudition is not at all the same thing as the fingerboard of allusions that is the true essence of culture. In "Conversation on Dante," an essay that is itself dialogue through and through, the protocol of a poet's "orbiting" a lifelong interlocutor from the distant past, Mandelstam writes: "A quotation is not an excerpt. Quotations are cicadas." They chirp and chirp . . .

ON THE QUESTION OF STYLE

Does thought make style, or is it actually style that has thought line up for it, in the manner of the hypercorrect ballet teacher and her pupils? It's not as easy as it may seem to translate this problem into the familiar schematism of form and content, content and form. Language itself keeps its participants believing in the not-at-all mythical notion that anyone who has mastered its rules may use it with equal rights. Learning the ABCs fulfills, ever anew, the promise of coevality contained in the vocabulary, grammar, and syntax of each individual language and already intuited in childhood. The variety of modes of expression is not only each language's life insurance, but it also guarantees that it will not, one day, fall apart as a result of the petty hegemonic games of the literate. On the hither side of its myth of origin, something cleaving to indivisibility survives within language. And it's not because those primal words that a poet's offended sensibility mumbles about really exist that every statement is bound to remain ambiguous at best, but, rather, because everyone is as close to and as distant from the dictionary's revelations as everyone else. Speaking means throwing oneself into a maelstrom of unpredictable twists and turns. Thinking and articulating come from one and the same source. What remains undecided is how exactly they condition each other in speech and in writing.

And so it came to pass that one day philosophy—being

dissatisfied with this kind of indifference inherent within language—seized the day and decided the matter in its own favor. The price of this coup was nothing less than the disenfranchisement of poetry. As a result of thousands of years of habituation to this unlawful usurpation of language for the purposes of prioritizing truth, style and thought seem completely distinct today. Philosophers are people who believe that thinking means disciplining rather than manipulating the will to expression. As if the aesthetic were merely of secondary importance here, as if the form of expression were slavishly beholden to the supreme rule of cognition. But, fortunately for us all, the aesthetic did get its revenge in the form of philosophy's dearth of imaginative concreteness. Nobody should think that what happened back then in Greece—the usurpation of language by philosophy and its betrayal of poetry—went unnoticed. There have been plenty of alerts both among the dispossessed and among the philosophers themselves warning us about the consequences of this arrogance. Anyone can look up where and how the tyranny began. If it's any consolation, poetry and philosophy have remained chained to each other to this day as a result of the primordial sin of their falling out. Even rudimentary knowledge of Greek suffices to preserve the memory of philosophy's coup—as if it had just happened. Language itself, in its genealogical stubbornness, attests to it: pre-Socratic thought took its first steps on the foundation of the oldest verse epic; it owed its existence to the vanguard of poetic speech. Heraclitus' and Parmenides' mental flights were preceded by Homer's and Hesiod's work as surveyors. Every new attempt to make us forget this is kept in check by our shared poetic memory. The realization that philosophy's emancipation from its origins in poetry had remained an empty promise—notwithstanding its frequent proclamation—compelled twentieth-century philosophers to make certain revisions. The best among them, the intellectually most agile ones, all came under the spell of art again—the dialectician Adorno is a case in point. They tried to repair the damage done to poetry by their ancestors by trying to obtain an exclusive lease on the language that belongs to all, in the manner of those oligarchs who wished to claim state and society for themselves. Their punishment consisted in succumbing to the treacherous supremacy of style. It's no accident that the renegade Adorno's philosophical testament begins with an encomium on Marcel Proust. He is the patron saint of Adorno's *Minima Moralia*. Most of its pieces are secretly dedicated to him.

THE POEM AND ITS SECRET

1

Asking about the purpose of poems and of poetry in general will not get us very far for the simple reason that each of us will define this purpose differently. That's how it is and that's how it's been ever since what is at issue here—what we call lyric poetry—became conscious of itself as a key constituent of the very notion of the modern in art in general. Since then, every answer to the unwieldy question of the purpose of poetry has disintegrated into a myriad of individual voices. No two poets would have committed themselves on this point, let alone shared the same position. A healthy skepticism is one of the natural laws of this profession. It is the invisible mark of recognition on every poet's brow. Any explanations poets may give about what they do primarily serve the preservation of a secret. Vague as this secret may be, all poets, in their own individual ways, will hold on to it and barricade themselves behind it.

This has been a purely protective measure ever since a certain Plato tried to uncover it. In his dialogue *Ion*, his stand-in and alter ego, Socrates, is teamed up with an artist who makes a living as a rhapsode. Through his subtle method of interrogation, masquerading as naïveté, Socrates aims at exposing Ion, a doughty interpreter of Homer, as a fraud and witless parrot. The point is to discredit not just this particular rhapsode but, along with him, all other poets as well. What

Plato comes up with is a kind of APB. On one hand, the poet is cast as a con man, who in his epics and hymns, his odes and dithyrambs pretends to possess expert knowledge he cannot possibly have. The poet doesn't think, he only receives what the god whispers into his ear. On the other hand, the poet reveals himself as a mere dreamer and airhead, a man possessed, a creature consisting of nothing but antennae and nerves. If you know one, you know them all. As Socrates says: "The poet is a light and winged and holy thing, and there is no invention in him until he has been inspired and is out of his senses, and the mind is no longer in him."

As much truth as there may be to it, the philosopher's description boils down to one aim: disenfranchising the poet. Even apart from the contradiction embedded in the supposition that one can be enlightened and completely clueless at the same time, this description lacks the most basic coherence. How does being inspired, a mouthpiece and medium of the gods, go together with having no professional expertise (*technē*, writes Plato), being ignorant in every respect, an eternal dilettante? Such is Homer, the argument goes, when he dictates the formula for a healing potion without being a doctor, when he describes a chariot race without ever holding the reins in his own hands. In light of such reasoning, one cannot but wonder how Aristotle, himself a philosopher and not a poet, could have felt justified in writing a treatise on poetics? Wasn't philosophy, as an abstract doctrine of ideas, more than anything untainted by the empirical? That jealousy was the real issue here is suggested by another dialogue. In the *Phaidon*, the very same Socrates prides himself on his privileged access to the Muses. There, unexpectedly, he explicitly claims the mystery of supernatural inspiration for himself. The intention is utterly transparent. Once the favorite of the gods, the poet is downgraded to a mere juggler of words devoid of sense and reason; the philosopher, by contrast, will from now on be the gods' true correspondent. The aftermath is well known, even though everyone realized that philosophy was originally a mere waste product of the great narratives that had been around long before it, handed down orally by rhapsodes like Ion, and that already possessed knowledge about almost anything. In these narratives' shadow, on the margins of the heroic epics and myths of origin, philosophy prospered in the guise of arabesque and commentary until one day it rose up in the form of proverbial wisdom and blossomed into a wild sunflower in the mysterious and oracular speeches of the pre-Socratics.

The fragments of Parmenides, for example, are still marked by their origin. Their hexameter form attests to their proximity to the rule of imagery and song, they begin with an invocation of the Muses, who inspire all knowledge. The prose fragments of Heraclitus, by contrast, already speak a different language: the language of conscious ambiguity, of mystery even, of relinquishing lexical strictures—the first precondition for all semantic hegemonies to come.

What happened? Nothing less than a complete usurpation. In essence, all philosophizing began harmlessly enough as clever textual analysis and interpretation. Soon, however, such hermeneutics gave rise to the theft of the message by its own messenger—in this case, Hermes, the nimble courier god who becomes the philosophers' patron saint by defrauding the poets of the fruits of their labor. It had to happen this way: "The Greater is namely knowledge," as Parmenides, with such traitorous iridescence, expresses it. And thus the history of a conflict takes its course, one that still has consequences today. It begins with the dispossession of poetry and ends with her complete disenfranchisement. After publicly questioning the ancestral authority of storytelling, it was but a stone's throw to Plato's perfidious suggestion that the poets themselves, this coterie of liars and illusionists, be banished from the city. The wordsmiths turned into washouts. A few thousand years of habit and discipline helped to repress the memory of this act of violence. The beautiful and the sublime had been subordinated to the rule of ideas once and for all.

For over two thousand years now, every poet's biography has witnessed to the success of this coup. The poets have come to terms with their stigma, with their status as exiles within society. They've had to learn to disown themselves, to camouflage their true intentions. What they call poetics—from Callimachus and Horace all the way to Cavafy, Eliot, and Rilke—is a game of hide-and-seek: defensive, cryptic, and clandestine through and through. Do not be blinded by such occasional counteroffensives as Friedrich Schiller's project of an "aesthetic education" of mankind, Hölderlin's philosophical hymns, or Novalis's ingenious *Pollen* reveries—ever since its early humiliation in classical Greece, poetry has seen itself demoted to a mere pastime. It was an art for art's sake long before it defiantly libeled itself as *l'art pour l'art*.

No sooner did he look beyond the confines of his craft than the typical poet—think of Lessing or Herder—was immediately confronted with the strictures of his genre, with questions of style and form, his own critic, more subaltern than modest, abstaining from any sense-bestowing intention. Out of their snail shells, however, most of them were eying transcendence. Their secret comfort was that, owing to the silent wings of words, their souls maintained a connection to the distant past and to posterity. Ensconced in the hideouts of their writings, they knew, like the members of a secret society, that their verses were what would outlast brass, the walls of Troy, and Rome's palaces. They required no more than a single aphorism to be able to shrug off the burden of their existence as a tiny minority in the diaspora of a shared mother tongue. And this is the situation: while the philosophers are happily immersed in their games of truth, paying utmost attention to one another, the poet stands to the side, left to his own devices. Each poet cultivates his own orchids. None of the all-powerful epistemologists since Plato's day has ever taken him completely seriously.

2

After being chased from the philosophers' banquets and excluded from the grown-ups' conversations and symposia, what could the poets do but rely on themselves for guidance? If they wanted to preserve their dignity, they had to renew their contract with the gods. And this is precisely what they did, inwardly and secretly. They did it by entrusting their most sacred possession, their psyches, to the gods. In order to be able to remain undisturbed and among their own kind they would pretend to be mad and deranged in public, infantile or autistic, according to their whims. Outwardly, they would alternate between sentimentality and naïveté, while appealing to their patron saint, Orpheus, who had long been dismembered, his body mutilated, his mortal remains scattered to the four winds. They tried to play for time; they all turned to what they did best. One wrote epigrams cursing his fellow men, another wrote elegies decrying his solitude here on earth, a third competed as a tragedian at the annual theater festival and afterward vented his anger at the wayward audience in malicious satires. One polished his tender, bucolic verses for so long he ended up inventing his own meter. One wrote noble hymns to the winners at the Olympic games because athletic male bodies filled his nights with wet dreams. And yet another worked off his desire for the obscene in bawdy comedies. Thus were the meters created—asclepiad, sapphic, alcaic, amphibrach, iambus, trochee, anapest. Thus did the genres emerge, competing with one another whenever they could.

From today's perspective, the advantage of the poets' newly won autonomy can be clearly discerned. What has since fallen under the rubric of classical literature owes its good reputation primarily to one characteristic. It could be called the primary quality of all true poetry and literature, its cardinal virtue. It is what keeps it alive across the ages: its vividness. If Hegel is right in claiming that the true philosopher has only one fundamental idea that he returns to over and over again, then the power of imagination, the twin gifts of vividness and plasticity, were the poet's levers for perpetually unhinging this one idea. His voracious eye and sheer rhetorical mastery were no match for a rationality that was, at best, capable of processing reality one phenomenon at a time. Philosophy could only theorize about the imagination. Its practitioners were virtually clueless as to its uses and abuses. Immanuel Kant, distrustful of his own guild, must be given credit for being the first to acknowledge this central lacuna in his *Critique of Judgment*. Respectfully, he cordons it off and pronounces it impregnable territory under the head of the "autonomy of art."

What artist, what poet, would not be obliged to thank him for that? Disenfranchised, but not disenchanted: What more can they ask for after their long odyssey, always on the dark side of history? Small wonder if over the centuries they have fortified their autonomy into a kind of fortress, a barely accessible network of catacombs. They themselves don't really know what's hidden in those labyrinths behind those walls. Perhaps what lives and breathes down there, subterraneously, is now only the specter of their former sovereignty. Every poet avers that he has seen it once with his own eyes. Certainly something is stirring down there. Every once in a while, in a poem, you can hear it keeping time beneath the cranium. Something diffusely mysterious, never wholly explicable, the remnant of an old family secret, jealously guarded by every neophyte who joins the secret society and goes down again into this inner labyrinth. It is surely the main reason why poems are still being written even today, in the face of slight and resistance, in an age of universal knowledgeability. Their elusiveness is the true cause for poetry's survival.

3

I may have shed new light on the conditions in which the art of poetry is created, but I'm still not a bit wiser as far as its radioactive core, its magical powers are concerned. It's one thing to understand its mental prerequisites, however we may choose to describe them, in archaic terms as *genius*, or in the terms of modern neurophysics. It's another thing to understand how these conditions bring forth an art whose entire purpose it is to set off fireworks in the reader's psyche. It seems to me after decades of practice that the truth of the matter continues to elude us, being shrouded in a sort of twilight. So long as a phenomenon cannot wholly be explained, however, it's only fair and just—for both expert and layman— to continue speculating about its secret.

No matter how different, how diverse in style and texture poems happen to be, the good ones stand out on account of a certain shared je ne sais quoi that can never be entirely unraveled. A poem may mesmerize us through special wordplay, the magic of punning, or the sleight of hand of technique and performance, it may captivate us as a congeries of peculiar oneiric fantasies and seduce us by conjuring a tableau of exotic creatures of the imagination—all this, however, says little about the surplus value of its mysteriousness. However one may define poems, and even if one sees them, as I do, first and foremost as musical scores that stimulate us into experiencing our psychic limits, their secret remains their secret remains their secret . . . and so on. And when stuttering is all that's left, humility is the only way out. And so I say to myself and admit it: all this talk about the secret of poems just keeps circling around a blind spot. And this blind spot can be just about anything: the very spirit of the mother tongue, for instance, that eludes the poet no sooner than it appears; or the certainty, in the face of repeated official denials, that beauty and natural harmony continue radiating on the inside, while on the outside any sense of them has apparently long been extinguished; or a kind of empathy—to be found exclusively in poetry in such spontaneous form—with one's posthumous interlocutor, with a "you" summoned from the future; or the movement toward an end, thus alive and heartrending only in poems, that is more than just the fading-out presaged in every line; or, perhaps, it is something like megalomania, of the kind that helps you become a better person. But as palpably as it may manifest itself here and there, no poet will ever get to the bottom of it. Some have known more about it than others; the best have noticed that it is something that leaves the author by the wayside, turning him into an anonymous creator. Metaphor is much more intelligent than its author, says one. Somebody must have dictated a few lines to me, exults another. Yet—unrecognized, this blind spot remains.

Personally, I believe that what is expressed in poems is the human devotion to the transcendental—together with a concomitant fidelity to this world's prodigious wealth of detail. Poetry's secret, it seems to me, consists of two ingredients: a love of this world and a curiosity about metaphysics. The proof? Only among the poets does one come across them, those successful moments of reconciliation between something purely ideal and its unexpectedly concrete manifestations, less often among theologians, and almost never among philosophers. The reconciliation offer tends to come from the side of poetry, rarely the other way around, from the ranks of Plato, Kant, and their kind. All the more precious are those rare moments when they break through the wall of silence.

Just recently, one of them, the American Richard Rorty, was given to such an act of mercy, when he explained: "It is in the nature of intellectual and spiritual progress that philosophers constantly shift back and forth between quasi-scientific argumentation and non-argumentative flights of the poetic imagination. They move to the one whenever they become frustrated with the other."

4

When the average intellectual today reflects on the artistic and cultural achievements of the last century, he first thinks of such names as Freud and Picasso, Stravinsky and Heisenberg, Hitchcock and Wittgenstein. Impossible to imagine that a poet should be among them. Not a single poet from the ancestral gallery of the likes of Pessoa, Cavafy, Rilke, Yeats, Mandelstam, Valéry, Frost, and Machado will cross the mind of the historically minded thinker, who claims to understand what modernity is all about. It is as if the art of poetry, of all things, were the blind spot in the cultural memory of modern man. It doesn't make too much sense to brood over why this may be the case. Presumably, it has to do with the fickleness of memory itself, which obliterates everything that hasn't been put to use in the service of power, technology, capital, ideology, or physical force. And so it is that the poets are still alone with their little secret. A secret so big and momentous that it could change the world one day, if only it were noticed.

Imagine a thinking that could penetrate into certain otherwise hard-to-reach places, like dental floss between the wisdom teeth or an endoscope into the stomach. It will make certain places visible for the very first time—individual branches of the otherwise intractable psychic cave system that runs through the bodies of all humans and can be discovered only by a resourceful imagination audaciously pushing forward into still unsecured galleries. This thinking is poetic thinking, and it is not the exclusive domain of poets and literati; rather, it is a method used by many small search parties that have started out from several directions unbeknownst to one another, an army of phenomenologists working on expanding the confines of our shared imaginaries.

WHY LIVE WITHOUT WRITING

Questions are remarks.   —Wallace Stevens

There are three questions that a poet is always asked once he's become reasonably well established, that is, isn't forever required to spell his name, and his CV is reduced to two or three worn phrases. Never mind the fact that these phrases come out of the platitudinous files of some press department. What matters is that he showed sufficient stamina in the pursuit of his solitary discipline, which might suggest pole-vaulting and dashing sprints, but probably has most in common with the monotony of the marathon runner. Whichever, one day finds him standing under the open sky with a few curiosity seekers in front of him. The air is thick with old ideas, fantasies about the poet's life unchanged since Homer's day. I'll bet you anything: they come out in the form of the same three questions. At the end of the reading, there's not even any hesitation or throat-clearing. It's as if the questions were always there, a kind of diffuse curiosity, a residue of admiration tinged with skepticism and a little bumptiousness.

"Can you really live off it?" is the first of them. It's always the one to start the dance, and it seems to be the one that's of greatest interest in a society governed by getting and spending. Money sets standards and settles issues. It's money that measures the worth of each individual, whoever or whatever he or she may be: a pole dancer at a nightclub, an auto mechanic, a seasonal laborer in the asparagus field, a military spy hollowing out an enemy dictatorship, or—out of whatever frivolity of youth or deformation of personality—a poet. *Can you live off it?* It's the quest for a common denominator, the slightly sneering imputation of a low motive that even the poet-fantasist daren't go too far away from without risking a stumble. Whoever holds forth unpaid is like someone preaching on one leg: he won't be doing it for long. The question is a conscious and malicious comment on that flamingo or ostrich position. *Live off it* is a way of saying these fruitless verbal stunts, prestidigitations, aptitudes must surely lack in market value what they claim to have in terms of significance. To sensitive poets' ears it will sound like a threat, a tactless reminder of a bad habit, a warning against something that will surely end up as parasitism, in the warm bath of a state-endowed hostel.

Usually the matter is quickly resolved by a reference to the fee for the just-over reading (which the poet will certainly declare to the tax authorities). The fact that such an obvious connection doesn't occur to most people is due to the public subvention of literature. It is rare for people to have to pay for the privilege of hearing their bird of paradise (and asking him such and other questions). Few would stump up, if required. Free admission to the bard is considered a right. The same art lover who would pay hundreds of dollars for a seat in the stalls to hear some pampered tenor makes the silent assumption that the recessive librettist, the wordsmith with the light voice and the fluttering gestures, if he insists for some reason on appearing in person, will do it for free. The question about earning a living is half accusation, half condescension, because the party questioned inevitably strikes them as a poor fellow on day release from his cell in solitary, sitting there quietly reading out his difficult messages, a little nervous, as though there were armed guards on either side of him, rarely straight-forward. His material is as encoded as the secret messages passed from hand to hand in prison, those crumpled scraps of paper that look as though their conveyor had smuggled them in under his tongue. The spittle that issues from the reader's mouth is a grim little echo of those sticky scraps—but not as much as the poems themselves, these minimal jerky missives, these coded appeals in a secret language. Do I have to accept this and pass it on? the skeptical listener asks himself. What's it for? First I want to know if it's even possible to live off these messages from longtime solitary confinement. Basil Bunting, angry English member of the circle of the equally angry Ezra Pound, offers a portrait of the skeptic in his poem-monologue "What the Chairman Told Tom."

> Poetry? It's a hobby.
> I run model trains.
> Mr. Shaw there breeds pigeons.
>
> It's not work. You don't sweat.
> Nobody pays for it.
> You *could* advertise soap.
>
> Art, that's opera; or repertory—
> The Desert Song.
> Nancy was in the chorus.
>
> But to ask for twelve pounds a week—
> married, aren't you?—
> You've got a nerve.
>
> How could I look a bus conductor
> in the face
> if I paid you twelve pounds?

Who says it's poetry, anyhow?
My ten year old
can do it *and* rhyme.

I get three thousand and expenses,
a car, vouchers,
but I'm an accountant.

They do what I tell them,
my company.
What do *you* do?

Nasty little words, nasty long words,
it's unhealthy.
I want to wash when I meet a poet.

They're Reds, addicts,
all delinquents.
What you write is rot.

Mr. Hines says so, and he's a schoolteacher,
he ought to know.
Go and find *work*.

If you think this scene from 1965 is a little dated—though I wouldn't know why—then you only have to substitute the many prejudices that lurk inside you about so-called modern poetry: incomprehensible, hermetic, elitist, socially redundant, indulgent, cerebral, and so on. And contrast that with the refreshingly blunt tone of the chairman in Bunting's poem, which, strangely enough, comes out of a collection called *Odes*. The poet himself evidently thought it sufficiently expressive to be included in one of his rare bibliophile editions, flanked by arid, dense nature poems, bone-dry histories of the rim of Europe. It seems to be a problem of poetry, before all formal questions: its right to appear at all before the serious world of work. A profession is the spine of life, says Nietzsche. By that token, a poet would be an endangered species, condemned to live without a spine. Maybe that's why he so often has recourse to alibis. When questioned, he refers to his other occupations. He talks about his day job as editor and translator, mutters something about articles in prominent weeklies, deflects attention to his work in prose and his production of reviews, which in his own eyes, too, brings him closer to the generality. He wants to show that he is concerned with principles, with his own speculative contribution to what contemporary philosophy calls "the logic of the senses." He, too, is concerned with a methodology of contemplation (and not just sunsets and stamens). He promises that he is about more than merely chance self-expression, that he is exploring the basics. Casually he brings in his Ariel-like agility, his Hermes-deft understanding of the sciences. If he's going well, he alludes to the unique possibilities inherent in his eccentric situation. Then, having politely stepped aside, he brings in the poet in general, the finely honed senses this species has had for pioneer work in many fields, long before psycholinguistics or art philosophy occupied their own terrain, and long since, too. Because it's still not settled, he says, finally, who is taking advantage of whom. Phenomenology and dialectical thought, journalism and advertising, the mushrooming proliferation of writing up to and including the very latest self-help manual, they have all nibbled on the oatcakes of poetry. They have received a gift that came to its creators, if they're going to be honest about it, as a gift in turn—a gift, according to the ancient Greeks, from the Muses. And so he asks, with for once barely a trace of irony, that all questions of duty and ownership be set aside. A little calmer now, he goes on to talk about the privilege conferred by writing—the privilege of using his

gift of observation and his verbal finesse to make explicit
statements on being human, to make notes on the real world
and translate it, at one and the same time, into metaphysics.
Perhaps it will even occur to him to portray writing as a specific form of understanding, or, following an original notion of
Novalis, as "progressive anthropology." Once in train, he will
insist that poetry is the most paradoxical and complex form of
contemplation, and thereby the most valuable contribution to
a natural history of thinking and sensation. If he finally succeeds in elevating this to a proof of existence, exalted over
every bank statement and of almost inestimable cultural
value, then, more exhausted than convinced, they may finally
leave him alone. But right away, bet you anything you like,
will come the second question, the starting signal for an expedition into the biographical hinterland. "How long have you
been writing for?"

This question seems to be more straightforward. It would
be enough to name some date or other, having recourse to
some childish lisping-in-rhyme, some fairy-tale scene after
which you were never the same. Or, following Proust, the recollection of that first sleepless night, when, instead of going
over your notes on photosynthesis once more for the biology
test in the morning, you started to tiptoe away from the present by starting to hammer out sonnets, for one whole week,
till you got to fifty. Or you refer to some early trauma, running
away from your family into a shrubbery that could be bent
under only a line at a time, the triumphal arrival in the clearing you could reach only by writing, with the divining rod of
words, and how you first came upon the Other, that Other you
finally turned into, the more you became engrossed by this
lonely game.

At first it sounds more innocent, this question of *when*, but
it's not without its subtext either. It's generally brought forward more shyly, by people who do a bit of scribbling them-

selves in their time off, or who have set up reading groups to speculate about the intentions of their favorite mages. These good people have some sense of how to proceed. When they've determined one day where writing comes from; how it became an obsession; what part was down to heredity, artistic education, regional culture, or personal handicaps; how helpful or unhelpful were family conflicts, early reading tastes, and greater or lesser deviations from the standard educational program—when they've finally cracked the mystery by indiscretion and no little statistical hocus-pocus, they'll proudly inform us. Feeling themselves to be like-minded or allies, they begin by politely but firmly inviting themselves around. The particular focus of their curiosity is childhood, its many unlit niches and attics, where *animula*, that little soul-butterfly, slipped from its larva and one day took to the air. In other words, what they'd ideally like is a spy hole into the past for them to peek through into the intimate setting where such transformations took place. And this is where their interest coincides with that of the author. Because he, too, wouldn't mind knowing how it all began—even if only to be able to tell his grandchildren about it. He, too, would benefit from a modern espionage technique that could show him some live footage of the dawn of his own consciousness. But unaided, all he can do is project generally unfocused and in other ways untrustworthy images from his memory.

For instance, the warm cave of bed, where he would read Jules Verne and James Fenimore Cooper by torchlight deep into the night, to be ambushed not by the Hurons, but by his father, whispering "Lights out!" and pulling away the pillow. Or his unusual habit, when he spent his summers at his grandmother's, of prowling through the apartment, done up to the nines, chanting, armed with the little daggerlike knife sharpener from the top drawer of the kitchen cabinet, imitating the pose he had seen in the illustrated Shakespeare edition,

modeled on the sinister figure of Prince Hamlet. Or the secret vow, given after reading *Buddenbrooks* in school, which
Thomas Mann wrote at twenty-four: By the time you get to
be that old, you have to have done something as good . . . and
what remained of that was the secret force of the word *vow*, to
this day. No, all that won't do to furnish a proper medical file
with a nailed-down, certifiable anamnesis. The status of this
clear and well-upholstered prehistory is fiction.

It appears that the opening chapter of any bildungsroman
is bound to be underlit, as if any artist had no option but to
situate his self-portrait among baby talk, nursery rhymes, and,
in Joycean manner, Dante and moocow. Because the *when*
only incites to a hectic search for original actions, and behind
every origin is another origin, every first cause masks another.
"Don't trust any of the anecdotes about beginnings" is really
the only good advice. What looks like the first time is actually
déjà vu, a gala premiere after a long rehearsal period, some
scene that memory has gotten expert at lighting. It can't help
reminding you of the museum-ready installations in writers'
houses, the rococo desk parked in front of the window—
everything, of course, the way it was, the site of inspiration
exactly as the master left it, still warm, papers untidy and
inkwell open.

Really, the only good thing about the question is its
undertone of yearning. The phenomenon it shyly inquires
after is obviously much bigger than anything that can be said
about it. In their heart of hearts, both participants know that
it's not much good waving a questionnaire at the mystery of
creativity. Because you will never catch the first murmured
aside in flagrante, any later attempt can be nothing but a well-
intentioned but ultimately vague reconstruction. Of course
you can follow Proust and take the road of greater and greater
refinement, sifting recollections into voluntary and involuntary and admitting only those that sidle into the photo album

unbidden. In this way, you will at least gain access to a kind of backstage, the place where the ur-images slumber in children's books, the characters evoked by the deft pencil, the ever-palpable ordinary objects. If you're canny about it, you can mingle with them again, place your body in their midst as once before. Maybe you can even find your way back into Act I, Scene 1, the original scene in the golden spring light, or at least resurrect one of those richly circumstantial moments, when you sat like St. Jerome in his cell, not with holy books, but at least a Roget's to hand among a slew of papers, and by the door instead of the sleeping lion the new bicycle, never so neglected as now, on this October day. Because the first time you were entirely oblivious to yourself, not in the wild harum-scarum way of sport and running, but in that quiet, cut-off way, fixed on something in the remote distance, recalled with a jolt only by a look at the clock.

⎯ But who could say if that was it, the moment that reflective understanding awoke, the immemorial and essential astonishment that is the precondition for all further writing? Just as you can't localize poetry in the brain—as the neurologists have long conceded—you can't date and trace its arrival in the life of an individual. The subsequent aim of the enterprise may be all about specification, the mot juste, precision of expression, objectivization, and so on—but place and time and the motives that launched it on its way will always stay in the dark. All that can be said is that the one thus questioned one day became poem-obsessed and that he has since then been avid for words; just as other individuals with deft hands may become craftsmen, or those with some sixth sense develop a feel for stock market movements or political developments. One day, something happened that would later awaken in him the desire for still more absurd retrospectives. After all, the question *when* violates a taboo, shooing the poet back into the early pastures of childhood, into the empire of grown-ups, or giants even, where he spent so long as an embarrassing dwarf. If it happened to him later that, Gulliver-like, he was confused by size and sometimes felt himself too big, more often too small, then that had presumably to do with distorted perception resulting from being an author. At any rate, such metamorphoses and reversals came with the territory for him.

All these themes—self-isolation, split identity, forms of memory—are just the chapter headings from the one book that every one of us, not just poets, is writing all his life, and not always with belletristic ambition. In the whole of world literature, only one person to date has succeeded in trans-forming this project into one luminous whole, that is, in mak-ing a paper cutout of his own life so crisp that it can be held up against the light. Once again I refer to Marcel Proust, the sublime researcher into matters mnemonic, who has supplied the most conscientious answer to the question *when first*. His lavish self-portrait in the form of a phenomenological study eventually came to seven volumes of minutely descriptive prose. As someone who generally confines himself to poems, I of course don't have so much space. But, above all, the time for such a venture seems to be differently allotted in each individual life.

For myself, at the moment, there is only a line-by-line groping, the snipping of various phases of life into skinny lit-tle strips with plenty of space between them, the chronologi-cal leaps bedded among the peaks and troughs of various meters. All I have for now, by way of the guerrilla tactic of a poorly armed memory, is avoidance, the jump from poem to poem. Here and there a swift raid, and then back into the woods, the protective jungle hideouts. *Zeit schinden*—"playing for time"—you call it in German, the language I cohabitate with in a monogamous relationship, the occasional extramari-tal affair notwithstanding, and whose intrinsic intelligence takes me on the most beautiful odysseys. To German I owe my most important insights and a few true moments of happiness.

What comes about in this way is at best a novel in fragmentary form. Something with the quality of a sketch. Then again, sketches have made panoramic paintings, given time. Each individual poem seems just to be a running-up; it starts over and over, only to withdraw quickly. It seems modest, fugitive, as though under a curse, as if blocked from the get-go by its tendency to end as a mere gesture, when it began with an aspiration to inclusiveness. But then, one day, you might ask yourself whether it's not the other way around, whether the poem isn't a product of extreme concentration, either on a sequence of images or movements, or a subtly articulated argument, or the pivotal scene of a period of life. Then its main drive would be semantic reduction. A few clusters of words express what the lavish epic draws out over hundreds of pages. Or to put it another way: Couldn't it be that poems, as long as they are alert and open to impressions, are novels by other means—and therefore do sterling service to readers short of time and hungry for intensity? What they have to offer are lessons in accelerated consciousness, machete slashes through a tangled world. For aficionados of the concentrated and powerful, they are distilled experience, abbreviations of existence, shocks and pronouncements in droplet form. It's not really surprising that people are curious to know where such a thing springs from and when it first makes its appearance in someone's life. In the end, the party asked, even if he has stamina and will continue to make his inquiries himself, will have to pass. Perhaps, as the lawyers say, he will agree to a settlement, in poetic form, of course. Then he will take the role of self-scrutineer as far as it can be taken and describe his first year. Perhaps a little like this:

(*In a different key*. "Sealed in air and summer / The blade of grass in the ice-block outside the refrigerator plant, / I looked around, very early, too early, / With eyes that would have frightened any mother. / *And I saw more than was good for me* . . . / My little joints made the sweetest music. / Really, I wasn't asleep, I was just pretending, / In the role of a child (played by a child). / Through the seedy meadow ran a yellow peril / trailing after butterflies and dandelions. / Close to the ground and without memory / thus passed my first year, / somewhere yonder.")

•

But the trickiest question is always the third one. It comes out only when the others have been shot off and hope sinks that there is any common ground of understanding instead of the deeps and trenches of idiosyncrasy. There's a hush as it is asked. It's a typical child's question. There are various permutations, but basically it goes like this: "*Why* do you write?"

As you can tell, the questioner has just taken a step back. He's been thinking about what it would be like to spend the livelong day sifting words. He can imagine it a little, from writing letters, maybe from learning French or Spanish at school. He is reminded of interminable lessons, blank expressions over blank sheets of paper, and the whole thing to him resembles something like an English essay for life—literally, a life sentence. The focus of his pity is the duress, the component of torture, he doesn't think of it as an adventure, sweet uncertainty, the atmosphere of sub-rosa assignations. He doesn't have a clue about the little discharges produced by rubbing electrostatic words together, the silent bliss caused by the imagination becoming so physical that it produces a tingle across the scalp, like a cranial massage.

Like all consumers, his view is rather one-eyed, either dominated by the question of effort (which strikes him as immense and incommensurate) or else by the question of outcome, which seems disproportionate to such an effort, a sprinkling of letters plodding around the arid desert of the alphabet, a hermit protocol concretized in a couple of printed pages of doubtful utility. In the worst case, he will be dismayed by the renunciation of a life of large, visible projects, a life, as he would see it, out in the open, wild and professional—rather like his own.

What he completely fails to see are the joys of production, the sheer pleasure of this strange alchemical process, for which there are only few, scattered recipes and that at heart is as old as anything in the world, including the sharpening of flint arrowheads, tattooing, and baking clay. If it can be said to be a process at all. Because, as all the insiders will tell you, the thing can't really be described as a craft, however physical and preindustrial that may sound. Perhaps because we are dealing with something that's not just preindustrial, but precraft. Poetry, inasmuch as it is still in touch with its origins—the senses and the voice—somehow eludes history, it antedates all known structures of history and economy. It was present in the corner of the Stone Age huntsman's cave, just as it is there now in the cafeteria of a factory that makes jet planes. In both cases, it is unobtrusively and consolingly there between people in its shy but natural way, claiming no attention. You could rest from the effort of the chase, or momentarily forget about blueprints and lead times, because it was in the air, or, as they say, free to air—either as the monotonous chant of the eccentric cripple lying on the mammoth skin in the corner, or as the droning chant of the latest hip-hop bard featured on the morning show. What I'm getting at is that its sheer being there lifts it out of the category of craft. In fact, this very being there, unobtrusively omnipresent in music and commercials, folk song and requiem, indicates that it needs to be legitimized by the other professions and crafts in the first place. Sometimes I think that the poets were the first to have to make their way through adversarial thinking and professional palaver, bickering in home and cave, in the office and on the factory floor. At least they had no choice but to listen to it closely, to collect everything heard and seen and then process it before it disappeared in the general confusion of voices, the chaos of—literally—the daily grind.

Which means that on the one hand poetry has always depended on there being a well-ordered society with a division of labor, ready to finance its festive bards, and on the other that in the interests of proper and concentrated recording, it has always had a tendency to stay off to the side somewhere. The latter has led to the insoluble paradox that it flourished in splendid isolation, cannily insisting on neutrality and right of refusal, while at the same time being always at the heart of things, in the middle of the banging and the slaughtering, there where the destruction of the temple was discussed, or the construction of the Trojan horse. Rather than chip in with advice, it has played the part of the observer, who would finally convert his collected silence into the one and only commentary that survived the wreckage, some unforgettable line of song, some key scene of an epic or heartbreaking elegy.

And so it can leave the question *why* unanswered and relax. Only a society despairing of its own destiny, devoid of any desires beyond economic reproduction, could allow itself to cast in doubt the so-called difficult art of poetry. I don't think much of a state that keeps badgering you for self-justification—whether intended as provocation, the final shred of theological doubt, or simply a request for practical advice. Of course, loss of a potential workforce, disorientation during purposeless time off, and the reduction of entire classes of the population into masses of passive spectators are all alarming prospects. Plato's poetic cleansing was an early indication of the way the wind was blowing. His plan to banish from his state those useless poets who did nothing but fiddle with pictures, and reach into the pleats of their togas for metaphors and phantasms, was not just an idle suggestion. So: What would have happened to them after their relocation to their Hyperborean island? They would have starved to death, for sure, and no one would have prevented it. Wrapped up in themselves, they would have done what they best liked to do anyway: bid farewell to the world in all its variety. The toughest would have lasted longest, iron sublimators of their destiny, reviling one another and recasting the chattering of their teeth into iambs and trochees. Perhaps some would have been turned by their dereliction into monotheists like the future Christians. Their tale about the extinction of their species, lamented between bouts of narcissism and cannibalism in artful psalms, would have continued to drift around the seas for a while, a message in a bottle. After a few decades, a young Apollonian bully on one of the coasts, a trained decathlete and arithmetician, would have fished it out and, after a swift nauseated reading, destroyed it before his eloquent and athletic comrades could denounce him in the gym for spreading unhygienic writings . . .

Society, at any rate, would have survived it, just as it has from time to time de facto survived the loss of its unbidden guests, the poets: either totalitarian-style, by formally condemning and liquidating those elements it deems noxious; or democratically, as a result of an exeunt through what it generously refers to as *Freitod*—"death by one's own hand" (read: suicide). In the twentieth century, the price for these losses was in either case the spiritual darkness of collectives, here the retreat into the shot-up ivory bunker, there the mass departure for self-destruction. Hardly a century has gotten through as many good poets as the twentieth. The conciliatory, if not exactly comforting thing about the question *why* is that, after all, it's just about a phantom pain. Such a question can come only from someone who has lost something, even if he doesn't know exactly what it was. So back, quickly back to the euphoria that awaits the writer. On some days, the pleasure is such that every poet flinches a little at the sound of the word *work*. And the *why* wants to know about that, too. Because *work*—a job—as defined in the dictionary isn't something that you would publicly put into question like that. Not even prostitution, beset by at least as many taboos and half-truths, ever needed to furnish answers as to its whys and wherefores, and the fact that it was a job was never denied, not even by those who would like to outlaw it as a form of exploitation. No one was ever stuck for a justification for this occupation. You just called it the oldest profession and pulled rank. At the same time, you forgot that poetry, satisfying similarly inexhaustible appetites, was surely at least as old. If not older still.

No other occupation seems as fraught with doubt. Anyone brave enough to risk his bourgeois contentment at an early age will spend the rest of his life wondering if it was worth it. His social acceptance will depend entirely on his growing influence—or his talent, in layman's terms. It's not enough if he assures you he's getting by; no, he has to convince you that he's fulfilling some universally explainable purpose.

That involves fighting on several fronts. The *why* will strike the poet as a hydra-headed monster; as soon as he deals with one head, another pushes up. Why, oh why? The question splits into loads of subordinate questions: Why do you write when no one can tell me what the point is? Why do you have to do something so dubious? Why are you so difficult that hardly anyone can understand you? Why do you stand there so calmly, presiding over all your neuroses? The one question stands in for a tangle of other questions. And why not, since there's no one more available for such public introspection than the poet.

Not that the poet, in his life, bothers himself with this most infantile of questions for long. He inevitably disregards it, begins, forgets about the future and growing up, and—if he's lucky, anyway—remains a child at play for the rest of his life. Is it the repression of this big question that allows him never completely to lose access to childhood and to such qualities as playfulness, love of home, curiosity about the world, hunger for myths and stories? In the end, you're always left with the individual's psyche, locked in its embrace with the sweet idiom of the tribe. That's what condemns poets to these embarrassing questions. People look to them to pull answers out of their hats, answers that are more digestible than those of the philosophers, more entertaining than those of the priests, and—with luck—more comforting than those of those cynics, the doctors. Complicity with the latter, a bad habit of poetry in the twentieth century, only few are able to take. Poets shouldn't always be playing devil's advocate. Their insistence on physiology, on blunt physical realism and drastic disillusion, must be a disappointment to those who prefer to see them still in the role of landscape gardeners.

Not that poets are altogether unprepared for all these demanding questions. Since Kafka's story "A Country Doctor," they are the ones to have been put to bed with the patient, right up against the gaping wound. But never mind what they do and what they write when they're there, nothing is self-evident. Very little makes sense, reconciles or heals, and only in the rarest cases does it help people through their tangled day-to-day life, which thanks to progress and *Civilization and Its Discontents* has become quite a cozy little labyrinth.

Later, they might look up from their notes, and their eyes mist over at the sound of a word like *futility*. In its polysyllabic lightness it somehow evokes the Sirens' song, the trill of frustrated mermaids. But to whom have they not sung in some hour of weakness? As is well known, poets are people who regularly get to hear their preorgasmic groaning simply on account of the work they do. Over time, they have learned to develop all kinds of defensive techniques against such tempting distractions. And that's how they want to help the rest of humankind. Odysseus, tied to the mast by his crew, openeared to these deadly sweet sounds, is certainly a better model than poor Marsyas, who loses his skin in the fluteplaying contest with big-headed Apollo. The only worse role model, no sort of exemplar, is Orpheus, who in the Greek version is the founding father of poetry. According to one variant of the story, women tore him limb from limb because he paid them insufficient attention. They nailed his severed head to his lyre, and threw it into the Thracian Sea, where it continued to drift about for a while, singing to itself. The other version has it that as punishment for his contempt for agriculture he was ploughed under by some peasants. Either way, he ends up in pieces. There's not much to choose between the two stories, they share one moral: the price of alienation, selfabsorption, disregard for sex and property is a martyr's death in the service of the Muses.

Probably that's why poets have become more self-critical and more modest of late. They are back in the real world, no longer treading astral paths. More skeptical than most rocket scientists, they look about their immediate vicinity, registering the tiniest quiver of a needle, the puff of quartz dust on their instruments. Still with that fresh, animal gaze—albeit as the natives of language—they escort each new flight and describe things the experts miss. Their task is no longer metaphysics and contemplation of the Pleiades. Even if love and death remain their preeminent assignments (because who else is there who would accept them?), their radius in the last few centuries has steadily expanded. No philosophical, geopolitical, or moral problem has escaped their sensitive soundings. There is no crisis zone on the globe or in the mind where you don't run into poets, no dirty work for which they consider themselves too fine or too romantic.

But by the same token, they will no longer stand for all the reproaches that are leveled against them. Someone who is spared nothing in what he does, who has no protection and no aesthetic privilege, such a person will at least lay claim to his constitutionally guaranteed space, as part of a properly constituted minority. So one shouldn't be surprised if these incessantly questioned parties start shooting a few questions back. Trained in self-doubt as they are, they know where the adversary's weak spots are. It takes them a while to launch into a counterquestion, but then they do it enthusiastically, and, as we will see, quite unscrupulously.

The representative question is the *why*. If you approach the matter unsentimentally enough, a meditation on the subject will surprise you. I don't want to frighten you, but have you thought about what happens to people who aren't artists? E. E. Cummings once gave a particularly blunt answer. His barrack-room tone was probably in imitation of some raw recruit. In the introduction to his novel *The Enormous Room*, he comes up to the reader with a pally "Don't be afraid" and gets a merry little dialogue going. In the course of it, the encouraged reader lets the fearless author talk him into the question: "What do you think happens to people who aren't artists? What do you think people who aren't artists become?"—only to be triumphantly shot back at by the author: "I feel they don't become: I feel nothing happens to them; I feel negation becomes of them." After that triple salvo—according to the author anyway—the reader has no more questions. At best, it's a whispered echo of the poet's final threat: "Negation?"

Well, one could probably be gentler about it. Delicate sensibilities may be hurt by a poet, of all people, arguing so ruthlessly and self-righteously. But why should he spare you a peek into his own box of prejudices, when he is compelled on a daily basis to inspect those of others? Moreover, everything with Cummings has to do with this one, ambivalent concept, *negation*, which signifies both the process of negating and its effect, the result of disappearance, namely: nothing. And it is precisely this annulling, this deletion, this causing to disappear that is at issue. Are those nonartists, always terribly busy but finally disappearing without a trace, are they not the ones who are condemned to negate everything that doesn't press itself on them in the form of reality? They are the ones who have no possibility of returning, who spend their lives in the service of their own removal, all for the sake of banality and materialism.

Anyway, they don't contribute much to spiritual variety. If it were up to them, there would only be the world as is, which means rough and ready, drearily underexposed, a place of torment and tedium, a global Golgotha without witnesses—and not because they are entirely devoid of imagination and playfulness themselves so much as because all their activities are essentially negative, a sopping-up of resources, a clearing-away of what existed previously, a destruction of terrestrial substance without a chance of any revision, let alone irregularity. In truth, it is they who are holding negation, the philosophers' rattly old machine gun, in their hands, and it is they, not the bearded wise men of stoa and academy, who have most frequent recourse to it. They don't have to be ill-intentioned, it's enough that they continue to do what nonartists do when they are bored. Which means behaving like normal consumers of the universe, always busy, always on their treadmill, a.k.a. "the real world," or "common sense," or "business as usual."

Oh, that's just resentment speaking . . . In fact, artists and nonartists have a wonderful symbiosis. Each side profits from the weakness of the other and receives its legitimization from it; see above. Only, one side seems always to have known why as a minority it always had a modicum of modesty, while the other was able to ignore it in its nihilistic philistinism. The wonderful thing about this little argument is the way it sharpens the issue of *why*. Instead of proclamations as to the function and purpose of their respective activities, it's an argument about who, bluntly speaking, is responsible for more of the overall pointlessness. Probably that's why the exchange is so satisfactory. Be warned: most artists, frustrated or otherwise, approve of this sort of thing.

Better watch out: artists are people who, unless they're feeling particularly hypocritical and ingratiating, would laugh to scorn the claim that there's an artist in everyone. Whether they appear in the guise of cool diplomats or cult figures or shabby drunkards, none of them is without that shred of vanity. Of course they are going to assume that someone without the lofty inner life suggested by art and poetry is to be pitied. Sooner or later he is bound to break up into aspects that may be connected to him as a legal entity, but that won't have the least thing to do with his inner world. They shudder at the notion that one day he will realize that none of this was him, and in all of it was hardly any of his. Then it's usually too late, and the person will dimly sense that for the whole of a selfless life he has been working in the cause of negation.

Writers are rarely as hard-boiled as they pretend to be. What drives them is their fear of the void everywhere. Hence the question that bespeaks dread rather than confidence, the long-repressed counterquestion that it will occur only to impertinent individuals, favored by some daemon or other, to ask. After two decades of habit, and barely a day without sarcastic self-communing, it goes: "Why live without writing?"

•

Living without writing means, first and foremost, not having an exorbitant paper habit. At least in that point, the blameless abstainer can look to be let off by the environment. But it also means, sadly, the wasting of one's only chance to break out of intellectual solitary confinement and become a little more communicative, more human—not just with the twenty-five relatives and friends with whom the average life furnishes you, but with all those who could really one day listen to you, tomorrow's unknown readers. I write for a reader who is as yet unborn. That sentence, misquoted from memory, can only have come from a manic writer. It's the sort of proclamation that shakes you, that sends a little shock through the naturally idle body. Because from the very outset it's the body that jealously keeps watch over writing and extorts ever new concessions from it. So, why write?

In the first place, I would say, you write to escape your dread of the sheer present. You fill page after page, as Nietzsche once put it with angry yearning, not to cozy up to your nearest, but out of love of those farthest away from you, and because the contemporary and the day-to-day will be all the more precious to you when you return to them in a wide arc over unknown terrain. Hence many people's habit of getting drunk in company: at close quarters only a maximum of inner distance can create moments of ease and relaxation. Hence the silent conversations everyone has with themselves, or locking yourself up in the bathroom to read undisturbed, or the distancing look in the mirror as soon as you know you're unobserved. Hence, too, the recurring need of lovers to go to the cinema and stare together at the magic screen, which for a precious hour and a half will make them forget their bodies. In writing, it is one's innermost being that tries to assert itself, paradoxically, by self-exposure. But publicity, as will soon become apparent, is nothing but a particularly tough protective shield.

And the second reason is a dilemma that concerns each individual psyche. You write, I believe, because you can't quite shake the suspicion that as a mere contemporary and biological cell mate, hopelessly trammeled up in your own limited lifespan, you would always remain incomplete, half a man, so to speak. Someone must have put you onto the idea that only your most individual expression gives you the least chance of one day being seen in any way other than in your mortal sheath—say, as a kind of ghost. Ever since that tormenting voice (whoever it may be) first challenged you in the name of metaphysics, you've been trying by all the laws of glassblowing, a.k.a. poetry, to fix a little window in your own diminishing time, in the hope that tomorrow or whenever you may be seen through that little peephole. If you happen to succeed in making your sweetheart, or one or two of your friends, or yourself in your peculiarity visible—the way Vermeer, say, showed his pregnant letter reader—then it will have been worth the effort. Writing, the voice whispers to you, is the least circumstantial method of breaking out of the given and the immediate. Its only requirement is a mastery of the alphabet, which, thanks to universal education, may generally be relied on, at least hereabouts. You don't have to be able to draw or set down notes like Bach, and yet, once you've passed your spelling exam, you've mastered the only method by which consciousness can be recorded.

From which it follows, third and last: you write because the brain is an endless wilderness, whose roughest terrain can be traveled only with a pencil. As soon as we are in the innermost dreamy connections, all other art forms are dependent on verbal synthesis. The dream, as you discover when you write, is the fully authentic self. You will never have amounted to more. The world will not appear any more variegated. Which means the notion of what really exists can, with writing, be comfortably extended by a dimension or two.

Let me conclude this flight with an anecdote. I suspect it may be one of those grisly parables by means of which Orien-

tal wisdom likes to offer instruction, often to the dismay of
the Westerner. In it, all the issues we have treated thus far are
settled, so to speak, by a stroke of the pen. The setting and
atmosphere are familiar from Kafka's *In the Penal Colony*,
where the grisliness also has a strangely mild quality about it.
In his diaries, Hugo von Hofmannsthal brings up the story of
a German officer in China who, following the Boxer Rebel-
lion, participated in a penal expedition:

> The officer sees a line of men sentenced to death,
> standing in a field. With his sword the executioner
> goes from man to man. There is no need for his assis-
> tants to tie or even to hold down any of them; as soon
> as it's the next man's turn, he stands there with feet
> apart, his hands gripping his knees, his neck stretched
> out, offering it to the blade. One of the last in line, still
> some way from coming due, is completely immersed
> in a book. The officer rides up to him and asks:
> "What's that you're reading?" The man looks up, asks
> back: "Why are you bothering me?" The officer asks:
> "How can you read *now*?" The man says: "I know that
> every line I read is something gained." The officer
> rides to the general who has ordered the execution,
> and begs him for the man's life for so long that he gets
> him off, rides back with the written acquittal, shows it
> to the officer in charge, and is allowed to go and take
> the man out of line. Tells him: "You've been acquit-
> ted, you're free to go." The man shuts his book, looks
> the officer in the eye, and says: "You have done a good
> thing. Your soul will have profited greatly from this
> hour"—and he nods to him, and sets off across the
> field.

ACCENTED TIME

Music only carries, like gas streaming in, the balloon (poetry) up
into the air.   —Johann Wolfgang von Geothe, letter to
Carl Friedrich Zelter, May 11, 1820

1

The oldest piece of music I've ever heard dates back to classical Greece—more precisely, to the heyday of Attic tragedy.
It was no mere accident, I think, that the composition was
found on a page that also contained a fragment of text from
one of Euripides' tragedies. I have to say right away that I was
completely taken aback by what I heard. *Music* would be an
all-too-euphemistic word for that archaic sound structure.
Cacophony is more like it, even if that insult surely does injus-
tice to the Greeks. The ugly dissonance was undoubtedly not
their fault but that of the somewhat abstract and archaeological manner in which the music was performed, with instruments reconstructed from pictures on vases. The ancient
composition reminded me of caterwauling, but that wasn't
due to changing listening habits so much as to the way it had
been restored.

Given that the few pieces of musical notation that have
come down to us from that age have been found partly on
marble fragments and partly on tattered papyrus rolls, it is
astonishing that they could be translated back into anything

ACCENTED TIME   117

like sound at all. To reconstruct a pitcher from a few clay fragments is one thing. It is something far more fantastic to make
a set of bland notations and some bare suggestions of rhythm
into sounds that might actually come off as music. The am-
phora from the bottom of the sea can be quickly brought to
the surface and glued back together—a musical world remains
forever lost. Why? The eye is simply the better historian: it
selects and compares and keeps space and time at a distance.
The ear, by contrast, is completely engrossed by the present,
bound as it is by its natural symphonic habitat. Which brings
us to the first major difference between literature and music.
Memory holds on to images, words, and signs; it draws on language. Hearing subsides with the passing of sound. Musical
impressions are transitory, they develop in passing. Music continually erases its own memory. Only repetition and constant
exercise can ensure its transmission from generation to generation. This is why the auditory experiences of classical antiquity can never become part of art history's and philology's
inventory and put on display like exhibits in a museum.
Reconstructing them is like trying to resurrect a flesh-and-
blood human being solely on the basis of the portrait his biographers have sketched of him. Classical literature, by contrast,
is as familiar to us as the condensation of our breath on the
mirror. Body and voice may perish, writing remains.

Literature hibernates in books—leaden rations of printed
letters. Music floats in the air for as long as there's somebody
who knows how to perform it. It requires a specialist to bring
it to life. A text, by contrast, requires only a reader—and this
means potentially anybody who happens to be literate. It was
not the *melos* of his poetry, its idiosyncratic verbal music, but
the words themselves in their very nudity, employed as
metaphors and synonyms, that tempted Horace to predict that
he would, one day, become immortal thanks to them. The
individual line of verse, not the jangling of the kithara, will

outlast brass, Egypt's pyramids, and the centuries' flight. This was roughly what was going through my head as I was listening to those ghastly dithyrambs. Like it or not—Horace can hardly be said to have exaggerated. For almost a thousand years, his wager was on. That was how long the musical tradition lay dormant—trapped in the state of its own illiteracy, multilingual yet without orthography, a child of free play and naïve improvisation. It was first awakened from its millennial slumber by the strictures of musical notation. Only in the service of religious edification did it eventually also acquire formal discipline. Then, during the heyday of courtly pomp, it fell in love with its own sense of play. But it did not gain sovereign status until the rise of the bourgeois concert industry, which helped it to blossom into the freest and most refined of artistic genres.

2

Let's recap: the first encounter between literature and music that can be accurately dated took place against the backdrop of an amphitheater. Musical and verbal art grew up in the same place and hail from the same family (and not only in the West). This, if you like, explains their ongoing rivalry. Literature may have an advantage over music when it comes to presence of mind, while music easily outperforms literature when it comes to higher forms of communion. As far as their powers of creating interpersonal connections are concerned, they merely differ in degree. In other words, music is simply better at evoking our common sense of humanity. It bridges the abysses that separate one individual from another, while verbal art foregrounds them by primarily addressing the individual. The question of who was there first is merely a reminder of the silly problem of the chicken and the egg. But in case of doubt, the perception of sound always precedes the quest for meaning. Still, this says little about chronology and even less about priorities. Nobody knows what the Neanderthal in his cave was first carried away by—the palaver of a heated hunting story or the monotone dirges of those who stayed at home. Either way, this complicated relationship presumably began with onomatopoeia. I know that this thesis is mostly self-serving. Poets simply put more store by onomatopoeia—verbal creation through sound imitation—than composers. Besides, most of them are creative enough to imagine that music didn't require language in the first place. On the contrary, it must have been in a moment of simple obliviousness that man first put a reed to his lips and made it resound by dexterously blowing into it. Let's assume he was alone at that moment, separated from his kin. What else could he do but try to keep the terrifying noises emanating from the world around him at bay with the help of well-tempered, heartfelt sounds?

Perhaps this was what secretly impressed me so much about my discovery from the distant past. Deafening and repulsively exotic as it may have sounded, there was something about its bleak phonic solitude that made me think of all those millennia when we humans lived unprotected and at the mercy of the elemental forces of nature. With all due respect to Nietzsche, the spirit of this music heralded not the birth of tragedy so much as the horrors of early geological ages. Its instrumental monotony had little to do with the tragic hero's rage in the face of imminent death, the chorus's shocking revelations, or the bucolic peace of pastorals. What it conjured was an inhospitable, prehistoric landscape, the silence of a world before man. Long before even the first paean or the first psalm had been intoned, long before music filled our hearts, there was nothing on earth but the croaking of frogs, the droning stride and the munching of dinosaurs, and the piercing roar of a solitary saber-toothed tiger.

3

Their common origin has kept literature and music tethered to each other. No one will deny that at some point they did go their separate ways. But whenever their paths would subsequently happen to cross (in the madrigal, the Romantic song cycle, or the operatic *Gesamtkunstwerk*), their kinship would again come to light. I know I'm not saying anything new by insisting on the equality of these two art forms. Myth itself has captured their familial ties in the image of the Muses. And even though the genres are unequally distributed among the nine daughters and some of them may seem more gifted than the others, nothing will change the fact that they all came out of the same Olympic liaison. Zeus was their father, but this means little more than that even they weren't untouched by the almighty's promiscuity. They all had the same mother, Mnemosyne, a.k.a. memory, with the lovely braids. To her they owe their most precious dowry. The primal scene in which they are all gathered in the same parental home has been preserved in human memory—in Europe, at least—to this very day, even though history was soon to separate them, thereby proving Hölderlin's sorrowful insight correct. Hölderlin leaves us in no doubt as far as we ourselves, his studious apprentices—long since emancipated from the Muses' tutelage—are concerned, when he writes:

A sign we are, meaningless
Without pain we are and have nearly
Lost our language in exile.

Our common language, the only realm in which we humans can truly express ourselves as creative and active beings, was beyond doubt. Confusing as the distribution of portfolios among the nine sisters may have been: except for Urania, the one conversant in astronomy, they were all musical, and each played an instrument. Each was also uniquely endowed with rhetorical gifts ranging from comedy to tragedy, from the dance song to the heroic epic. What they all had in common, though, was a shared feeling for language, a shared musical sensibility, which predestined them for the guardianship of the various art forms.

If we trace the genealogy all the way back, what we find, *pace* all blood ties, is but this one relationship: that of music and poetry—my present subject. It was Nietzsche who insisted on the birth of Athenian tragedy from the spirit of music. But the inversion of this genesis, too, has a lot to say for itself. It could just as well be that the same lips that produced the very first flute sound had previously murmured a few poetic lines into the wind. The word *song* still retains its double meaning today. Do not be deceived by such a thoroughly philological coinage as *lyric*. Nobody can prove what came first: the lyre, that stringed instrument, curved as beautifully as a peacock feather, or the half-spoken, half-sung text in stanza form. If in doubt, consider the voice the older instrument. It was one and the same human self that melodically coordinated its feelings in word and sound. Both hand and voice belonged to the same body, and the same sensibility set them in motion. This may explain why to this day poetry is the only art form that straddles every threshold—the threshold between language and intonation, *pictura* and *poesis*, and, last but not least, writing and signification. Its innate discreteness forbids it to make too much fuss over the differences; striking a balance is its difficult day-to-day business. Its self-confidence stems from the certainty that in its own quiet way and undisturbed in its own realm it humbly follows the same rules as all the other arts. Not only on the authority of the Bible ("In the beginning was the word . . ."), but on the authority of aesthetic genealogy as well does it deserve the appellation of firstborn. No less a figure than Igor Stravinsky claimed that music was the youngest of the arts. "If we go back further than the fourteenth century, we encounter so many practical obstacles that even in deciphering musical scores we have to resign ourselves to conjecturing." Fortunately, as far as all this is concerned, poetry is a veritable Sunday child. First of all, its written tradition reaches much further back and with as much fidelity to the original as can be desired. And second, in its case, all condolences come too late anyway. It doesn't need first to be told what to do and how to behave musically; it knows it already, just as the body intuitively knows how to move. How a poet lives his life is of no significance: what determines the structure of a stanza and the particular thrust of a poetic line is the very singularity of human existence itself. Music, by contrast, will—unless it is reduced to its bare essentials—always strive beyond the individual and toward the universal. Like a force of nature it sweeps past our heads. How it manages to find its way back into the individual heart is one of the secrets of its trade. It would hardly be unjust to claim that music likes most of all to dishevel our souls the way wind does hair. Only in the rarest of cases, in Bach's case, say, or, quite differently, in Schubert's, does it engage in a rational and intimate dialogue with the listener. If all the names of all of the composers were reviewed, each of them could easily be subjected to this litmus test. As a rule, what counts as classical in music today boils down to the power of overwhelming, be it through fullness of orchestration or through elaborate harmony. The whole minor-major system of the past sought the same effect—the goal was to inundate the individual listener completely, to make him defenseless, to raise his invisible hackles through chords and then leave him alone with his goose bumps. By now, all of us have been submerged so many times we can simply no longer remember the silence of the world before this great symphonic seduction. This alone—not to mention the fact that our eyes have at this point been so overstimulated by photographs and films—would sufficiently explain why most people find a plain epigram, a haiku, or a line by Hölderlin so feeble and bland, so pathetic and unspectacular. It is as if the eyes and the ears were hopelessly doomed to go hungry on poetic fare. And this although it was poetry, more than anything, that, from the beginning, wanted to have it all—a maximum of synesthesia. In other words, when Melpomene, Calliope, Thalia, and Erato put their heads together, everything was prepared for sensual experience.

4

Whoever expects the arts to overwhelm him externally with the force of thunder, whoever prefers the brutal methods of cinema-cum-Wagner to the modest amphibrach will never get his money's worth from poetry. For such a person, every metrical foot is too lame. For this much is true: compared with all other artistic genres, poetry will always be the least Mannerist. Its means of expression are simply of a more subtle nature. It does take more than a little bit of sensitivity and intuition to be able to follow its tricks to the point at which they become insights. Quite late, at a time when the poetry of the Greeks and the Romans was hardly more than a rumor, a pastime for educated aristocrats, a poet named Ausonius formulated the paradox of poetic refinement:

> I am the daughter of language, of the air, the mother
> of empty evidence, entirely voice even without spirit.

This could be interpreted as self-incrimination, as a confession to a specific flaw. But before anyone complains about birth defects, it should be understood that it is the echo itself that talks like this. More than that: when it comes down to it, all poetry is its own echo. Its middle name is still that of that unfortunate nymph who left behind nothing but her voice. Never mind the pun: her daughters were actually named Iambe and Iynx—read: scandalmonger and howler. Poetologically speaking, these two—veritable orphans—are the simplest modes available to man no sooner than he finds himself on his own and with no other instrument but his own voice to give testimony of his existence, be it in keening wails, in bare interjections, or in the form of carefully crafted verse, in this case, iambs made up of short (unstressed) and long (stressed) syllables. This was the form preferred by Ausonius when he tried to capture the essential paradox of poetry in an epigram: as soon as it echoes in the reader's heart, its physical absence is coupled with intense presence. Of course, poetry (and, more broadly, all literature) is hardly more than the echo's echo. It plays with the invisible. It takes the form of sound only for those who lend it their voice. This is what the late Roman poet meant when he talked about the difficulty of drawing a face that eludes the eyes. How else than through an acoustic image can what has long since melted into air be conjured? Here, only one thing can be of assistance: writing, which moves the lips anew; writing, which remains in suspended animation until it is found by somebody who can be its sounding board. Viewed in this light, letters are to sound carrying images in its wake what notes are to music. Thanks to the alphabet with its infinite combinatorial possibilities, the poetic text can work as a score. Even if it only rarely blossoms into polyphony (as a rule, the poem, following its monological nature, remains monophonic, and often even melody-bound), it does—just like the score on the conductor's rostrum—arrange all its vocal components in the spirit of its overall composition. Language itself brings the echo to life. It lives, Ausonius says, in our own ears. Through the ages, it remains within earshot, omnipresent. It seems as if it really could detach itself from the pages of books and buzz up at any time as the *vocis imago*, as Virgil once quite metaphorically dubbed it. The idea of a copy of the voice may sound like necromancy, but such apparently nonsensical similes are necessary if the ambiguity of lyric poetry is to be captured. For the poem is a composition in waiting. It contains the demand to be read, quietly or out loud. It wants to be engaged from within, to be translated into the resonance of a kindred soul. Incorporeal, its call will have already reached, line by line, the corporeal reader's ear: intone me, recite me! Or at least read me, so that a string may silently begin vibrating inside you.

5

This precisely attests to the above-mentioned originary kinship of music and poetry. Both art forms depend on having someone turn to them one day and bring them to life. On this issue, at least, all composers are in agreement. Music remains a mere concoction of notes, rests, and time signatures on paper until somebody meets its challenge with his virtuoso playing or golden voice. In a different, perhaps even plainer way, the same is true of the written word. Even if the technical investment needed to reanimate it seems smaller, the emotional and intellectual effort is comparable to what a piece of music demands. As far as perception is concerned, the two operate on the very same level. What allows them to transcend the conditions of reception of the visual arts is something else, though.

Poetry may indeed stick to meaning like the fly to the flypaper—to its content, as philosophy dubs this handicap— but what gives it wings, as much as music, is its groundedness in time. With every initial sound, with every breath, poetry follows time's fluctuations and meanderings—it is an intimate companion of the invisible and the ageless, as its insistent murmur makes clear. The fact that its pathways from body to body don't seem to take up much space, that it prefers to move horizontally, at eye level, while music, more high-handed and grandiose, tends to take off more quickly—the fact, that is, that a structure of words is far more likely to remain true to human mortality and not to bury it under a flood of sound is certainly not the worst of poetry's characteristics. In poetry, too, intervals (here understood as the distance between successively sounding syllables) determine the relationship to time. As time—infinite, manifold, and sweeping—unceasingly inundates the individual, what can the poem do but break it down into endless moments? Time cannot be grasped or negotiated with, but it can be given accents. If its measure cannot be taken, at least it can be translated into our own measure. And few measures, discounting the measurements of physics, are better designed for such work than the measures of verse. They provide us with the modest norm that we, as individuals aware of our finitude, can hold up to the supreme norm of time. Allowing ourselves to be guided by the modulations of our voice and vouchsafing our entire spiritual existence to it, we transform time into a transparent fabric of stressed and unstressed moments.

6

Poems are pauses in dying, at least on paper. Transcending the layout on the page, they displace their author's individual life beyond bounds. They transport you into a kind of anti-time, in which you become everybody's contemporary no sooner than you engage in this uncircumstantial practice—be it as aficionado, reader, or poetic interlocutor. Irrespective of their rootedness in the sensual world, poems are—and at this even philosophy cannot but prick up its ears—vessels for the metaphysical. Owing to its semantic absolutism, poetry is a memento suspended over the abyss of existence. For the duration of a few breaths, the brain defies its own transience.

It is hard to say to what degree this is also true of music, at least for a musical amateur like me. As I said before, music seems to pursue different goals. Music is far more sublime, not only in its aesthetic effect but also in how it uses its means and techniques. It is also oddly overdetermined, incomparably better armed, with all its pedal points, fortissimos, crescendos, and diminuendos. By comparison, literature always stands naked before time. Nothing in it can be compared to scales. The whole wondrous apparatus of harmonic series, chords, timbres, and key changes just doesn't apply to literature. (The only exception I know of is Hölderlin's doctrine of "changing tones," which defines *poetry* as "song" and operates with contrasts deriving from the use of original Greek forms: lyric, epic, tragic.) Apart from such bold ideas, literature is left with prosodic equivalents at best. Astonishingly, however, such poverty predestines it to a special kind of intimacy with time. Aphoristically speaking, poetry almost always maintains a second-person-singular level of intimacy— a *you*-to-*you* relationship—in its engagement with time, while the power of music, its transpersonal magic, can be said to derive from the third-person impersonality—the *it*-to-*it* relation—of objective confrontation. Both are about transforming neutral time—be it physical, historical, geological, or even, more generally, planetary—into shaped, individualized time, into the discontinuum of *accented time*. Given, however, that subjectivity gets expressed so differently in poetry and music, the lyrical chronos and the musical chronos cannot really be compared. A composer will inevitably use joy and sorrow, boredom or anticipation differently than his versifying colleague. In the end, the composer's ambition is almost always total. His unspoken agenda is nothing less than the total transformation of what philosophical idealism called "forms of intuition." Power-hungry Wagner merely ratted out what is, after all, the clandestine goal of all music: "Here, time becomes space."

Hardly any writer would subscribe to such a formula in good conscience—not to mention the fact that he would, most likely, lack the means for such a totalitarian aesthetic. And not for lack of desire, mind you—after all, hasn't many a poet tried to put the word into a dream state? Poetry comes from inside, its practitioners claim by way of justification—it is an endogenous creation, a game of telephone between psyches. Yet, no matter how timeless and how nearly impalpable poetry may be, it will always remain infinitesimally small compared to space. Its asylum is the moment of meditation, an *intermundium* inhabited by the psyche and not the external world with which the sound spheres of composers compete. Poetry always takes place in the next room, no matter how great the radius of its appeal may be. Language is its medium, standard pitch its natural sound space. Neither clamor nor the verbal thundering in the soccer stadium, nor even the wielding of megaphones can make you forget this. How touching the jealousy of certain modern-day bards who joined the fray, as if the goal were to drown out all of Beethoven's symphonies. Compared to the breakers of music, the spoken word is that solitary shell you have to pick and hold up to your ear if you want to hear the distant murmur at all.

7

While I put all this down on paper, a laser beam in the magical hi-fi box behind me is scanning a small, shiny silver disc. This procedure transforms thousands of digital signals into a series of electronic impulses that are then translated into vibrations emanating from my speakers and spreading across the room. Even if I don't pay close attention to it, the timbre of the soprano gets to me. She is singing a song cycle by Gustav Mahler. Breathing lightly, I witness, not without respect, the majestic sound carpet being unrolled for a poet's few spare words. It is hard to believe that an entire symphony orchestra has to go to work here. The prelude is set to a poem that begins with the elegiac line "I am lost to the world." Friedrich Rückert is the name of the fortunate man in whose honor the English horn paints a melancholy landscape—the tempo, as befits a distich, purest adagio. Every now and then, the strings shiveringly switch from minor to major, dignified treetops lining the voice's distant path. "I am dead to the world's bustle," the voice sings. Suddenly, I realize: the music alone is en route—the voice, it seems, was left behind long ago. Isolated, lost to the world, it is now but its own echo. It dwells neither in the frozen landscape of Schubert's wanderer nor in Eichendorff's sylvan solitudes, but in the otherworldly space of the memories of life, at the farthest remove from humanity. There it rests in a realm of stillness, as the poem has it. Separated from the body, it remains stationary. Once more, the orchestra circles around the forsaken place, then the voice withdraws, vanishes into higher registers, up into delicate regions. There, with the last line, the riddle is solved, and we find out who's been speaking here all along: not some alter ego, but the poet's own voice at the very moment of fusion with its subject—its own song. As soon as it becomes one with it, all sorrow ends. Ennui and melancholy yield to the recognition of mortality: "I live alone in my heaven, / In my love and in my song." And this is good, very good, the music seems to be saying, as it joins in with the concluding verses and buries whatever doubts we may still have.

Why this apparently arbitrary example? Simply because it says it all. Poets are said to be naïve. At least, they like to pretend that they are, if only so as to be able to assert their competency when the successful moment does arrive. Here, we have such a successful moment. Admittedly, hundreds of others could be found in the treasure trove of Romantic art songs—from Schubert to Schönberg, say. But this particular song demonstrates in the most exemplary fashion the synthesis of the poet's word with the composer's art. Melodic inventiveness meets poetic depth of character, and during this summit something else is generated, something that is still unknown and surpasses the inspiration of both. Keeping in mind what I said earlier about the origin of song, you might think that the result must necessarily fall within the purview of tautology. Not at all, however—all those centuries that have passed (not without a trace, as every new renaissance in instrumental style attests) since the shepherds sang in ancient Greece made sure of that. If evolutionary leaps are less visible in poetry than in epic, it has to do with its specific, congenitally static character. Music, by contrast, is by definition a dynamic affair. That it has more than lived up to its reputation is evidenced by the scope of its evolution.

But, no false modesty, please: literature's influence has always been critical. Nowhere can this be seen more clearly than in the colorful history of melodics. After the unisons of the classical chorus—literally, its monotony—and the dark ages of Gregorian chant came the madrigal, which cultivated, from its very inception, casual relations with a poetry well formed and sure of itself. But it took Romanticism to make the breakthrough of genuine synthesis possible. Elevated emotion, nostalgia, ennui, fairy-tale bliss—if these catch phrases long thrown at Romanticism are even halfway accurate, then no epoch was more conducive to the grand marriage of literature and music. It took no more than reminding both of their common origin for the knot to be tied. Suddenly, everything fit together; suddenly, everything fell into place. Only recently blown across the mountains from Italy into the languishing north by fresh winds, melody—that bastard child of folk song and Italian aria à la Rossini—could use the Saxon and Viennese music industries as its landing pattern. Suffice it to name Weber and Schubert as proof. As different as they were in temperament, each made his own contribution to the renewal of melody, and the audiences—in their naïveté, some say—have been thanking them ever since with frenetic applause. Here, the circle is joined. And it should not trouble us that it has been broken many times since. Even if most of what has since emerged from the encounter between word and music sounds like crash, collision, and cacophony—what lives on in the repertoire are songs like the one by Mahler. As you can hear, it owes as much to the lines of the poet as to the ambiguity of the music, which leaves us speechless.

THE BARS OF ATLANTIS
On the abyss of the imagination: A descant in fourteen descents

MESSAGE IN A BOTTLE

If a poet has been at it for long enough, he will find his work picked up by those factory trawlers called anthologies, and even in textbooks. And then, if not before, he will find he is in for a bit of a shock. He will be approached for information, explanation, thoroughgoing elucidation of this or that aspect of his work. Lecture podiums will throw themselves at his feet, newspaper supplements will keep themselves blank for his self-analyses. A flood of questions will rain down on him: Will he comment please on this or that phrase that may have escaped his lips eons ago. In Germany, it tends to be schoolmasters who come knocking, and after them the keen amateurs of poetry, the type that sign up for guided tours of museums and even go so far as to spend their time browsing in archives. Retired professors will beat a path to his door, footnote fetishists, newspaper clippers, bibliomanes. And all of them, with their forensic curiosity, on *his* traces. You may have guessed by now that something of the sort has befallen the present writer—but no one who writes and publishes nowadays will escape such treatment. Not since we've had media that shrill and chatter around the clock, and that in the context of a society that is only ever briefly *not* in interactive mode, in a concert hall for classical music (let's say, a performance of Debussy's opus 109, *La Mer*), or in a formal lecture, where old-fashioned rules of silent listening still apply.

I want to talk to you today about a line of mine, one single line. It's one of those tricky cruxes in an author's work that draws readers' letters, and the occasional personal approach, after a reading, say. At such moments, an author is liable to be covered in confusion. It's possible he'll admit that certain lines of his authorship don't make sense to him anymore. There are places that, years later, make him uneasy, and seem—even to him—to cry out for explanation. He can't revise them or buff them away, but all at once he understands why a poem is sometimes likened to a message in a bottle (it sounds so hackneyed, but there's something to it). It spends a long time out there in the sea of books, that sea of silent print, and now it's been washed back to his feet. *Message in a bottle*: a scrap of text sealed up, with no addressee, except for whichever chance beachcomber picks it up, uncorks it, and starts to read it. Well, the poem that launched the following meditations is one of that sort.

A single line in it, as I say, but one that kicks up dust aplenty. And it's returning to it, and seeing it hanging there in its web of unspoken implications, that seems to demand a more fulsome account of it from me. Very likely I'll end up crossing state borders and leaving the domain of the contemporary poem altogether. I won't be able to do it without thumbing through other literatures, visiting previous cultures. Also, the nature of the subject might make the whole thing seem like an odyssey on the ocean of symbols. I may even suffer shipwreck. But I'm afraid you can't have it without taking a risk—that wildly exaggerated claim contained in the following line: "Travel is a foretaste of Hell."

POETRY AS SEA VOYAGE

Odyssey? Ocean? Shipwreck? Aren't those just a figure of speech? And what have they to say to the advanced and accelerated world of today? Even if one insists that simile and metaphor, comparison and analogy are widely differing expressive resources that need to be carefully distinguished in the interests of conceptual clarity, we are still left with the conundrum of their traditional nature. And since most of these forms are getting a little long in the tooth, we must wonder which of them still work today. Or is it that poetic images outlast theses and theories? Are the basic foundations and fundaments of human imagination not what they always were, for all the acceleration, modernization, globalization? Might that not be a cause for the astonishing durability of poetry? One notices that there are certain occasions where humans still (or even more than ever) trust to the fixity of words. They mark the great, singular, tragic, festive moments of life—the proposal of marriage, the grief for the departed, the international treaty. It is there that the poetic quotation is dropped like an anchor into the racing tide of time. It sounds a little abstract, perhaps, hence an illustration is in order:

The sea voyage is actually one of the oldest figures for poetry. The ship, of course, stands in for the soul, and for the state; but it was the poets who, mindful of the metaphor's dynamic qualities, extracted a maximum of drama from it. The ship as symbol of setting out, of life's hazards, was one of the most widely used metaphors, from Homer's *Odyssey* to *Moby-Dick*, current as long as Western civilization was in an expansive phase. And not just the Western tradition either: Chinese, Persian, and Arabian literature is full of examples of maritime heroics, as witness the adventures of Sinbad the sailor. It's second nature for Horace, in one of the early odes, to beg the sea to spare his friend and colleague Virgil, who is on his way to Athens—to celebrate sailing as a hidden triumph against the gods. As if the Mediterranean hadn't been a ships' graveyard even in those days, he writes in cool mockery of Neptune:

In vain did a wise god
Separate from dry land
the inhospitable ocean when a bold ship
Risks the leap on forbidden terrain.

Would it occur to anyone to say anything quite as exalted
when shuffling onto a plane nowadays? Or is it that we've gotten a little more reticent as concerns the celebration of our
modern means of transport? Why, you wonder, are there no
odes to that abecedary of Airbuses and Boeings and Chinooks,
not so much as an elegy to *Concorde*, the only supersonic passenger plane in history, now shunted off into a museum?

Presumably the general technophobia of poets has its origins in a profound ambivalence that is already to be found in
the primal image of the ship. The heroic risks, the incredible
bravery of the conquerors of the seas in the *thalassic epoch* have
morphed into the continual calamities of our *oceanic culture* (to
use the terms that the German geophilosopher Ernst Kapp
devised in 1845). Who, thinking of luxury liners and Atlantic
crossings, doesn't straightaway think of the *Titanic* and its ice-
berg, even a hundred years after that catastrophe, which has
long since been dwarfed in terms of human victims' numbers,
if not of narrative intensity? Our fantasies of sailing and cir-
cumnavigating the globe have all turned into their inverse.
We've lost the enthusiasm that only yesterday greeted the
most highly evolved machines in the evolution of transport:
the jets and rockets and space shuttles and railways. The
slump into dysphoria, of course, was predicted by another
poetic fantasy where submarine technology and science fiction blended to an extreme form of eremitic flight from the
world. Captain Nemo in his *Nautilus*, Jules Verne's hero from
his novel *Twenty Thousand Leagues Under the Sea*, is a prototype
of that development. Disillusioned with a humanity that has
relentlessly colonized the planet, he became a mountaineer of

the underworld, a despiser of terra firma. But even the sea—captured and conquered and finally scored to a crisscross of sailing routes, by mariners from Odysseus to Ahab, the sinister whaler, by pirates and empires—is no place he cares to stay. This radical misanthrope seeks out the lower depths. The critic of industrialization is left with the seabed. But down there, among the giant squid and a primordial human-hating range of fauna, living without light or love, the song of poetry as sea voyage doesn't have much purchase. Down there, all the celebratory phrases collected by someone like Ernst Robert Curtius (in his magisterial work *European Literature and the Latin Middle Ages*) are defunct—images such as the "leaky ship of the spirit" (a commonplace in late antiquity already), the "sails of interpretation" in Hieronymus, the "lonely mariner at sea," and, finally, "arrival in the safe embrace of port." The ship as metaphor of existence—the subject of Hans Blumenberg's great and subtle study *Shipwreck with Spectator*—is beached. Shipwreck itself turns out to be merely an episode; never mind how frequently it recurs. We are no longer standing on the beach in the classical attitude of the philosopher in Lucretius, calmly observing the travail in front of him. Even that "joy of shipwrecks" that Giuseppe Ungaretti evoked in 1919 after the first global calamity are not what they were—not since we've had television to pipe horror into our rooms on a daily basis. The limits of metaphor and euphoria, all the intoxicating stimulants that from time immemorial have been based on travel. At this point literature experiences a hiatus, and starts toying with the idea of a breach, begins to question itself. Faced with the trenches in Atlantic and Pacific, antiquity and modernity alike tend to shrivel away. Tradition and improvisation, seen from there, are both equally rootless and obsolete. All you hear is Captain Nemo and his revulsion at the horror of terrestrial life, the babble of the escapist: "The sea is beyond the reach of despots . . . A supernaturally marvelous existence stirs in the sea; it is nothing but movement and love, a living infinity, as one of your poets once put it . . . Oh, sir, come and live, come and live in the bosom of the sea! There and there alone is independence! There there is no master's voice! There I am free!"

To be abstract again: At what moment does a metaphor become effective? Is it, as some philosophers contend, its utter autism that makes it so enigmatic, so seductive? Are metaphors purely verbal products, introverted pictures with only a vague connection to the outside world? We know how it operates: you take a this for a that. One notion, by sleight of hand, by legerdemain, is substituted for another. This, as we know, is the meaning of the original Greek *metaphoros*: and the greater the distance between the two components of a metaphor, the further the leap from *quid* to *quo*, the more powerful the surprise. In an Athenian side street once I saw a moving truck with that on its side. It stood there, with its back down, and on the pavement were people's belongings piled up. From that moment on, I've never forgotten the practical sense of the term. A metaphor is a moving truck, it drives significances from here to there, and in the cabin are the poets chatting and driving. But it's the *Inbild* (an Idea, Plato would have called it) slumbering within us, coming from who knows where, that gets the metaphor moving. Beginning with such an *Inbild*, I would now like to set out on a little poetic cruise with you. In a series of brief descents I will try to triangulate a site that Plato was actually the first to name, and that we owe to him. The subject is the myth of Atlantis, that ur-topos of the sinking of civilizations, their natural disappearance, associated with one's fear of the indifference of the sea. Then, flight from the world as a recurring, if disguised, motif in modern poetry, as witness the striking deep-sea fantasies in a number of poets, for instance, Jules Verne, Lautréamont, Baudelaire,

T. S. Eliot, and others. Also, we will be talking about Dante, their forefather, and his surprising cruises in prominent places in the *Comedy*. Then, complementing Gaston Bachelard's *Poetics of Space*, I will briefly stop at the isolated image of the bar, the model for the stretching of time in a small space, according to the motto: poetry is rare. We will talk about the figure of the cosmopolite, that is, the hypermobile whirligig man of our times. And finally we will repair to the dream of an underwater museum, the ideal final assembly point for poets, once everything has been lived, and everything spoken. We will proceed by leaps and bounds, but each brief trip will contribute to the trip as a whole, which was launched by the line of poetry referred to above.

The speaker of the poem is changing planes at an international airport, and thinking about the long distance he has already traveled. A pretty standard situation, since by now those who have experienced the condition of global flotsam are presumably in the majority, all those, so to speak, equidistant, sociologically declassified, travel-neutered individuals. To put it another way: the speaker of these lines is one of the army of the globalized, part of the fifth column of the unwillingly cosmopolitan. Looking out bravely, spinning on his own axis, he finds himself in one of those strange, despecified places, that in the language of the planners is called a transit lounge. Perfectly natural that he should feel a little giddiness, coupled with a sudden sense of his own tininess. This is not to extenuate or justify, but it may be one of the reasons for the metaphor that now abruptly surfaces, put by the author in the place where it will get most attention: at the end. "There in the transit lounge," you may read,

> Where downtime remains conscious to no end,
> The proverb from the bars of Atlantis swims
>   into ken:
> Travel is a foretaste of Hell.

POSEIDON'S TEMPLE

And once I, too, got to see him in his Technicolor glory that stopped me in my tracks. I'm referring to that naked, tanned figure of a man that a Greek hand brushed onto the lid of a sarcophagus, some two and a half thousand years before I, a tourist in the south, came along to look at it. The place was Paestum, a dry-as-dust spot in southern Campania in Italy, the time a paradisal summer in the early '90s, back when I was young and venturesome.

My recollection of said man is so vivid I can summon it up at will. I'd spent hours traipsing among ruins, pursued by the sun, by the electric chirruping of thousands of cicadas, intimidated by the majestic dimensions of the three mighty temples. I felt a little of what Goethe felt in that brown-yellow desert. After the green landscapes of the Bay of Naples, I found myself in a barren plain, a desiccated, rather discouraging-looking landscape that wasn't quite of this world. Dusty roads, cornfields, a few pines. No signs anywhere—"Antiquity, look out!"—to prepare you. Quite abruptly you found yourself, hundreds of miles to the west, facing the colossal religious sites of Doric immigrants, like incredible tangles of some alien architectural vegetation. It was as if you were hiking in the Black Forest and suddenly stumbled upon tropical lianas. I sweated up flights of stairs, my hand unthinkingly resting on the wide rills of elephantine pillars, testing the solidity of the stone flags, taking off my flip-flops, only to put them straight back on again because of the tarantula sting of the burning ground. There was something swamplike in spite of the dryness; in the heat haze the pillars were like bundles of reeds that threatened to break under the weight of the beams. *Entasis* was the magic word that explained the impression, but it sounded more like *elephantiasis*. You could see how a paranoiac like Piranesi would have been in his element—elephant—here. Above all, the temple of Poseidon, that mighty breathing body, carved out of tufa muscle, had silenced me. In my stunned brooding I would have offered myself to those porous pillars, suffered myself to be crushed by them.

It was imposing, no question, particularly later on, as dusk fell. But monumentality isn't everything. Past worship leaves not only empty space, but empty spaces of memory. There's nothing to grab hold of apart from the pleasing terms of architecture: *epistyle*, *tympanum*, *cella*. But the real sensation of the place was elsewhere.

DIVING INTO ETERNITY

Just opposite, in fact, in a corner of the local Museo Archeologico, in the form of a simple sketch. It showed the outline of a man diving from a tower into the water, forever frozen in profile. It depicted the split second when a man no longer has solid ground underfoot, but hasn't yet reached the new element either. His gaze was aimed unwaveringly at the strip of blue below him, and yet it looked curiously animated: there was almost a cunning twinkle in the pupil dabbed in the corner of the eye, that gave him something approaching a squint. The good man was hanging suspended in space, as if to illustrate Zeno's famous likeness of the arrow. If his dive was into the next world, then—just as the arrow never got from A to B—he would never make it. The picture was on a narrow stone trough, unearthed from one of the necropolises in Paestum. A sign named it "Tomba del Tuffatore"—which for a long time was translated into German as "Tomb of the Underwater Swimmer." But I suppose it would be more correct to call it the tomb of the high-diver. It's easy to imagine how the confusion came about. On fleeting inspection, the picture depicts an underwater scene. The two trees with their feathery palm fronds would be some zoophyte or other, some giant coral outcrop, the tower might be the remnant of a civilization sunk in the sea. The seeming weightlessness of the man will have done its bit. Also his posture was a swimmer's, diving down with powerful strokes: a diver for pearls, or sponges.

There could be no question as to where he was headed. The sarcophagus itself gave it away: here was someone on his way to the underworld, Orcus, the Isles of the Blest, or whatever the Greek names were for the unknown land. It was a snapshot, a Polaroid showing a mortal on his way to immortality. Or rather: it captured him halfway. Just like those freeze-frames that a jury at the Olympics consults to determine the outcome of a long jump or a hundred-meter sprint or a high dive. According to Orphic doctrines current at the time, it was the way of the soul, brushing off the body, to assure itself of life after death. Such a dive would have been an effective representation of such an idea. Plus, Greek philosophy from Pythagoras to Plato to Plotinus was obsessed with the idea of cleanliness. The dying Socrates could think of no better topic for his last dialogue than this. The separation of soul from body is the main purpose of the journey of life as far as he was concerned. The fact that the man was jumping into the water was perfectly right; further proof of the otherworldly import of the little painting was the diving tower—an almost abstract construction, slightly skewed, of stone slabs piled up on top of one another. Some specialists have seen in it an allusion to the so-called Pillars of Hercules. That would mean the man had pushed off from the bounds of the habitable world, to dive into Okeanos. The little scrap of water surface at the painting's bottom edge would then be a representation of the ocean on which, according to Plato, the earth was merely an island; somewhere beyond must be Atlantis, the fabled sunken world. In other words, the figure was on the point of falling out of the picture. Admittedly with consummate grace, reminiscent of Attic vase paintings or Etruscan frescoes. The athletic posture was astonishing and exemplary, the body taut as a plucked string. It *looked* like someone suspended in some unearthly medium. As if, squinting at eternity, he had already quit the earth's atmosphere.

It's not hard to explain my enthusiasm of that time. It was the first time I had beheld a piece of Greek mural painting. And then it depicted a scene that, in every respect, had something weightless, floating about it—it was between significations, between elements, between land and sea, between this world and the next. Another indication of its sublimity was the fact that you forgot what the painted surface was intended to cover. The mortal remains of a big shot, presumably some stinking-rich sybarite living in the lap of luxury, an inhabitant of ancient Poseidonia (which later became Paestum). The little rectangular painting had obviously been made in a hurry. It had to be finished within a day, and then placed in the ground along with the dead man in his comfortable, richly ornamented container. Hence the impression of freshness, of enthusiastic departure, hence the whiff of eternity in a highly concentrated moment that made me involuntarily hold my breath.

THE COUNCIL OF PRAWNS

Back to that day. I remember a blazing, truly imperial day in August. The museum closed its doors, the halogen lamps over the grave paintings of Paestum were turned off. The sea wasn't far, just a few minutes by car, with windows down to cool off. The air was so clear, I thought—but there I was mistaken—you could see Capri, the island I owe my first impressions of the undersea world. The sea was of a dazzling ultraviolet blue. It was that part of the Mediterranean today called the Mare Tirreno, a last dying echo of its Greek past. At the sight of it I felt a deep peace flood my entire being, the sort of feeling that favors eccentric decisions. And that was the summer I learned to dive. By which I don't mean holiday snorkeling in shallows by the shore, nor yet that popular pastime of going out in an excursion steamer, through whose glass bottom you can, if you're lucky, glimpse small fish and seaweed. I mean proper diving, with that impressive, if faintly ridiculous, tackle familiar from James Bond films. Now, I have every sympathy for anyone who finds this amateurish clowning around under the sea stupid, but I have to say I fell for it right away. Probably something to do with the steep learning curve. Because no sooner had I completed the course for beginners, padding across the sand of a small cove in Anacapri—having, of course, pulled on my flippers much too soon—weighed down by the heavy gear, sweatily weaving in and out among fishing boats, no sooner sat through a couple of hours in a humid classroom close to the water, than it began. My diving instructor, a cheerful Italian, had so little English he didn't spend very long on theory. Already on the second day we drove out to Faraglioni, the jagged cliffs off the southeast corner of the island, to practice a descent there. And so it went on, the full program, as an hors d'oeuvre. I flippered through the Blue Grotto—the kitsch capital of Capri, where Emperor Tiberius installed his hidden nymphaeum—in the wavering light of waterproof torches, and saw the rubble of the villa of the author Curzio Malaparte at the foot of the cliff, at a depth of more than forty meters, where as a greenhorn I had no business being. Between the chunks of cement, I encountered my first moray eel, which came silently hissing at me out of its hole, mouth agape, as appalling to the newcomer as the skeleton on a ghost train.

And then the following scene: The whole class is kneeling down on the seabed, clustered around the instructor in a semicircle. Breathing noisily in and out—it sounded almost as if we were gurgling our last—we each concentrate on the man with the status of mage in this underwater empire. He has a

pointer with him, which telescopes in and out, and with that
he is gesturing at a little seam in the seabed. There, in the
white silicate sand, straight in front of us, but just now invisible to us newcomers, a quiet natural wonder is taking place.
About a dozen prawns, tiny, glassy, soft, resembling pieces of
tubing in a chemistry lab, are assembled in a silent, somehow
Asiatic ceremony. Like us, the intruders on their domain, they
have formed a semicircle and are just in the process of feeling
one another out with their antennae. Had we not been wearing goggles, we would have rubbed our eyes in disbelief at the
extraordinary illusion. We saw a parodic version of ourselves,
an anticipation by some millions of years, performed by these
frail, dignified beings in their serious conclave. What was in
session there, ancient and dawn-of-creation-like, was the
council of prawns.

ON DIVING

It's true, the perspectives at the bottom of the Mediterranean
weren't exactly what a nature lover like Jules Michelet might
sing in his hymns to the coral groves in the Indian Ocean, but
it was at least a pale imitation. It did as an inducement to
carry on, whenever opportunity offered. Sixty dives later, I'm
still not cured of my little maritime mania. Experiences the
professional would greet with a yawn at worst, or a tired smile,
are a precious trove of memories to the occasional visitor
underseas or the author in him. I have remained an amateur,
hence a few more remarks of a general nature.

Anyone who has foresworn the connection to the atmosphere's universal supply of oxygen for a longer or shorter time
will know how exposed one feels. For all the equipment
involved, it entails giving oneself over to another element,
reverting to a previous phase of evolution, and that has something frightening about it. However sweet the poet's siren

call, "O that we were our ancestors: / a clump of slime in a warm moor," that sort of *nostalgie de la boue* isn't for sensitive souls. It's not where humans belong, and you feel it with every muscle fiber. I will never experience the feeling of losing gravity as one quits earth's embrace. But at least I know what it's like to hang around at a depth of twenty meters without gills and swim bladder in places with such evocative names as Shark Bank, Pirates' Bay, Gorgons' Reef, or Thousand Steps.

It's surprising to what far-flung places diving takes you. I've been to the Caribbean, the Dutch Antilles, to islands with names that suggest scents or gaudy cocktails, like Bonaire and Curaçao. The Indian Ocean has gulped me too, sites on the Seychelles, the island of La Digue, for instance, famed for its powdered-sugar beaches—backdrop for rum commercials. It wasn't just there that I had the feeling I had wandered onto a film set. I expect it was a consequence of seeing too much Jacques Cousteau on TV as a young person. Probably that's where one should look, too, for an initial infection with the subsequent disease—there, and the call of the gaunt commandant: *"Il faut aller voir!"* Let's take a look.

What is this desire to stay underwater for hours on end? What possesses you—me—to step into the water with a steel cylinder on your back and flippered feet? Only yesterday anyone thus garbed was called a frogman—and with good reason. Only a very small minority of those who set out from the myriad diving resorts scattered over the planet have any of the attractiveness of mermaids, nymphs, and Nereids that myths and cartoon films dangle before us.

Diving demonstrates the thalassic regression of *Homo sapiens* in its most blatant form. We are not equipped to live in the water; therefore we try, with every technical means at our disposal, to simulate that capacity. Diving is an echo of those lovely womb-weeks. To put it another way, it's a technically enhanced meditation on the condition of our lost paradise: that before birth. To see grown men in colored rompers (neoprene), gumming the mouthpieces of their breathing tubes like pacifiers, rolling their eyes blissfully the while behind their silicone masks, that's what diving is. Only unenlightened persons would confuse such an essentially magical activity with an ordinary pastime—any version of faster, higher, farther (or deeper). To talk about diving as a sport is to the initiated a sacrilege. Any other pursuit while underwater, even one as popular as underwater photography, remains a mere distraction.

That's maybe half the truth; the other is hinted at in Baudelaire's poem "Man and the Sea." There the master stands by with one of his dizzying analogies that he was pleased to call "correspondences." The sea, with its unfathomable deeps, became an equivalent of the human soul. Was it therefore not logical that one day a man had to plunge into the mirror? And don't you look into yourself each time you dive?

> The two of you are shadowy, deep, and wide.
> Man! None has ever plummeted your floor—
> Sea! None has ever known what wealth you store—
> Both are so jealous of the things you hide!
>   (Baudelaire, "L'homme et la Mer,"
>   tr. Roy Campbell, Pantheon Books, 1952)

Enough of diving. Everyone has his own hobbies, and I'm not out to make recruits. This is just to indicate some of the new possibilities of exploration that twentieth-century technology has brought within reach. The Aqua-Lung permits the layman to set foot in otherwise inaccessible places. No wonder millions of people make use of the opportunity to convert themselves into amphibians for an hour or so. What does the poet say? "All is shore. Eternally calls the sea—"

COSMOPOLITE

Which brings me to the title of the little piece that has served me as a diving board: "Cosmopolite." It's a word with its own sonority, not just the three *o*'s joined together like railway cars (the consonants like buffers between them). For someone with a childlike relation to language such as a poet, that would already be reason enough to use it as often as possible. But then if the person in question happens to have a past like mine, there's a further appeal to it, a whiff of the forbidden. *Cosmopolite* is a term with a long and checkered past. In the parts where I was born and grew up, it was almost something like a charm. Admittedly only for part of the populace: the other straightaway sensed the devil, sniffed betrayal and conspiracy, reaction and subversion, and whatever else from the class enemy. In the ears of system believers, faithful and burning Communists, *cosmopolite* was a cussword, along the lines of *Trotskyite* or imperialist *Dreckschwein*. For an average person like Dzhugashvili (a.k.a. Stalin) it was simply a class of criminal. Siberia was full of cosmopolites. These were people who were punished either because of their doubting the idea of communism or, just as likely, because they clung to the belief in its universal spread, like certain old Bolshevists. Or because they were too slow to grasp that the Soviet Union had a monopoly on communism now. Some also because they were Jews, which meant they were cosmopolites by birth. In rarer instances because they were free men, citizens of the world, members of a greater cosmos than the Soviet—such as the poet Mandelstam. For these, very few in number, *cosmopolite* was the secret word by which they might recognize one another (a shibboleth, as it might be). Be this as it may, for seventy years the word was charged; to some it was a credo, to others the name of a dangerous and highly infectious intellectual disease.

The grounds for this are familiar enough by now. Socialism was an affair that functioned only with sealed borders, Berlin and other walls, and the measures against any form of transgressive love or global consciousness were correspondingly sharp.

Clearly, the cosmopolite was the most dangerous type of being there was. Hadn't Socrates taken the wind out of his Athenian accusers' sails by claiming that his polis wasn't Athens, but the cosmos? The solitary individual, ducking his duties as a citizen by identifying with some bigger home, was always a thorn in the side of the mighty. Bad enough that the idea of the cosmopolite, which was first conceived by a Greek, Diogenes Laertius, grew into the purely utopian concept of world citizenship as it passed from the Stoics all the way to the Enlightenment thinkers Kant and Wieland: by the end of the nineteenth century, it gave off a strong reek of imperialism. The suspicious Leninist thought he could detect capital flows and expanding markets lurking behind any seemingly innocuous League of Nations arrangement—in a word, the machinations of some Western empire, whether British, French, American, or other. The cosmopolite, therefore, was a creature who, on the wrong side of all those protective fences, served the interests of the exploiter in the land of the proletarian. The tragic aspect of this is that the very Russia that was so thorough in its extermination of any world-citizen consciousness had once begun with idealistic notions concerning that same citizenship. For a while it looked as though the word *cosmopolite* might have made its way back through Russia to Western Europe long after its Greek roots had been buried there.

The present writer is himself a survivor of the world revolution. He is able to confirm its failure, and now reckons himself among the travelers of all countries who ask nothing more of history than that it spare him any more such experiments. One thing he is sure of, however: that cosmopolitanism is now

in a decisive phase as a practical policy. In a period of globalization, or, if you prefer, of international crises in short order,
the word has acquired a further layering of meaning. From
now on every man is a cosmopolite, willy-nilly. After all, globalization comes down to this: there are no more faraway
places, the planet has been opened up to its remotest corner,
colonized by media and money. Every inhabitant of the earth
is now the center of this world, stuck in the same fix, with the
fine distinction that the fix is a heated swimming pool for
some, and a desert, flood zone, earthquake region, or bloody
quagmire half the size of Africa for others.

ATLANTIS AS MODEL

Gentle reader! Please forgive me for taking so long to answer
you. You inquired about the penultimate line of my poem
"Cosmopolite." You'd racked your brains for many days, trying to work out what those "bars of Atlantis" mean. You're
right, it is an ominous-sounding line and a great leap of imagination—at once utopian and anachronistic, if you like. Since
the riddle of Atlantis comes up just about every other night on
television, let me keep my remarks to a minimum.

The principal source of the legend of the drowning of the
island of Atlantis is Plato. He in turn was drawing on the
ancient Egyptians; he admits as much in the two dialogues
called *Critias* and *Timaios*. The latter refers to a great island
situated far beyond the Pillars of Hercules (in other words, as
I'm sure you know, beyond the Strait of Gibraltar), "which
was bigger than Asia and Libya put together," as he says. This
island of Atlantis, whose armies, it is said, had attacked the
countries around the Mediterranean long before the times of
Solon, whereupon the united forces of the ur-Greeks fought
them off, later on was sunk by an earthquake, an entire civilization thus vanishing into the sea (Okeanos, if you will). The

decline of Atlantis was not a chance event. The population had made itself guilty of something appalling that caused the wrath of Poseidon to fall upon them in such a terrible way. For this story, too (like the wanderings of Odysseus, the collision of the *Titanic* and every tanker accident since), was the sea god's doing. Had it not been so, humankind would have been forced to reflect on its own reckless and expansionary conduct—especially, with Atlantis in mind. In any case, the name lives on in that of the ocean lying to the west of Europe. The Atlantic Ocean, the Atlantic alliance, transatlantic flights, et cetera, are all things you hear about every day. Occasionally books are written (there are actually several hundred of them), and documentaries made, that tackle the story of the sunken island. Leonardo da Vinci has bequeathed us a so-called *Codex Atlanticus*, a folder of drawings, scribbled on with all sorts of notes in his characteristic mirror writing.

Now to the word *bar*. It is intended to bring a whiff of big city and modern nightlife to the myth, and with them a shot of irony. Think of the whiskey bars in Brecht's *Mahagonny*, and all the dives and harbor pubs of the city poets. I suppose I might have evoked the bars of Babylon instead. But that would have been a place that is clearly described in the Bible, and that, thanks to the archaeologists, one can inspect in the Asia Minor collections of the museums of Berlin or London. No, the author of those lines of yours wanted to be more mysterious. He was thinking more in terms of places like that Orplid of which Mörike sings, or Hölderlin's *Tinian*, which abruptly surfaces in the fragments, where it is used to designate one of the Mariana Islands in the western Pacific, which had recently come to public attention through the memoir of the British admiral Anson. But if it was to be Atlantis, then in the continuation of the legend as set out in Francis Bacon's little masterpiece of surrealist invention, *New Atlantis*, where one may read about Neptune's sex and the triumph of the

Greeks over the Mexican fleet. To this day the myth of Atlantis has something alluring and mysterious. It's the riddle of a culture that exists in a couple of textual references, no more. However many millions of dollars are sunk in searches, only a fool would seriously think he would one day look at it through his periscope.

P.S. The summer before last, I went with a friend to the coast of Asia Minor (modern Turkey). Around the island of Kekova, facing the fortified village of Simena, we inspected the underwater ruins of an antique town from a fishing boat, steered by a laconic old Turk for not much money. The exciting thing was that we were in an archaeological exclusion zone. There was no chance of getting out, much less of going down. Snapshots show the enraptured amateur lying on his tummy on a rug in the bow of the boat, head over the gunwales, gazing intently at the underwater architecture, almost close enough to touch in the crystal clear water. Afterward, we went snorkeling in a little bay that was the only place far and wide where one was permitted to drop anchor, and that in antiquity had been a port for galleys. The seabed was littered with the shards of thousands upon thousands of amphoras. A solitary octopus accompanied us for a while. He obviously shared our curiosity concerning the remnants of the old harbor walls, the red brick from the erstwhile thermal baths. At that moment, all my accumulated Atlantis fantasies were brought to life.

SAILING WITH DANTE

One poet whom one would hardly think to connect with marine voyages and storms at sea is Dante. If you read up on the life of the bustling, subsequently exiled Florentine, you encounter scenes from daily life within medieval city walls. You see thrusting towers and swanky palaces, the geometrical horror trip of Gothic architecture, long winding corridors, discreet galleries. You are put in mind of the hilly landscapes of northern Italy, with swift-flowing rivers, and glimpse the starry skies the wanderer would see over Tuscany and the Marche when he tipped his head back. From the fresco paintings of the time one knows the steep rocky borderings of vineyards and gloomy forests, the stony fields, the great piles of turned earth that make the work of the plowman with his team of oxen seem related obscurely to the miner's. It's a closed world, with clear structures and multiple levels. The perspectives are always those of the earth-dweller, telluric fantasies, connected to the earth, or at the most to what happens within it.

In other words, Dante's descriptions give back what would have been familiar to an Italian of his time—only translated into subterranean, avernal regions. If you picture that gigantic wall painting with its hundred cantos, you will see lava screes, mountain passes, and serpentines. The protagonists walk around a vast crater, its original the volcano lake near Naples, which the Greeks took to be one of the entrances to the underworld. They creep past swamps, stare down into abysses, lose their way in prison-cell-like spaces and torture pits. The difficult trek up Mount Purgatorio brings Alpine landscapes to mind, a climb up rocky paths. Even the description of Paradise and the final peek into the concentric arrangement of Heaven owes something to the familiar topography of the times. Aside from a few brief spells of unconsciousness, the poet always keeps terra firma underfoot. Taking up a pair of notions from Goethe's time, the Neptunian and the Vulcanic, Dante's spatial sense unquestionably owes more to the latter. And yet there are exceptions in the *Divine Comedy*. Three or four times, the horizon abruptly cracks open, and the imagination leaves the familiar behind. In at least four places, the story goes over to the Neptunian; in various ways, all four places are to do with the invention of the sea voyage. The solemn tone makes the reader sit up: the advance into the open sea by single adventurers like Jason or Odysseus is simultaneously condemned and celebrated. These are among the most impressive, and also the most mysterious episodes in the poem. They always challenged the interpreters. The fact that these passages have a central importance is something that has struck other writers. Borges remarks that Dante couldn't have known the *Odyssey*. However difficult it is to imagine that Homer's epic was terra incognita for him, his ignorance would explain a thing or two. Above all, the boldness with which, in his continuation of the tale of Odysseus, he deviates from all that his antique predecessor left us.

Like every other poor sinner in the *Divine Comedy*, the great wanderer, too, lands in Hell. There, he is languishing in the place for false counselors—punishment for the wily stratagems he was famous and notorious for in his lifetime, chief among them the coup with the wooden horse. Or was the idea, after all, Laocoön's? Either way, there are plenty more counts of indictment on Odysseus' docket. As Dante has him confess in the course of a long monologue, he deceived even his own crew until the last moment. After he had had enough of his home port of Ithaca and wife and children and servants, he talked them into one last voyage across the open sea. This was a voyage of no return, out past the Pillars of Hercules (leaving Seville to his right and the present-day Spanish exclave of Ceuta on the coast of Morocco on his left, as Dante, with geographical precision, records), and on and ever on, into waters where no man had sailed before, now under the constellations of the southern sky—true to the heroic watchword of all subsequent navigators that what matters is not life but the voyage itself. We aren't born to loaf around like beasts; only the man who seeks out danger will make discoveries.

Finally, on the horizon they see a vast cone, not unlike our spoil heaps. This is Mount Purgatorio, the obverse to the funnel of Hell, the Antipodean mountain that in the *Purgatorio* is described so windingly. Odysseus, though, is in Hell, because he plunged his men into destruction, because he was unable to stop. A storm comes up, three times they sail around the mountain, then a maelstrom opens and swallows the ship. If you like, you may think of the Mururoa atoll and the French A-bomb tests, the overturning of all spatial and temporal circumstances. A sad death, because Odysseus' departure has achieved nothing. Dante wants us to understand that this was a meaningless end, that it did nothing for mankind. The eternal wanderer had sailed over the edge of the maps of the day and had vanished without a trace, never to be seen again: "Then the waters slowly closed over our heads"—*"Infin che 'la mar fu sovra noi richiuso"* (*Inferno*, XXVI, 142), as it says in one of the most lovely tercets in the entire poem. (I admit, it's one of my favorite lines anywhere.) "Here we come to the miracle," comments Borges, "a legend invented by Dante, a legend that exceeds anything in the *Odyssey* or the *Aeneid*." It was a sudden vision that overcame the poet in his twenty-sixth canto; even today you can feel the frisson at the astonishing way the material is condensed. It has been suggested that Dante here combined two legends that were current in the Middle Ages. The one is the etiological myth of the founding of Lisbon by Odysseus (the shared sibilants reinforce this), the other is the belief in the Isles of the Blest, far out in the Atlantic Ocean. The Egyptians, the Greeks, the Romans, the Celts, they all liked to tell the most fantastic stories of a vanished civilization far out there, the ur-version of all subsequent utopias that was either floating or else sunken out at sea. One must imagine Odysseus in one of the tavernas on such a dream island on the seabed, boozing day and night with his chums.

Basically, all Dante does here is take the motif of the voyage beyond to its logical conclusion. In another place, he tackles the Argonauts: Jason, the first man to hurt the sea (according to the fifth-century Latin poet Dracontius). In the eighteenth canto of the *Inferno*, Virgil points out a man of unmistakably royal bearing, and that's Jason in the pit with the seducers, enduring terrible torments with dry eyes, the model Stoic. The listing of his crimes (most of them perpetrated against women) doesn't change the fact that he is someone whom Dante secretly admires: the man who with a few followers set off on the quest for the Golden Fleece. The alert reader will notice what warm, brotherly feelings the poet has for him. Dante is speaking on his own behalf here; yes, he sees himself as the bold voyager and discoverer. At the very beginning of the *Paradiso*, he warns the reader to stay behind in his little bark, sooner than risk the open sea with him. The choice of the metaphor of the sea and its great masses of water is perfectly deliberate: "I take my course over uncharted waters"—"*L'acqua ch'io prendo gia mai non si corse*" (*Paradiso*, II, 7). Which reminds me a little of a certain dive. In his wonderfully temperamental way, Dante compares his hearers with the intrepid Argonauts headed for Colchis. The ones who, watching Jason plowing with fire-snorting bulls, weren't half so astonished as the reader will be ere long. You won't believe what's coming next, he shouts out to us, before heading off on his vertical journey through the celestial spheres into the empyrean.

But before the final chorale there is one more sea passage to come. It's only three lines of the thirty-third canto, easily overlooked, but also terribly prominent. In such a mathematically—or if you like, arithmagically—composed work it can surely be no accident that the name Neptune falls in the last few meters. Dante is almost at the end of his fourteen-thousand-line voyage. He has seen into the heights of Heaven

and seen how everything there hangs together that in the universe beyond falls apart: bound, as he says, in a single book of
love. To make this moment of synoptic vision clearer, he
instantly swoops all the way down to the bottom of the sea.
It's one of the boldest changes of perspective ever risked by a
poet, one of the most astounding metaphorical leaps. Turning
the topmost under, he puts himself in the position of the sea
god, and with him looks up in the seconds that the shadowy
form of the very first ship glided past, the *Argo*. It's the
moment when myth and history meet in a sort of changing of
the guard, a nodal point, marked, as ever, by rhyme. The
Romanist Ernst Robert Curtius has found the probable source
for this astonishing swing of perspectives. He locates it in the
Achilles of the late Roman poet Statius. In this case, it's the
hero's mother, the sea nymph Thetis, who views the fateful
ship from her low vantage point far below the waves. In the
case of a poet of such absolute memory as Dante, the com-
parativist may assume he has scored a bull's-eye. Curtius
observes: "This tercet is unmatched in Dante's poem; perhaps
no other has such pathos." Amazed, the god takes in how the
future catches up to him and passes him.

> One point can cause me more remoteness
> than twenty-five centuries on the reel,
> that Neptune stiffly beheld the *Argo*'s shadow.

> *Un punto solo m'è maggior letargo*
> *che venticinque secoli alla 'mpresa,*
> *che fe' Nettuno ammirar l'ombra d'Argo.*
>
> (*Paradiso*, XXXIII, 94)

The Christian apotheosis is the dethroning of the sea god, his
naval relegation. There is no return to the prehuman astonishment, once Beatrice, the beloved, has smiled at the poet

and turned back to the eternal source. The rhyme on *Argo* in this case is *letargo*, for which recent translations offer "remoteness." It suggests the coming alongside of two basically incomparable ages: the moment of forever holding one's breath in mystical oneness with God—and the other, that linear, historical time in which the wheel is invented, and the loom, the ship, and the book, and still ahead then, the airplane and the moon rocket. Dante's comparison, according to one way of reading, is clearly to the latter's disadvantage. It's as though he were saying one moment of inattentiveness before God will cost you more than if man had slept through a couple of centuries of progress. It's Neptune who here is plunged into astonishment, not man, and for that reason already, there is a need for other readings. Or, put differently, a poem of such modest complexity will always require new readers.

This obscure, oft-commented-on passage elicited the following commentary from one of the more unusual Dante translators into German, a man with the pseudonym Philaletes (King John of Saxony) in his 1865 edition. "For one instant in Dante's soul the memory of divine vision was lost, bringing with it more forgetfulness than the course of the centuries from the earliest-known events in world history . . . The 2,500 years from Dante's time until then may be calculated as follows: 1,300 back to the birth of Christ, a further 750 years to the founding of Rome, 431 years to the destruction of Troy, 42 years to the *Argo*'s expedition: total, 2,523 years." The appearance of the *Argo* marked the beginning of the space revolution, later confirmed by the voyages of adventurers such as Columbus, Magellan, James Cook, and Vitus Bering. Step outside the Mediterranean, the home of the Homeric gods, and the world stood revealed in its orbic form. It was the beginning of globalization. The fathers had slept through the uprising of the sons. In a millennial upsurge, the age of maritime limits is shaken off, the whole earth taken into possession. Because, as we discovered only then, it so happened that Atlas was the son of Poseidon.

MODERN HELLS

Permit me one last little digression. It concerns one of the unsolved problems of poetry that have gone on burning since the end of Romanticism, the question: Where does the poem speak to us from, and where is it at home? Seeing as so many of the possible places have been wrecked and abandoned— the forest, the solitude of the churchyard, the seashore, any sort of *locus amoenus*. Where can the poem still unfurl its echo? Is it now confined to the soundproofed recording studio, the radio station, and underground seminar rooms of cultural studies, one of many victims of a restructuring of public space? Where can it still go? Does its arena and its anonymous concert hall bear any resemblance to the so-called transit lounges in international airports?

There are several possibilities. Some say a page in a book is enough; that's where a poem really belongs. The book is where language gathers itself, concentrates itself on itself—the honed speech of the poet as the absolute master of expression. That would have been the view of someone like Mallarmé, and not a few have followed him there, armies of immanentists and poet-linguists—all die-hard anti-semanticists—to whom linguistic combinatorics means everything and the external world nothing. This party at least knows what it is about. It seeks to free writing from anything external. As far as they are concerned, there is nothing outside the book, and the exact butterfly-wing movements of each individual, precisely calibrated combination of syllables.

Something in me resists such linguistic self-sufficiency. Just as I am convinced of the double existence of every human being, of his simultaneous physical and spiritual being—which gives all his manifestations something of a pas de deux—just as clearly I know (but alas, cannot prove!) that when we speak, we are at one and the same time here and there. Language already contains quiddity in the shape of its grammar. The thing that enables it to live is the permanent oscillation between active and passive senses. It's the constant switching of operative, perceptive, and reflexive elements, the way that language is both simultaneously world-creating and receptive to the things of this world. A poetry that fails to give me a sense of some outside, something beyond lexis and ictus, doesn't grab me. Because I do understand this much about the whole thing: what ultimately matters is the difference between the epidermis and the page. Of course, the poem lives and waits quivering between the covers of a book. As soon as that's thrown open, it should take to the air and begin its flight, in spirit brushing all those places where it rested as its author was working on it, before—from whatever height and distance—it alights in some stranger's heart.

OF AIRPORTS

These are the places that you hurry through, walking
    on air,
Not noticing: as if here were almost tantamount to
    being there.
You got to heaven's gate in the nick of time.
There were escalators, travelators, tour groups
Swilled this way and that through a system of tubes.
Everything was transfer and transit, even the bistro
For a quick cappuccino on the go.
Nothing suggested any mystic threshold to the
    beyond.
Neither the glance at your passport picture, nor the
    X-ray,
All those chicanes and sunderings took place on
    earth.

There were locks, and you handed in your keys, your
    watch.
The soul suffered, because someone was messing
    with it.
In the waiting room, already incommunicado, you
    changed sides.
And between arrival and departure the light liquefied
To a generic twilight that suggested nothing so much
    as shopping.
The body, before jet propulsion launched it skyward,
Consoled itself with cosmetics, chocolate, rum.
Pure chance that it wasn't swaddled and taxed like a
    mummy.
A whiff of Babylon blows through the halls. Variously
    disoriented
And disorientated, people had trouble reading signs.
In such a place, the present evaporates like a fresh
    scent,
Leaving behind only the future, callously calling out
    names like numbers.
Then you caught a glimpse of it, through the plate
    glass (Christ!)
The ferry with the giant wings, the big bird, the
    people-carrier,
The stewardesses, smiling sibyls full of awful
    knowledge,
The black rubber streak on the airfield. *Viva la
    muerte.*

EUROPA POINT

Maritime routes were once paths of the imagination. The voyages of discovery were preceded by flowering fantasy. Tales of
vast empires beyond the sea (gold and spices, cannibals and

bipeds with dog heads) followed in their wake, and soon reached the stay-at-homes, and then in turn nourished the imaginations of the poets. The Atlantic had been crossed numerous times before Columbus. Vikings, Basques, Icelanders, Normans, the ranks of early-sailing peoples are extensive. They, more than all who followed them, were what they called the "wanderers of the seas." The trouble is, it was all such a long time ago that our collective memory has kept only scraps and notions of their exploits.

For a long time, the Pillars of Hercules were accounted the absolute limit, as Dante has shown us. What was once the sound barrier for rumors regarding the earth is today a busy isthmus, which the architects of the new Europe are pleased to call Europa Point. It sounds plausible, like any other geographical coordinate, but it can't help betraying some of the erstwhile yearning. Doesn't the name suggest that this is where you gain access to an entire continent? Isn't it a fevered optimism trying to sound cool and modern?

Just recently another freighter sank in the narrows. Like so many of the rest of them it was sailing under the Liberian flag, when a gale drove it against the rocks of Gibraltar and it broke in two. It was the usual predictable catastrophe, which meant the press didn't even bother to sound surprised. The crew were lifted off by helicopter, the ship was left to its own devices, and of course the tanks emptied their oil into the sea, causing the ecobrigade to protest. Aside from the local fauna and flora, no one came to any harm, certainly not the owners, who have presumably long since cashed their insurance check. Over it all watched the lighthouse of Gibraltar, and day and night the heavy traffic steams by on either side.

The difference between a ship and an airplane seems to be that one can't leave a message in a bottle from the latter. At most, in a catastrophe, you'll be able to text your loved ones one last time, or leave a message on the answering machine from your mobile, with the vague hope that the recipients will listen to it before erasing it.

THE TEARS OF ODYSSEUS

As so often, it was Homer who cast the first stone. A recurring line from the *Odyssey* comes to mind: "And with tears in his eyes he gazed out across the great desert of the sea . . . ," it says in reference to its hero, once again stuck on an island, imprisoned by an amorous woman (in this instance, Calypso). Translated literally, the line goes: "Across the sea, the infertile, looking, while the tears to him flow." What interests Homer here is a subtraction of liquids. The lesser libation, the veil of tears, is enclosed by the greater, the salt sea, and indifferently absorbed. The sea says nothing, but one can sense what it might say if it could: Cry away, little human, it's not going to do you any good. I'll drink the rest of you later at my own convenience. Of the countless monological moments that carry the epic along, it's one of the loneliest and most moving. The poet must have been so struck by the line that he used it on several further occasions. It's the secret refrain of all the adventurers of whom the *Odyssey* tells. There are the wanderings of a man whom Poseidon subjects to ever more chicanes: an analogy of life, at many moments a comedy, as we see in the frustrations and setbacks of the unhappy hero. But only the remorselessness of nature, in the guise of the measureless sea—allegedly the tool of the gods, but in reality its own willful, fickle element—gives the travelogue its tragic quality. No amount of cunning can help Odysseus against the fact that man consists largely of water himself, he is a collection of fluids. It is this that makes his body so utterly vulnerable to the cycles of the elements. His own vital fluids destabilize his psyche, confuse his emotions—blood, sweat, and tears, as it says, with biblical pithiness. In that way, the likening of sea and desert makes its point, infertility or no. The decisive thing is the mismatch: in one corner the ocean, the vast sodium chloride reservoir of the world, and in the other, a few traces of salt in the eyes of a single mourning man.

DEATH BY WATER

Among the phobias of poets of all the ages, marine fantasies and sea-mares are surely among the most prominent. We can only guess at what draws the poet's imagination down to unknown submarine spaces, and to those shadowy creatures that eke out their existence in those great depths. In many cases such concrete hallucinations are traceable to a vague fear of drowning, forming part of the great complex of fears that animates so much of writing and that has given rise to such different genres as epic, detective story, sexual confession, travel writing, and adventure story. It took a mixture of dream analysis and hermeneutics to figure out why authors, of all people, should be so ambivalently drawn to water. To go under in the gloomy deeps, to swallow water to the point of asphyxiation, has become an idée fixe to more than a few, with the result that what they most feared was what finally came to pass. The yieldingness of water, the way you lose the ground under your feet, makes it attractive to people with a professional interest in crossing borders. It might be a deep pond in the countryside somewhere, or a river that wends its course through a large capital city. But of course the biggest draw remains the ocean, with its abyssal depths only dimly guessed at from behind the high sides of a ship or the upper deck of a passenger liner. If the sea is the emblem of an adjacent infinity, an elemental geographical space where all traces of individuality are dissolved the instant one takes the plunge— then going down in the waves is the perfect Romantic death bar none.

Shelley's sailboat adventure, his drowning in the Gulf of Livorno (and the ensuing burning of his corpse on the beach) belongs here. Also Lord B.'s natatorial feats in the Bosporus, poetic image of his symbolic union with the sea. The fact that the notorious expatriate and Venice worshipper met his end in the lagoon town of Missolonghi on the Gulf of Patras suits his image as bard of freedom and bridegroom of the elements to a T. But the absolute acme of such sea-directed death wishes is unquestionably the appeal to the ocean in the *Chants de Maldoror* of one Comte de Lautréamont. This enigmatic youth spent almost the entire crossing from his maternal Uruguay to his paternal France gazing into the Atlantic breakers. The impression of the all-swallowing water was so annihilating that he never forgot it. "Hail to you, old ocean! . . . You are the symbol of identity: always true to yourself . . . Often have I asked myself which is easier to plumb: the depths of the ocean, or the depths of the human heart! . . . Tell me then, are you truly the abode of the Prince of Hell. Tell me, Ocean." His sinisterly preposterous, dithyrambic prose poems read like a rhetorical charm against the nihilism of the element and its threatened destruction of everything human. He describes how Maldoror, his alter ego, the villain from principle, having viewed a shipwreck from the height of a cliff, and shot the single survivor, throws himself into the sea to mate with a female shark.

And so on and ever on. There is Baudelaire, who, making for India on the one and only sea voyage in his life, suddenly stops and decides to return to Paris. On the island of Bourbon (known today as La Réunion), famed for its vanilla, he falls off a rope ladder into the harbor, and is hauled ashore, with his precious books still tucked under his arm. "Only his hat fell prey to the sharks," was the droll conclusion in an anonymous Parisian newspaper report on the incident. Then there's Jules Michelet, a romantic of erudition, the first to attempt a biography of the sea. In it he describes not just the colors and consistency of the inhospitable, bitter brine—milky white, and a little sticky—but also all its denizens, which will forever remain alien to us, beginning with the jellyfish and invertebrates, through the terrifying giant kraken to the whales, those gentle giants in their terrestrial solitude. Female whales, it says bizarrely in one chapter, which is a textbook example of anthropomorphism, are fish on the outside and women on the inside. Also Coleridge, who owed his "Rime of the Ancient Mariner," the ghost ship locked in Arctic ice, and all the trimmings (water snakes in traces of burning white, the phosphorescent water, a ghost bubbling up from the deep) to a friend's dream. At that point Coleridge hadn't even crossed the Channel. The voyage across the Pacific or his vivid description of it was pure imagination. And yet all the usual poetic phobias were implicated in it.

Marine fantasies are common in the British tradition, as they are in any other maritime nation. In America they are slow to surface, but then they do so with a vengeance, in Melville's epic of the white whale, or Walt Whitman on the Brooklyn ferry, famished for contemporary reality. There are almost none in Russian. In a poet like T. S. Eliot, thanks to his slim oeuvre, they are all the more striking. There are so many sea-related phobias and phantasms in his work that one can talk about a complex. The unconscious always sends its signals from underseas—one doesn't need to be a Freudian to see that. Even in his early work there are suspicious flickerings when his poetic doppelgänger J. Alfred Prufrock pines for a pair of ragged claws scuttling across the floors of silent seas. London society life is impossible for him, and he yearns to be in sea caverns where mermaids wave to him, and "human voices wake us, and we drown." Eliot begins, seemingly, with dry satire, but before long his verse is peopled with nightmare creatures sprung from the briny element, at first still in minia-

ture format. In "Rhapsody on a Windy Night" it's a city fountain, in which an old crab, his back armor stuck with barnacles,
irritates the wanderer by clutching at his cane. Eliot's teacher
Jules Laforgue, a poet of decadence, who once had the pleasure of reading aloud to Queen Augusta of Prussia, beckons.
In one of Laforgue's prose pieces, there is a description of
Salome's palace that derives from the Berlin aquarium: "A
labyrinth of grottoes . . . luminous sections of subterranean
kingdoms . . . arenas with basalt steps, where crabs in stolid
and awkward cheer knit themselves into pairs after supper,
squinch-eyed funsters, who would pinch you as soon as look
at you." The instances in Eliot's later work are thickly strewn.
His most famous poem, *The Waste Land*, revolves compulsively
around the trope of submersion and drowning in the waters of
the Thames, Ganges, and Mediterranean. It was for the most
part written on the shores of Lake Geneva, where the poet
had retreated with a nervous breakdown. Its most striking
section, the fourth, "Death by Water," is about a drowned
Phoenician merchant. In classical epigram form, as witness
numerous instances in the *Greek Anthology*, he remembers one
Phlebas, who found a watery grave in the open sea, a long way
from any port. When his life flashes before him as he goes
down in the maelstrom, it's not just a popular belief, but also
one of the poet's idées fixes speaking.

There is a long list of writers who came to a watery end.
Virginia Woolf's grim suicide comes to mind. Her pockets pre-
emptively weighed down with stones, she crosses the boggy
river meadows behind her house to the river, where she is not
found for several weeks. She had been prone to visions of
floods and dissolution of self, of being threatened by gigantic
waves. There is Georg Heym's breaking through the ice on
the Havel while out skating at night, Paul Celan's leap into
the murky Seine. Accident or suicide, it seems to be something to which poets are prone; the statistics speak for them-

selves. In that respect, as in every other, Orpheus is the ances-
tor. Whoever seeks death by drowning, thus the tawdry psychological inference, wants to get back to the womb. But what
if there's more to it than that, a nostalgia for the cradle of evolution—the original home element of every individual mortal
cell?

UNDERWATER MUSEUM

There is still more to be said about our advance into hitherto
inaccessible geographical spaces. Jules Verne's fantasies in
Twenty Thousand Leagues Under the Sea are much less fantastic
than they were, now that we are capable of sending manned
and unmanned diving bells to all depths, and cameras send
back information about the life down there. The pictures
from that dark or barely lit world are getting ever clearer. Ever
new strange fish shapes emerge from these fairground horror
shows, such unpleasant creatures as the bristlemouth or the
saber-toothed viperfish. Oceanographers and marine biologists announce new excursions into Captain Nemo's world
practically on a weekly basis now, and often they come back
with something, too: new species, huge quantities of minerals
and chemical elements (chunks of manganese lying on the
ocean floor). It's all still happening offstage, so far as the globalized earthling of today is concerned. Thus, while the moon
and even Mars are heaving into potential colony range, as far
as the settling or even the complete discovery of the sea is
concerned, man still doesn't quite trust himself. But the deepest trenches and remotest stretches of water have now been
measured. There are deep-sea charts with precisely delin-
eated regions from 3,000 to 10,000 meters below sea level.
They are the obverse of the Alps and the Himalayas, upside-
down mountain ranges, with the difference that the water will
presumably never flow off them as it did from Mount Ararat at

the end of the Flood. Facts like these and many more can flash through your head if you look too deeply into some lines of some poem. But instead of speculating further on what the French call *mondialisation*, let me conclude with a dream scene that takes me back to my starting point.

Once again, I was on my travels, in a hotel bed, where it's probably easier to give oneself over to hallucinations, in an alleyway in Naples or within sight of San Francisco Bay—at any rate, in some place that offered a nocturnal connection between the subconscious and the sea. I find I can tolerate the meanest hostelry, so long as there's that certain whoosh— full of promise—behind the curtains. In my dream, I entered a spacious but fairly murky establishment, bathed in greenish light. It turned out to be a dive in both senses—as witness the fact that outside the windows, which were great big round portholes, schools of fish moved this way and that, jellyfish throbbed past. Also the vegetation recalled seaweed rather than palm or pine. Then I knew I was on uncertain ground. I had entered one of those night places where the marginal, cre- ative part of the populace has always tended to assemble, a meeting place for gamblers and writers. As I looked more closely at them, I saw that all the customers looked—well, rather bleached. They sat on barstools looking strangely stiff, celebrities from literature, though not quite so rosy as at Madame Tussaud's, say. The room was bewilderingly fur- nished, full of the usual clutter and plunder of harbor bars— tusks, ships in bottles, stuffed crocs—and on top of that it was also kitted out with various relics from antiquity, baroque and belle époque. Along the walls were marble spittoons, along with antlers and halberds; the low ceiling was supported on caryatids. Over the bar was a sign with the scriptural quotation "Man is a stranger on this earth." At least the undead poets could agree on that, as they sat together, each in his own pall of solitude. They communicated in a language that might have been Hebrew. There's not much point in listing them all; there was as decent a cross section of the literary celebrities of all the ages as any reasonably well-read person could come up with. You can find them arranged into a group portrait in the decor of bookselling chains, copied from encyclopedia portraits styled like handmade film posters, not good likenesses, but still easily recognizable.

The dream had a crack in it, and so this naïve *tableau vivant* kept playing the same scene over and over, with Platonists and Aristotelians shaking hands across the ages, teetotalers, opium drinkers, and alkies, those who hugged the deeps and acrophiles. There were women among them, too, their hair plaited into braids or cropped short, and a blind man (Greek or Argentinean, I couldn't quite tell) was the focus of a different symposium. Former duelists, mutual critics, and deadly rivals sat in stimulated discussion over alcoholic stimulants. In a word, I was in an underwater museum. It was one of the bars of Atlantis. Without having to think about it, I knew that we were far below the surface, in an oppressively posthumous, spiritist atmosphere, hazy and smoky. After I woke up, I tried to determine what they had talked about during their night at sea, but it was more than I could do. All I could recognize were certain elements of the composition, bunker rooms I had browsed through, stylized cocktail bars, the crew's quarters in a nuclear submarine, claustrophobic interiors of various sorts, paintings of Max Ernst or Jörg Immendorf, the Berlin aquarium. As far as the poetic effectiveness of such places goes, no one has written about them better than Bachelard. His *Poetics of Space* contains everything worth thinking about, to do with the spatial imagination, the metaphors of domesticity in a dizzying cosmos, the hopes and fears latently expressed in various images, their crypto-uteral aspect. It's astounding how little dated his ideas are, and how much they reveal about the workings of the poetic mind. The poet appears as a curious octopus, who occasionally peers out from the rigid shell of his bathyscaphe. In one place, it says: "The poetic image is a surfacing from language, it's always a little above the language tied to meaning. Whoever experiences a poem, undergoes the curative experience of coming to the surface. It's not a surfacing from any great depth. But such moments recur; poetry puts language in the state of coming to the surface."

IV

MADONNA AND VENUS

I looked forward to leaving Dresden with a more definitive attitude towards Giorgione . . .
                    —Samuel Beckett, letter to Thomas MacGreevy,
                                                February 16, 1937

1

When I close my eyes, I see photographs from the 1970s. The
sequence of images is always the same, though perhaps a bit
overexposed. A group of schoolchildren, gathered for a field
trip, is passing through the center of the city on the Elbe.
Heading straight for its main landmark, the charming
Zwinger, the children slip single file through a gate shaped
like a stony crown, or, approaching from the other side, they
walk past Semper's Opera House with a loud gaggle as they
cross Theaterplatz. Either way, they stop in front of the
museum entrance and, as well-behaved and impressed as
always when they are here, read the Russian inscription
scratched into the wall by a soldier at the end of the last war
to say that the mines in the area had been cleared. As a result, they don't notice the statues of two men high over their
heads in a niche in the triumphal arch. After jostling up the
steep stairway into a swirl of marble floors, arras, and golden
frames, they quickly push through the rooms with the Dutch
and the Italians, neither glancing at the suggestive scene in

Titian's *Tribute Money* nor stopping short at the blackberry brambles in Jan Wilden's winter landscape with the rabbit hunter and his dogs. Not even Rembrandt can bring them to a halt with his young Ganymede tearfully struggling in the eagle's talons and so afraid that he can't help wetting himself. Then they finally arrive at the goal of their expedition, the focal point of everything on the east side of the main floor. And there she is, the lovely virgin, shining in her simple glory, stepping lightly over white puffs of cloud, the angry child in her arms.

The class stands devoutly before Raphael's *Sistine Madonna*. The teacher mumbles something about Renaissance, absolute masterpiece, and high point of Italian oil painting. But because the subject was art education and the country where the scene was taking place saw itself as a worker-and-peasant state, her enthusiasm soon turns into grim pedagogy. Now the talk is of feudal rule, of paintings commissioned by that terrible kraken, the Church, and of religion as opium for the people. Next, the Soviet Union is mentioned, our brothers' unselfish nation that, as it did with many other art treasures, rescued and restored the *Madonna* at the end of the war—read: stashed it away for years on end. As is well known, the Red Army had its own trophy brigade, even if that sounded different back then. I still remember how I thought nothing of imagining the tender virgin as a Russian prisoner of war. In a certain sense, that just heightened her allure, making her even more attractive than the fairy-tale princess who survived the adventure in the dragon's cave. The two or three genuine Christians among us lower their eyes; as for the rest of us—whoever can, simply "tunes out." Some glance surreptitiously up at the canvas, irritated by so much history taught through a mere painting. The others are bored and try to kill time with little games. Most of us look strikingly similar to the two little angels at the bottom edge of the painting, who seem just as bored as they gaze over the parapet. What nobody seems to know: the parapet is actually a coffin lid and the painting a memorial to a deceased pope. And everything is suffused with a peculiar magic that forces the adolescent philistines (as shaggy and uncombed as the two in the painting) to whisper and mute their giggling.

2

Their complete lack of religious feeling notwithstanding, they were kept in check less by piety than by the effect of multiple reflection amid the surrounding canvases and by the very fact that they had all come to rest here. For this much was clear: this one painting was the quintessence of all the others around it, the very concentrate of their individual uniqueness. On a purely superficial level, what we gawking observers saw there seemed like the summation of all the surrounding groups of figures. We were not even wrong about that, for ultimately this painting *was* the core of the story all the other paintings also told, even if our little crowd, mostly nonbelievers, didn't know it then. It was not the format either—there were too many Rubenses and Tintorettos right beside the Raphael for that—nor the altarlike composition of this magnificent painting (all by itself, it re-created the absent atmosphere of a church interior). For despite all the cutbacks on the erstwhile Canaletto prospect, we, Dresden natives, were still rather spoiled when it came to spaces. Each of us had at least a dim, rudimentary idea of the power of grand architecture gracefully to suspend gravity, even if the buildings had gotten a great deal smaller and were now obscured and pockmarked, so that we had only the sky above them to serve as an aid to our imaginations.

So where did we get the sense that this particular painting was superior? It may have had to do with the authority assigned to it as much as with our own willingness to submit to authority. Its spatial position and subliminal staging clearly established it as the city's secret center, its inner sanctum. Besides, there were the many legends that had been spun around it, as well as the countless reproductions that were already insistent back then and have since become omnipresent under the sign of tourism and commercial advertising. But I think that our vague sense of being moved had something to do with ourselves most of all. Consider just how virginal we were back then. Our young brains had not yet experienced the double or even triple exposure every ordinary adult goes through, plowed up over and over again by television, movies, and the pictures in the daily papers. This is the only way to explain why we did not mistake the woman up there for an attractive actress, Gina Lollobrigida or Sophia Loren, glimmering in soft-focus light, and why, even though she was five hundred years old, she appeared to us in all her freshness and otherworldly beauty.

And yet she was not the one who preoccupied the Dresden boy back then. It would be an exaggeration to claim that Raphael's great hovering figure pursued him into his dreams. He was actually irritated by another woman, her neighbor, Giorgione's *Sleeping Venus*. Perhaps this was due to the general prudery of a country without peep shows and men's magazines, where pornography was a dirty word used to describe the other side, the dreadful capitalist world—but a sleeping nude, and one of such monumental size, that was something! At any rate, Venus's closed eyes fired the imagination much more than Mary's wide-open eyes. Against Venus's reticence, against this inscrutable dreaming face and the flawless, apricot-colored body offered up to the observer's gaze with no ulterior motives, the barefoot country girl on her high pedestal of clouds had no chance at all. Both paintings sported the same head of an Italian woman with the same austere part in her hair, yet, as both women's facial expressions suggested, they were worlds apart. The one was deeply distressed, gazing past the observer into an abyss of misery; the other was more than relaxed, with a countenance so unapproachably aristocratic that no voyeur, big or small, would ever get any ideas. There she lay, in front of a landscape rising like a green mons pubis, stretched out, lost in reverie, trapped underneath the varnish, poised between dream and anticipation. And the river of her limbs, *naturally*, had to do with the other river outside, beyond the museum walls, but back then I still knew nothing about that.

Only much later did it dawn on me that she may have had a special affinity for the place she had found herself in thanks to a king's collector's passion. *Affinity* is a many-sided word— here it means the power of attraction that certain things and people, even cultures, exert upon each other, based on certain essentials they happen to share in common. Fired up by his impressions of Venice, King August the Strong, that ladies' man and baroque cavalier, desired nothing more than to replicate Italian conditions in his own Saxon domain—this explains his veritable addiction to lavish paintings and all that amorous luxury at his court for which a Venus from the workshop of the most enigmatic Venetian would have been an appropriate symbol. And since like attracts like, the slumbering nude was allowed to reveal herself as fully and with such effect nowhere but in the valley of Dresden, within earshot of the Elbe and its hills. Her appearance fit harmoniously into the image of an old river landscape whose hills had their own feminine curves and contours. Only now do I understand her, and with her the peace that came over the landscape in her voluptuous presence. Back then, I hardly saw the context for all the particulars. The eye was only glued to the details: the blue plateaus in the distance (reminiscent of the landscape below the Elbe Sandstone Mountains), the deserted homestead behind battlements on the right, the tree stump on the grassy hill over her hips, at the level of her closed thighs. That is, he saw and yet he did not really see—that little Dresden boy. As was normal for his age, he thought about the concealed sex covered by a protective hand (what a pity) and naïvely ignored the delicate, dark-red velvet pillow with the lined opening on the left edge of the painting. Only years later did the forbidden fruit of this allusion become clear to him.

3

Madonna and Venus, what an odd pair. Perhaps my memory deceives me (with a little help from my unconscious), but I could have sworn they were still in the same room back then. In my memory, the vertical one looks down at the other, who lies horizontally at her feet, suspecting nothing. True, they never dignified each other with a glance, and they would surely not have had much to say to each other, either. Yet they were painted at the same time almost to the day, at the beginning of the sixteenth century: the one in Venice, in the studio of the eccentric Giorgione, a risqué alchemist of the canvas; the other in Rome, with the brush of the gifted Raphael, who began working on commission early on and with great success. Each is the work of a man in his thirties with some similarities in manner, and each is a product of the most extreme painterly subtlety. Giorgione was known for his soft, "lyrical" style, and Raphael for his colors, while the famous sfumato of both enraptured whole generations of painters. The instinctive assurance with which the two transferred their visions to canvas is phenomenal. In search of grace, which is so hard to capture, they worked all the way to the limits of immateriality and penetrated beneath the surface. Shimmering edges of bodies, hazy contours—each in his own way mastered and

even perfected the instruments of the "art of painterly love."
The worship of the feminine in the form of the donna, the
noble and noblest lady, was the focus of their best works. For
both, the magic charm was *bella figura*, and it is striking how
their women accrue ever more spatial presence over time
simply by virtue of their self-contained stillness—an artistic
device their creators learned from antique sculptures. And yet
they could not be more different.

The images of femininity and its attributes in Giorgione's
Venus and Raphael's *Madonna* were as different as night and
day. Raphael's chaste Mary was a story of veils and curtain
folds, clouds and devout symbols; the only things it revealed
to the interested observer were snippets of religious history.
After the Council of Trent, during the Counter-Reformation,
the cult of the Mother of God was once more strongly encouraged throughout the pope's sphere of influence. For many
artists, it was more than merely a compulsory exercise, a welcome fashion, or simply a lucrative business. Raphael's beautiful woman was a piece of ecclesiastical propaganda, using the
tools of illusion to make dogma seductive. Commissioned by
Pope Julius II and painted for the Church of St. Sixtus in Pia-
cenza, it was designed to overwhelm the observer like an
apparition—a natural creature of supernatural charms. Her
first owners and worshippers were monks—that is, unmarried,
tonsured, mostly older men in black cowls. It is not hard to
imagine what use they made of this painted paean to Mary.
One can still smell the clouds of incense rising up before her.

In contrast, Giorgione's *Venus* (with her dutiful hand on
her pubis) was just a seductive female nude. The color of her
skin, so earthy, with a dull shine like a heat source in the darkness, served but one purpose: the adoration of the flesh. She is
said to have been commissioned as a nuptial canvas by a
wealthy Venetian and was thus unambiguously intended as
a fertility charm and aphrodisiac. The little Cupid who was

originally in the painting and later fell prey to a *retoucheur* suggested as much. (Thank God at least *she* was left unscathed.) In her quintessential magnificence, she recalled all the sleeping nymphs of Greece at once. Her nakedness was so direct and concrete that even the most obtuse layman understood its intention. Giorgione was one of the first to make short work of all that Christian secretiveness. The painting was his idea, a reclining nude in an Arcadian landscape, and it was a dangerous subject that sent a breath of new paganism through European art. Even today, we still feel the force of liberation emanating from this *Venus*, the ultramodern thrust of its recourse to pagan mythology. With his audacious deed, Giorgione summoned all the others: Velázquez's *Venus at Her Mirror*, Goya's *Nude Maja*, Manet's *Olympia*, and so on. His unveiling act encouraged them all to create their own nudist enigmas, from Rubens and Ingres all the way to the last of the surrealist photographers. From him, too, comes the secret of the trade, that je ne sais quoi that nobody really knows how to interpret: the touch of magic in the representation of feminine nudity. What actually offended, though, was the format of his Venus: her real scandal consisted in being presented to us almost life-size. It seems as if she could open her eyes at any moment, hurriedly wrap the white sheet (a work of Titian) around her as if caught by surprise, and rise to her feet. The observer would be left standing there looking sheepish, exposed as a Peeping Tom and not at all just a harmless museum visitor.

4

What is this homage for and what does it have to do with Dresden? I don't know why, but these days when I close my eyes and think about the treasures of my hometown (which I left twenty years ago), it doesn't take me long to see one of these two women. And since nudity tends to leave a deeper impression, the *Venus* always appears first. Even when the heavenly body of the same name is mentioned, I don't imagine some abstract planetary surface (glowing red seas of ash, moon-rock-like scree) but, in all innocence, the woman in Giorgione's masterpiece. The most spectacular astronomical event a few years ago was a so-called Transit of Venus in broad daylight, which it was especially easy to see in the northern hemisphere; and at the sight of the little black pinhead crossing the face of the sun, the bygone beauty from the days of my youth immediately crossed my mind again. Only then did I understand how omnipresent she was. In a scatter plot that by now includes planetary orbits in outer space as well as childhood playgrounds in the sad-and-famous city on the Elbe (or what was left of it), she is one of my memory's hot spots. This may sound a bit strange, but this is, after all, how they work—our adult brains. Apparently, that small boy has never stopped firing up my imagination.

Incidentally, I've never been able to find out why she is always referred to as the *sleeping* Venus in catalogues and even on the museum plaque. Like so many of the liberties we take with works of art, this has simply become common practice. I am glad, though, that she was spared what, in the *Madonna*'s case, can only be called the Saxon idolatry (or ideology) of Raphael. The literature on her is relatively limited. Her reputation is a bit like that of her enigmatic creator, who died young. Vasari tells us that along with his pronounced sense of taste and his musicality (he liked to sing, and he played the lute), Giorgione was an easygoing fellow with a penchant for amorous adventures, one of which had a fatal ending. During a particularly heavy plague epidemic in Venice, he contracted the disease from a lover he could not keep away from.

In other words, the master of the Dresden *Venus* was a hopeless erotomaniac and troubadour who preferred to die in beauty rather than go stale with abstinence. All of this, however, fits right in with the historical image of the baroque residence itself, with the legends told here of its Muse-struck princes with all their unbounded power. Interpreting back from the work to the artist may just be an extremely popular illusion (in Raphael's biography, words like *virtue* and *humility* appear far too often), but with Giorgione, the signals are unambiguous, and they were received in Dresden by a court that looked to Versailles for inspiration—mistresses, boudoir magic, and all. Even more telling than many of the anecdotes about masked balls and concealed doors at the Dresden court is the fact that Giorgione's *Venus* was purchased during the reign of King August the Strong, who acquired the little gem in 1699 from the French art dealer Le Roy—that is, two years *after* converting to Catholicism in the hope of acceding to the Polish throne.

Only half a century later did the more straitlaced devotional painting follow her, at the instigation of August's son, King August III (surely the more conscientious collector, if only because he was aiming at completeness).

Madonna and *Venus*: side by side, like sin and forgiveness. Whoever goes on a binge will one day seek forgiveness, and this calls for a grand gesture. Could it be, one can't help but wonder, that the acquisition of the *Sistine Madonna* was also a way of purchasing a few indulgences, even with all the good taste in art and beyond any Saxon seesaw diplomacy? It may not have worked right away, of course—back then, more attention was paid to Correggio's *Nativity*. But the worshippers were quick to switch sides, and eventually they could no longer be held. It was the tireless Winckelmann who opened the eyes of his king to the goddess's radiance. If there is something like personal liability for collective autosuggestion at all, then Winckelmann is mainly to blame for Raphael's subsequent cult status. To him we owe the double reflex of the misty-eyed gaze and the silver-tongued sensibility invariably triggered by the *Madonna*. Since then, many a visitor is reported to have experienced spontaneous catharsis at the sight of her. In these reports, the rhetoric of revelation pulls out all its stops. Always wordy, they cover everything from stammering spiritual ecstasy to the sublime moment of conversion à la Damascus. Connoisseurs, hucksters, concubines— they all felt as if they had been struck by lightning and had had their very souls transfigured. Looking up at her, they would try to outdo one another in experiencing awakening and clairvoyance. Around her, even the nastiest Machiavellian and the dirtiest Epicurean became better people, if only for a few moments.

Could this be the reason for the endless stream of visitors (many of them philistines, as we teenagers were back then) who keep marching through Dresden and its Zwinger and crowding into a particular room? As fortune has it, they cannot avoid passing by the lovely sleeper lying outstretched on the way there. With a mixture of schadenfreude and jealousy, I steer the tourist masses past her in my mind, toward their primary goal, away from the stark naked one and over to the altar of the one chastely veiled. Then I, too, am overcome with clemency, and I say to myself: Whatever dangers and adventures the two of them may have had to go through, both ended their journeys in Dresden. What they have in common is their northern exile, on the other side of the Alps, in a city that, like no other in Germany (with the possible exception of Munich) brought forth an almost Mediterranean cultural efflorescence and in whose sunlight they both never had to freeze, at least. And here they now reign, keeping the reputation of the city, which had so much taken from it, as a place of pilgrimage alive. Here, they were cleaned and made over, taken apart and virtually restored to death. Here, they were treated with alcohol and X-rays. Here, they embarked on their rise to world fame.

5

Undoubtedly, the *Sistine Madonna* has come out on top as far as the public at large is concerned. Like the proverbial light at the end of the tunnel, it is she who today moves toward the visitor along his line of vision through the suite of the museum's main rooms. Her prominence, discreetly acknowledged by all the other paintings around her, makes a tabernacle of Dresden's Gemäldegalerie. For the exhibition industry, she is a phenomenon to be thankful for, surpassed in her singular status only by one *Mona Lisa* in the Louvre. Phenomena, however, can best be tackled by statistics. I assume that she—so full of promise, so often reproduced—is mainly responsible for the sheer number of visitors. Brand-name articles such as this one trigger comforting shudders of déjà vu in the observer, short-circuiting the South Seas poster with the most sublime vacation impression and guaranteeing that tourism rhymes with tautology.

I recently visited her again. And wouldn't you know it, even this showpiece had lost a great deal of its radiance. When I last saw her (on a rainy December day with slush in the streets), I was astonished at how dull and dried-out her colors seemed, darkened beyond what one would normally expect. Or had my eyes just gotten worse? Beneath her heavy layers of varnish, the poor *Madonna* looked as if she had spent a long time hanging in a chimney beside other hams. Her face had turned gray with sorrow. Perhaps she had just fallen out of the golden frame of early youth. I had remembered her differently. More than ever, her brown veil, puffed up into the shape of a mussel, seemed like a mourning veil. The unreal little angel heads in the background looked like skulls piled up in an ossuary. The velvet curtain in washed-out green, the dirty-white, dry-ice fog she was walking on—all of this was oppressive. "A loving mother with her firstborn, her only child" (as Goethe put it)—no, not really. The little one in her arms seemed disoriented, as if she had just dragged him out of bed. I saw a strangely grayed infant and marveled at the breadth of his lower back, at his athletic upper arms and his insanely stern look. Perhaps it was the lighting that gave everything the dreary atmosphere of a crypt. This *Madonna* could no longer be harmed by either enthusiasm or acid attack in word—as in the brazen Leon Bloy's case ("gymnast in bathrobe")—or deed, and least of all by a museum-shop industry with its tacky *Sistine* souvenirs. She had put it all behind her—centuries of fame and mystification. I'm sure that the song of the death of art (that catchy old tune) would have come to my mind, if it hadn't been for her feet and well-wrought ankles. They made my thoughts wander again, over to her who was already waiting for me. What could Nietzsche have meant when he spoke of a certain physiological falsity in Raphael's paintings?

No sooner did I again stand in front of Giorgione's *Venus* than I knew the answer, and all the gloom was suddenly gone. In front of her—peacefully sleeping, casually posed (*Venus pudica*, just out of the oyster shell)—no longer was there a reason to draw conclusions from the painting about my own aging, or vice versa. How sublime her sleep was; no twitching of the eyelids betrayed the horrified cry that had preceded it: "Pan is dead! Pan is dead!" A painting of a sleeping woman always draws attention to something concealed, luring your gaze away from its surface to its depths. You want to know what's on the sleeping person's mind, all the more so if that person happens to be naked and a woman. And all of a sudden you are somewhere else entirely, having lost track of time. Now and then, such things do happen in Dresden.

ONE SUNDAY OF LIFE

As far back as I can remember, I always found it the easiest thing in the world to suspend time. I needed only to raise my conductor's baton and just like that all the bustle—the busy streetcars, the grotty diners, the advertising posters and the profoundly meaningless to-ing and fro-ing of city streets would freeze; then, calm as you like, I could stroll into the *tableau vivant* and disappear in it, while everything around me kept still. In this way, the most tawdry places became sites of memory to me, and these sites in turn exclusive vantage points on the indifferently turning world. To pick a few at random from the oversupply, it might be the temporary premises of a used-car salesman in Berlin, under a silver-glittering banner, with his shady customers, who could effortlessly have made grade-A scarecrows. Or a sorry hospital in the sticks with its staff and the usual pitiable wretches in dressing gowns, among them myself. Or the crowded fish counter on the epicure floor of Berlin's most renowned department store at Christmastime—the drama of crowds of humanity sweatily pressed in front of the ice-cooled display cases full of tempting sea creatures. Or the deserted concrete forecourt of one particular church in the suburb of Wedding, where a few young Turks who would never dream of stepping within are curving around on their boards. Or the middle strip of Unter den Linden, under deep snow and a blue night sky, with a lonely herd of heavy cable drums, a few of them still pocked by snowballs. It's a random assortment, but what all these places have in common was the momentum of time passing arrested in me. And it wasn't just the present that was the object of such interventions. What I did there could just as well be done with the near and remote past, always provided it offered itself to contemplation on a nicely arranged platter.

One such was painting; a certain kind of painting, to be precise, the one that came under the name School of Vision— an expression that communicates gratitude and astonishment. I never had the least difficulty introducing myself into one of these old Dutch masters that hang in museums the length and breadth of Europe. Any sense of claustrophobia was dispelled the instant that I leaped through the narrow or broad gold frames—like a tiger through the burning hoop. And it's true, I always felt a tingling, burning sensation on my neck when I jumped, and it was easy to get goose bumps. In a trice I found myself locked into a winter scene with ice skaters and collectors of firewood (I myself was one of those dark forms at the back of the picture in baggy pants, standing dangerously close to the hole in the ice), or through a back door I stepped into one of those comfortably wood-paneled rooms, ignored by a collection of black-clad aldermen with heavy gold chains around their necks. Effortlessly, I could join that group of riders out hunting heron in the enchanted setting of green meads. Or I might suddenly find myself at a village fête, in the middle of a group of rowdy peasants in the lee of a dike, before slipping through the open cellar of the Half Moon and returning to the future. For some reason, no one seemed to notice these visits. None of the people in those long-past existences seemed to take the least notice of me. I was as unimaginable to them as most of their remote daily life was to me. And even so, each time I crossed into those gaudy and palpably near miniature worlds was a source of great delight to me. There wasn't much to compare with it.

Once in Vienna I found myself in the jolly company of some prosperous burghers in a painting by Jan Steen. What it showed was a household in a state of pandemonium (to say it with Milton), and the admonishment "Beware of luxury!" stood there as a motto over this topsy-turvy world. The strange thing was, I felt at home in it right away. Jan Steen, that elusive pimpernel among the Dutch genre painters, had figured the space where everything was going so wild, with such attractive hospitality that you couldn't but feel right at home among these cheery types. And such types they were: the young woman in the foreground almost swooning with lust, the villain next to her with his unbuttoned tunic, stretching his white-stockinged leg across the lady's knee; the cheeky-looking children, each occupied with some prank of its own; the wild fiddler with his flushed face; the nun raising her finger in admonishment; a man in a stovepipe hat, carrying a wild duck over his shoulder, engrossed in his catechism; and in the very midst of the chaos and its secret focus, the sleeping housewife in her chair, wearing one of those little velvet jackets with fur trim that Vermeer has in every other painting of his and that were all the rage at the time. And I, in the midst of that commotion, could easily guess how this comedy had come about.

The first thing that caught my eye was the monkey on the ledge above the coat hook, a little squirrel monkey—he was to blame. Because of the way he was tugging at the chain of the wall clock, time moved forward in jerks. With each jerk, a thought was lost, an action interrupted, and this so many times that nothing fitted anymore, and each human desire was dislocated. Topsy-turvy world. The two divines had lost the thread of the argument with which they meant to persuade the young people, and the young people in turn were doing whatever they felt like, only they straightaway forgot what it was, and seemed torn between desire and exhaustion. The delectable maid, aglow in her silk dress, was holding up a glass of wine in the direction of the playboy and had come to a stop a handbreadth from his codpiece. (The obscenely opened lid of an adjacent pewter pot offered its laconic commentary.) The fiddler's head was spinning to the degree that he no longer knew where to look. Another jerk, and the little boy takes a puff at the tobacco pipe, the little girl helps herself from the honey pot she has taken out of the cupboard, and the child waving its spoon drops a string of pearls into its potty. Meanwhile, the pig had wandered into the room and was sniffing at the rose on the floor, along with the proverbial hat and playing cards. Last but not least, a dog had jumped onto the table and was setting about the venison pasty that, it seems, the humans were done with.

Do I get involved? What business is it of mine, the invisible visitor from the future? I know the time of these oblivious burghers is over. The daylight squinnying through the leaded panes with its noonday pallor won't be back. And yet it's palpably there, plausible, habitable, resurrected in these colors that suddenly restore it in the memory of mankind when they threaten to forget it. They are vivid colors, insect colors of butterfly and beetle, rubbed and mixed by experts, purest chitin luster. There was the floury yellow of the brimstone butterfly, and the impression of the cabbage white's wing had starched the tablecloth. In the background from the fireplace—it seemed to be a cool spring, or maybe an intemperate late autumn—a vanessa shone with its drop-of-blood pattern. Here and there a dragonfly had loitered in midair, and left a shimmer. Or was it a trick of the lighting in the museum? Every shadow, every penumbra came—via the palette, of course—from moths and their myriad browns and grays. It was the colors that kept this household together; flickering before your eyes, they animated this delectable burgher world so enticingly opening before you, so completely equipped with everything, down to the last half-eaten pretzel.

The painting depicted one of those Sundays of life of which the sobersides philosopher spoke in his lecture on aesthetics. What did disorder mean there, though? Hadn't the little one been given a turban to wear expressly so that his soft little head wouldn't get hurt if he bumped it? They had baked and washed, ironed and heated, each had done his appointed task. There was the house key in its place, exactly at the vanishing point. Why should the elderly housekeeper, embodiment of Calvinist duty, not take a nap?

Neglect, pigsty, *porccheria*, *vanitas*, say the exegetes, who think they have solved the riddle. But all they do is read emblems. Themselves excluded, they sit behind the fourth wall, theater spectators who ignore the individual tremulous brushstroke because they are themselves gorged with meaning. I, though, having seen all this from the inside, wandering ghostlike through the room, I say: They are mistaken. In the stopped moment, along with the other people, I know that what is depicted here is the triumph of domesticity, a celebration of uninhibited utter being at home. Why bring in the saying? Farmers and burghers had sayings for almost every situation in Old Holland. If the pig in the room bespeaks waste, according to the proverb "to throw roses before swine," then one can offer the rebuttal: Where you drop your heavy head on the table is home. And the table is where you foregather and give yourself over to food and memories. And it's the place where the mice dance when the cat has dropped off. One saying, like the one on the slate table in the bottom right corner (*"In weelde Siet Toe!"*—"Beware of luxury!") is applicable in every situation. But the fact that it is at the bottom of the stairs doesn't mean that this household is about to go downhill. Some Dutch masters liked to round off their work with a proverb of choice, a verse of a Psalm, a comic rhyme, a wise saying from an almanac, whatever came into their heads.

Let's imagine the whole thing is a scene from a fairy tale. Then the next jerk of the clock would be another hundred years. The flies on the wall are still sleeping. The nun has raised her index finger to wag it at the Don Juan, who, incidentally, bears some resemblance to the painter himself, Steen. The lute is still hanging on the wall, unplayed, and the nail holds. Then the monkey lets go of the clock chain and down will fall basket and matches; rattles, stick, crutch, and sword will go tumbling to the floor. The fire in the kitchen range will flicker into life. There will be the sound of a smack—and no way will the seemingly uninhibited girl throw herself at the tiddled visitor, even if the bitterly pouting lips of the Quaker are forming a word that, as in a silent movie, permits itself to be lip-read: *whore*.

Topsy-turvy world: in a mirror everything is wrong way about, even life itself. *Topsy-turvy world*: in some Dutch paintings it is portrayed as an upside-down globe. The emblem lovers speak of "inversion," its result: a moral picture puzzle. The globe is upside down, the brothel is a chapel, et cetera. *Thrice topsy-turvy world*: Jan Steen liked to appear in his own paintings, quite often in none too flattering a guise, as a glutton, a sot, a Don Juan, whether in rich or poor company. Among his favorite tropes were such saturnalian excesses as carnival, bean feasts where the beggar becomes king, and the trouser-cacker, the prince of fools, Twelfth Night. He had nothing against appearing as a scurrilous type. His cheery doughy face, identifiable by its kind, pendulous cheeks, powerful nose, and broad double chin, kept floating on the surface like fat in the soup. He triumphed over bigotry and hypocrisy. I will never forget how once, when I was prowling around in one of his pictures, he put out his leg and tripped me up, and leaned back and split his sides laughing. Just then he reminded me of Charles Laughton. Someone must have said something about allegory, some idiot who could no longer see the world for symbols. I kept my cool, grabbed hold of a lemon that was sitting there half-peeled, thinking it was in a still life, and bit into it. I've never tasted anything so sour. How everything spoke to me and showed itself to me and yet remained somehow obscure, unfathomable, out of time.

I spend a lot of my time in paintings. And sometimes, when I forget to leave them in time, it can happen that the museum guards lock me in at night. It's happened to me more than once, in galleries from Amsterdam to Los Angeles. As it gets dark in these extensive premises and so quiet you can hear the smack of a playing card on a wine barrel, then I know: I've forgotten time again in one of my rambles. Then I remain standing for a long time on the brink, leaning into the frame, an intruder caught in the act. Then I turn over, like a sleeper who, briefly woken, rolls over onto his other side, impatient to carry on dreaming.

THE VANISHED SQUARE

1

Much too seldom does one have occasion, as a mere syllable-smith, to think publicly about architecture. I am well aware of how fantastically distant my métier lies from that of the shapers of space at their drafting tables. It goes without saying that each brings its own specific problems, those of craftsmanship and the command of form, those of creative force and the power of imagination. In both branches (and only as such can they be compared), there is a certain predilection toward autocracy. Architecture is first and foremost the mastery of space. Of all the creative arts, it is the most masculine, not in the sense of virility, but in the sense of domination. The architect makes his mark on the environment itself. Who would think of comparing his activity with that of the poet, whose impotent habit builds upon daydreams and airy fantasies and for that reason alone appears as something feminine?

It would seem as though poets are more entangled in idiosyncrasies and fixated on titillation than architects, who appear rather to obey the laws of design and to have at least one foot firmly planted in mathematics. That's the way it is: poetry at its most highly developed is merely philosophy plus coloring and decoration; in short, thought moving on a sensuous basis. All things considered, it amounts to the same thing every time: an object made of words. It makes little difference whether they are chiseled in stone, breathed onto onionskin, or learned by rote and engraved in memory. Two thousand years later, the prophecy of Horace finds itself brilliantly confirmed. Political systems come and go, monumental buildings lie in rubble, entire cities disappear and are reduced to mere clues for archaeologists—Pompeii or the harbor facilities of ancient Alexandria jut into the present only by the merest chance—but what has truly survived in its original form are the odes of a certain Horace: *aere perennius*.

Even though the efforts of every architect are thus tossed on the scrap heap, since in the end all that matters is their worth as ruins, let us admit without grudging that his labor is founded first of all on calculation, that is to say, on a cooperation of contrary forces: those that inhere in the material itself and those that result from the various interests of clients along with the functional determination of most designs. Long gone is the Golden Age in which contract work determined the development of literature. Sophocles was a case in point, as were Shakespeare and Tasso. In the case of a born loser like Mayakovsky, one can examine where this principle led in the modern era, as soon as it found itself in tyrannical spheres of influence. What remains certain is that architecture is unthinkable without dependence on wealthy clients. Regardless of what the constructive genius may dream up, the actual result of his thought will always be shaped by a preexistent situation, by ideas that will be Pharaonic, private-industrial, or republican and that will reach him in the form of certain inflexible provisos. The greatest pressure of all exerted on a building continues to be public taste. By contrast, novels and poems bounce along relatively carefree, assuming one disregards the social and psychic straits of the writers themselves. In the case of the architect, the actual topping-out ceremony is still celebrated by the zeitgeist. The reason for this is simple enough. Writing requires less space—say, a couple of hundred pages in a book. It occupies little more of the so-called real world than the reader's momentary consciousness. What it demands is really a certain quantum of the reader's time.

Though this may be the most valuable thing we have, still, for most people, such a consideration carries little weight. The time one has spent reading the latest chatty bestseller may indeed be irrevocably lost, but it can be decades before an ugly shopping mall or the eyesore of a convention center is finally torn up and the space to which it had so long and so high-handedly laid claim finally made free for the gaze.

If for no other reason, novels and elegies can be distinguished from the incontrovertible products of architects because the space they take up exists only in the mind. Architects, by contrast, make facts, actual objects, consisting of steel girders and glass façades, brick walls or concrete slabs, all of them obstacles and hurdles. While the human body has no choice but to find a way around walls and columns, the brain can proceed straight through a text. Unlike the flesh, which is everywhere subject to stone, the mind has a choice: it can shut off at any time, step aside, withdraw into its interiority. For the body, by contrast, frustrated by the superiority of architecture, which dictates its steps and hinders its progress, nothing remains but subjugation. That's just the way it is: even in the smallest prison cell, a single book page allows one to preserve a feeling of imaginary freedom. Take the wall of any house, to say nothing of a pedestrian zone or the labyrinth of a parking deck: already one is taken hostage, if not to say prisoner, by space. Accordingly, the most general definition of the difference between architecture and literature would be the transparency of their respective products, the contrast between physical constraint and metaphysical freedom. The fact that one can penetrate poems but not a row of houses might do for now as a criterion.

2

In general, the human being has his first experience with architecture as a child in the freshness of summer, building sand castles on the beach. We all know the deep satisfaction that grips one, first during and then after the completed deed, as one contemplates the finished work of art. Everything down to the last battlements painstakingly executed. The sea licks and foams up at the gates, the towers, moats, and even bridges delight the eye, the grown-ups are astonished. Nothing has been left out: there are wide avenues of approach and bucket-shaped cupolas, outer and inner fortification walls and window holes at every level. Not even the delicate tree-lined boulevard is missing, fashioned of tiny twigs about which one has spun seaweed just like the man with the stick of cotton candy. Mussels and bits of flint crown the structure, which dries in the sun and, alas, will soon show the first signs of collapse. But for now the builder can sit back and enjoy it, his elation in no way distinguishable from that which made Brunelleschi, upon first seeing the completed dome, the happiest citizen in all of Florence. What's really going on with this special game, so incomparably more complex than all others? Even if the child never returns to the spot, even if by the next day the whole thing lies in ruins, willfully trampled by a horde of envious barbarians or by some distracted beach stroller— even then, the occasion as such remains untouched. In it, a certain drive manifests itself, which is apparently latent in every child. The first constructive stirrings of the restless hands, of the measuring eye, these we call the innate building instinct. Two components seem to be at work here psychologically. On the one hand, the longing for security, a basic need for shelter, as is awakened by the sight of a snail's shell; and on the other, the will to mastery of space, the desire to erect a barrier against the elements and their destructive rage, using their own resources. Not by chance does the sand castle set itself against the open sea with its terrifying endlessness. The struggle plays out precisely where materiality appears with brute, overwhelming force, with tides, breakers, and erosion.

Building sand castles is thus paradoxically a well-considered act of defiance, an early exercise in futility: *construo quia absurdum est*. As far as its half-life is concerned, it's incomparably faster than that of the tree house or lean-to one erects later, in early adolescence, and mostly in groups, that is, using division of labor. In the lonely business of sand castle construction, one learns that everything built by human hands is ephemeral. Accordingly, architects would be those people to whom the early experience of loss failed to stick and who by contrast and with ever-increasing patience must challenge the sea and shake their fists at the elements again and again. In each of them, this early childhood building instinct has remained intact. They stand there still, as on the beach long ago, with their red plastic buckets and little molds, defying space itself and the erosion that swallows all. And the writers? To all appearances, they have renounced the fight and cast their vote on the side of the sea. With their evanescent imaginary buildings they have become complicit with mutability. At home in the metaphysical, they wink at the void with every second line. The trampled sand castle taught them relinquishment once and for all.

3

Most discussions of architecture suffer from the fact that they are predicated upon idealizations. The ideal city, the thoroughly planned neighborhood, the building that offers itself in neutral light on the presentation table, free of influence from any real environment. And yet, as every child knows, and not just since the twentieth century with its bombing campaigns, we are always dealing more or less with piles of rubble, with wild architectural scrap heaps that in the best-case scenario resemble a knickknack shop (thanks to the reigning heteronomy), and in the worst-case scenario (and more realistically) a concrete thicket in which the weeds have long since choked out the orchids. From this, one might draw the conclusion that the countenance of public space has been marked more deeply by arbitrary disfigurement than by any clear aims of city planning and construction. Demolition and a blind zeal for building have been far more consequential than any history of styles. As for my own sense of civic space, it has been stamped less by the arcades of the old European cities than by the well-intentioned rebuilding that took place after their destruction. One can easily imagine how mixed this feeling is. With every walk, the resentments that nothing can assuage swell. One is familiar with the confessions in which the crime, all too seldom, is called by name. Naturally, the talk of murdering the city comes from conservative tongues. Who else but the traditionalist could be enraged and melancholy enough to break with the general optimism? And yet, the lyre of lamentation has long since begun to sound hollow and noncommittal. There's a skip in the record, since all the hideous new condominiums are made from the same stuff as the indifferent dreams of their occupants. Even Nietzsche's contemporaries merely shrugged at the complaint of this sensitive critic of culture: "Stone is more stony than before." Since then, the issue is no longer even about stone and the collapse of its aura. To the building materials used today, despite their most scrupulous selection and fashionable fetishization, there adheres a peculiar sterility, such that the buildings appear like so many rouged corpses, mummies cosmetically tarted up. "What does the beauty of a building mean to us now?" asks the nineteenth-century philosopher at the highpoint of the *Gründerzeit* era, which gave us some of the particularly monumental display cases, city halls, parliament buildings, and palaces of justice, for example, typically in the city centers. And he answers himself, "The same as the beautiful face of a stupid woman: something masklike."

This haphazardly spoiled space, the product of industrialization, and wars of annihilation, plus bureaucratic population policy, has forever banished all thought of constructive beauty and rational creation. In the glistening light of the urban conglomerates, almost every kind of architecture appears as nothing more than a squalid patchwork. It is itself the problem it purports to solve, a deficit in principle, never again to be redeemed, least of all through innovative planning. In a hopelessly disfigured space, what can literature do but defend itself with tooth and claw? The city square that once belonged to everyone, the piazza, the forum, the agora—no eulogy can bring it back.

4

And now, on to the business at hand: an architectural work after my own heart. Oddly enough, single buildings—except for certain cathedrals, temples, mausoleums, and a few successful villas—have mostly left me unimpressed. The reason for this has almost always been their special status. Their exceptionality stood all too clearly written on their sublime façades. Above all, what made them appear so unsympathetic was the manner in which they set their frontage against all surrounding communality, an attitude one sees in certain people as well. The real welcome greeting always seemed to emanate instead from ensembles; only they—loosely gathered groups of buildings—were capable of welcoming the guest with open wings. A small village, a random dice throw of huts on wooden stilts, the bamboo palazzi of an indigenous forest tribe simply affect the viewer in a more solacing way. Since the beginning of human settlement and civilized social life, nothing better has been invented than the village square, ensconced among its houses, as one finds it in all cultures and in every corner of the world. It can therefore hardly be a matter of Eurocentrism and ethnic discrimination if I now declare my preference for a particular square that has inspired me more than any other. For me, the most beautiful square, the single work in which are united, like the rays of a fan, all the requirements that I, as a layman, would place upon architecture, lies in the center of a Renaissance city in Tuscany. It is the Piazza del Campo in Siena.

One could dub it the Square of Earthly Peace had not the emperor of China already monopolized all such mythologies. Of all the public squares I've ever encountered, including Trafalgar and Times Square, the Piazza San Marco and the elegant quadrangle of the Place des Vosges, this one seems to me the most astonishing. Only historical malice, that East-West dizziness that accompanies me wherever I go, called up for a moment the absurd memory of Moscow and its Red Square. Perhaps because of its convex surface, which causes one to grasp its expanse only gradually, while the lovely Piazza del Campo curves inward like an oyster shell. In both cases, one is dealing with a metamorphosis, or better, an anamorphosis of space: in the first instance its distension into a domed plain; in the second, its gathering into the form of an intimate vale. In this respect already they distinguish themselves like two absolutely irreconcilable political systems: empire and republican city-state. Whereas the point in Moscow was to abase the human being by intensifying beyond all measure his agoraphobia, in the case of the Campo, one can speak of the deliberate reduction of this same fear by lowering the common ground. Red Square is likely always to remain a monument to despotism and arbitrary rule, while the piazza in Siena brings to expression more clearly than many a national constitution the ideal of European civility. As a concept, democracy may very well be riddled with cracks and cavities, yet it is in city squares like this one that the idea of an open society can be verified at any time. No Mussolini

could have put on a show here, though several times he made
the attempt. Hitler's Hero Square speech in Vienna would
have piffled out like a farcical operetta in places such as this
one. It took the dimensions of ancient Rome to reduce the
modern masses to a sea of teeming ornaments before the
grandstands.

From a bird's-eye view, looking down from the tower of
the Palazzo Pubblico, say, the square resembles an open fan,
consisting of nine segments whose points meet in the middle
of the lateral side, representing the Nine Councils, a form of
administration prevalent during the Middle Ages, which
included merchants, craftsmen, and bankers, each with their
place marked out on the ground like the rows of seats in parliament. The square was the heart of the former republican
city-state, and, accordingly, an urban clearing that every city
quarter opened out onto as if to symbolize a system of estates
and that dramatized its segmentation as a common gathering
place with equal casting. Everything hierarchical was as foreign to the builders of this open-air conference hall as the vertical deformities of a tyrannical national architecture. That
said, it is not so much the proportions of its layout that are
decisive—in fact, like everything organic, it is based on a
rather inelegant ground plan—but instead the inviting gesture with which it receives the new arrival. Everyone who
comes here experiences the surprise that communicates itself
to the body as the sudden feeling of "being in good hands."
It's as if one were to step into a large baptismal font, as if the
space offered not only the opportunity to linger, but also the
possibility of self-reflection and purification. A great peace
descends upon the people gathered here. Even spoiled
tourists pause and recollect themselves when they emerge
from one of the narrow lanes and ring streets onto the Campo.
One sees all kinds of people in relaxed deportment, older
ladies resting from their boutique rounds, sleepy fathers giv-

ing their youngest a long leash across the wide-open space. Even the *ragazzi* with their gold chains and mirrored sunglasses have been transformed as if by magic into sluggish cats that singly or in pairs doze away on one of the bollards. Nowhere else would any of them sit down so insouciantly on the ground, as if this were the most natural place for tired hindquarters and aching bones. Presumably this is the hidden meaning of the designation *piazza-salone*, that is, "salon-square," a term that is kept on hand among experts for just such facilities. In the middle of the city, a reception room opens up. Nor is this all: the acoustics approximate a well-proportioned concert hall. One hears every rustling, and the voices that rise here and there, far from one another, mingle into the atmosphere of an orchestra briefly tuning up its instruments before poising itself for the beginning of the overture.

Within the mussel-shaped ring of stone, the floor is paved with white and ocher-colored tiles. At the upper end, there rises the bowl of a fountain with marble relief tablets called the Fountain of Joy because during its unveiling in 1349 the populace is said to have broken out in jubilation. Still today, there hangs over the entire square a certain solemn expectation, as if a chivalrous tournament could begin here at any moment. Connoisseurs of course know that twice a year this is exactly what happens. I'm speaking of the Palio delle Contrade, a horse race to which the seventeen parishes of Siena, each with their own insignia bearers, cavalry, and infantry, add a mock battle in historical costumes. But so much has been written about it that I need not expand on it any further, especially since, as a day visitor, I've only ever witnessed the preparations for this folk festival. It may be that, for the gawkers, any architectural work comes alive and opens itself only through spectacle, but the quiet flaneurs get by just fine without it. There's something else, though, that continues to give pause. It has to do with the interdependence of architecture and the forms of power. Of all places, one finds in Siena, drastically portrayed on a mural in the palazzo of city government, that is, in the immediate vicinity of the piazza, the precise way politics affects architecture for better or worse. A fresco by the Siennese master Ambrogio Lorenzetti concerns itself in minute symbolism with the consequences of civic administration for public construction. One grasps immediately in this allegory of the good government and the bad that the fault lies only partially with the knights of the drafting table, and in any case least of all with the craftsmen under contract. The true originators, the ones responsible for the collapse of cities, are those high-handed decision makers who treat common space the way the seven-headed fairy-tale dragon treats its lair. It seems apropos, therefore, to return again to the enormous distances hidden in that single, neutral word *space*. Even the Latin language recognized the difference between *locus* (a specific place or location), *area* (an undeveloped, open expanse), and *spatium* (articulated space). A square, one could say, is therefore that valuable something that from a random, often enough threatening *area*, from the sheer desert between individual buildings, creates, by way of *spatium*, a *locus*—and in the most felicitous cases, a *locus amoenus*. Surely it is no accident that the ones most thankful for such rendezvous points are lovers. But even the contemplative elders know, like their grandchildren, the skate rats and Rollerbladers, who these days have switched to concrete parks—even they know what a gift they have in such meeting places. It isn't difficult to imagine what would happen if once the urban characters among the city's populace—the corner jockey, the flaneur, the strollers immersed in intimate conversation—were driven hence. The real squares would cease to exist, plain and simple. Just as in modern architecture, with its vast expanses for consumers and drivers, there is hardly any room left for the individual, so the necessity disappears of saving some larger parcel of land as organized free space. Thus one no longer reckons with the wishes of a posterity in need of rest and recuperation. Rather, one imagines the future as a mere continuation of the hyperbusy present that has long renounced the freedom of assembly and contemplation under open city skies. But who knows, perhaps cause and effect are merely inverted here? In reality, it was rather the case that the squares disappeared first, and only later those who might possibly have enjoyed them. Regardless, a public work even approaching the Piazza del Campo would never be built today. One must make a pilgrimage to the biennial architecture festivals in order to dream along a little while, at least on paper. But what's the use of such daring sketches? One might as well cleave to literature, if for this reason alone: that only here one encounters the species that first turned a public square into a stage, the proud or scurrilous loafers, the keepers of the genius loci.

5

And so I arrive at the end of this little tour. Nothing works anymore—at least, not until the next doctrine from the halls of the city planners. Let the child go on building his sand castle. The ruffled beach suffices for him to stand back in satisfaction at the end of the day and rest from his work. In him, poet and architect are gathered into one person. Only later will he come to know the way things look when the two dispute their rights to the same space. By then, he will have heard much of history, of carpet bombing, and the necessity of breaking up the old city centers for the convenience of armies on the march. Like the modern traffic network over the metropolis, the grid of insight, consisting of nothing but memory gaps and communal junctions, will have laid itself over his restless brain. In the end, the newest city map will come to seem the natural matrix for his daily steps. Then the constant wriggling in the network of streets will make him think he has only ever walked in the same place. And in the end, when he has finally achieved some perspective on his artificial biotope, even the higher justice that lies in the disappearance of the public squares will become apparent to him. That there are no more squares is the veritable revenge of the city planners and architects on the writers and dreamers, who since time immemorial have been in league with *il popolo*. They've drawn their doctrines from what comes to pass when the people take control of the inner city and spread themselves out there as if on the living-room couch. Mountains of garbage were the result, revolutions and bloody drumhead courts, and the horror of a ceaseless carnival. Henceforth, every square inch shall be guarded. No one shall block or cripple public traffic in the name of some folk festival or other, or some church service under open skies. Whoever has a hankering to congregate can take it into the public parks, or better yet, into the convention centers and conference bunkers. Open spaces must belong to everyone and no one—which, owing to airtight planning, in the end meant rather to no one. Isn't it enough that here and there the ghosts still wander around? Enough, as long as the useless fallow of the graveyard beckons the living as the last fairground. In the meantime, it's the space for the dead that continues eluding all grasp, in the midst of the industrious city.

V

A LITTLE BLUE GIRL

For once, the spiteful Gottfried Benn expressed himself clearly in his judgment of Rilke's verse. It rather burst forth from him, and he spoke of the belabored, glutinous putty of rhyme with which a poet like Rilke—obviously the epitome of all affectation and impotence—liked to plaster his subjects. And so mean-spirited was this assessment that in certain quarters it was immediately picked up with relish and a furtive schadenfreude. Among the eccentric Prague poet's friends, however, there erupted a wave of mourning. But then a new age began, and all of a sudden it was as if all of that had never been said and was nothing more than the peculiarly ambush-like vulgarity of a colleague who was fighting for survival in the Darwinian jungle of poetry. Then it became possible again to gaze without shame into the depths of these poems, where, like an excavated Roman mosaic seen through the clear waters of a swimming pool, they glimmered anew.

Rainer Maria Rilke: sometimes it seems as if the name alone were enough to provoke animosities. For a long time now, I've puzzled over the source of this aversion, this stew of blasé brutality and strangely sexist spitefulness that ever and anon boils over among German authors as soon as the name is dropped. Certainly there are precedents here: Heinrich Heine's mockery of August von Platen, scarcely distinguishable from plain old meanness. But why Rilke, of all people? Benn considers him a miserable, unappealing figure; Brecht detects signs of homosexuality every time Rilke mentions the word *God*; and W. H. Auden surpasses them all with his bon mot straight out of the glee club: "The greatest lesbian poet since Sappho." Or, for the official record, in his long poem "New Year Letter," from 1941: "The Santa Claus of loneliness." The last in this line was Ernst Jandl with his cycle *The Ordinary Rilke*; but this was already tacit atonement, in the manner of concrete poetry, which accepted Rilke, this side of all rhymes and spiritualisms, as a pure brand name, a talisman as disconcertingly homey as "pickle" or "milk." That's the way of things in German literature: no holds barred. All of which is far removed indeed from the paeanlike flights of, say, Marina Tsvetayeva: "Rainer Maria Rilke! May I speak to you thus? You, the embodiment of poesy, must know that your very name is a poem. Rainer Maria: it sounds so pious—and childlike—and chivalrous."

To such heights, into such dizzying orbits, then, had the author of "The Panther" and the *Duino Elegies* been catapulted. Obviously, something had been granted him that few poets enjoy: an idea of his lyric world that is both easy to grasp and comprehensive, if somewhat indistinct. Another way of saying it would be to speak of cliché; and to be sure, partisans of the poet must somehow come to terms with the fact that there is, in Rilke's case, a whole colorful bouquet of clichés. Nowadays one must travel to distant lands, to Russia, France, or the English-speaking world, in order to learn something new about him. Rilke is one of those poets who actually gain in clarity when beheld through the veil of translation. His poems are like sculptures that have been wrapped up for shipping: their contours, exaggerated by the packaging, leap forth all the more boldly. But this lies already in the nature of his writing itself. It is hardly an accident that so many of his poems had their genesis during the poet's travels, nor that their subjects (Russian, Spanish, or French motifs and places) are for the most part borrowed from other cultures related to Europe. Consequently, their referents often lie outside the conventional field of the German language, though not beyond the reach of Rilke's natural poetic idiom. What many who share Rilke's mother tongue find so difficult to bear in his poetry, namely, its lyric plasticity (others would say its softness, like chewing gum and Play-Doh), turns out for his non-German readers to be a source of endless delight.

Like few other poets before or since, Rilke mastered the art of the significant clue, the wide-ranging association, the long-delayed, oft-broken echo. His verse possesses a mimetic smoothness that borders on the corporeal, generating a eurhythmic wake (or knee-jerk reaction) in the reader: a concurrence of synchronized ripples of the kind well known, for example, to the audience member at a ballet. And, in fact, choreography, the structuring measure by which fields of semantic play are here ordered and disposed, turns out to be the primary technical characteristic of this verse. Accordingly, it is always animals, children, angels, biblical and mythological figures, that is to say, archetypes of an indelibly pictorial kinesthetic, that the Rilkean poem seizes in its *tableau vivant*. His work is a veritable compendium of such movement sketches transposed into language, comparable to the sketchbooks used by painters to capture their own fleeting ideas. Here one finds portrayed once and for all the way a captive panther tosses back and forth in the cage; the way a gazelle pauses, listening; the way a swan glides without effort over the surface of the water. One need but read the description, in *The Notebooks of Malte Laurids Brigge*, of an epileptic on the Boulevard St.-Michel. The representation of an illness is pursued even to the very threshold of pain: a body exploding in slow motion.

Rilke's poems are privy to the body's involuntary stirrings, to the play of muscles while mopping or mating, to the spasm in the moment of self-abandon, fright, or embarrassment. Their strength lies entirely in the mimetic act of description itself: in that the poems, too, abandon themselves completely to their object, be it animal or human, a landscape or an artifact. Before the reader's eyes the motif celebrates its resurrection: verse-for-verse—as if observed from all sides or turned around in the hands—it is created a second time. One could produce an entire inventory of images of movement from his poetry collections. Nor is this all: some of his poems could be downright transposed into diagrams to illustrate their dynamic process. One of the most impressive examples of this kinetic art of description is the piece "The Arrival," from *New Poems: The Other Part*. It reads like a tracking shot in sonnet form, and it is of interest here because it attunes us perfectly to the fundamental movement of yet another poem, to which I will turn in a moment. The description is of an arrival at a Bohemian castle (*"Au Château de Janowitz,"* as Rilke specifies to a lady friend). What remains intentionally undecided is whether we're dealing with an automobile or a carriage; but of decisive importance is the gaze out of the compartment window, the double exposure of architecture and garden grounds. In the sweeping approach, futurism and feudalism are contracted without further ado into a moment of timeless arrival. Nor is the requisite animal left out. A greyhound, symbol of kinesis and elegance, eventually wraps up the syntax in a counter-movement. Here is the poem:

THE ARRIVAL

Was this momentum in the wagon's turn?
Or in the gaze that caught and held the baroque
angel figures standing full of memory
among the bluebells in the open meadow,

held and then released them, as the park
before the castle closed around the drive
and brushed against it, overhung it, till
it suddenly slipped free: here was the gate,

which now, as if it had called out a challenge,
forced the long front out into a curve
that brought it to a halt. In a flash, a gliding went
down the glass door; through the opening,
a greyhound pushed its way, bearing its thin
sleek flanks straight down the shallow steps.

Turn and momentum, drive and curve, gliding and opening—
the nouns in this poem express everything we're dealing with
here. Rilke's lines, once again, find their perfect balance, their
dreamlike certainty in the sense of movement. This is especially true of the pieces collected in *New Poems*, which rep-
resent a turning point in Rilke's aesthetic: their newness
consists precisely in the concentration on simple processes of
movement.

It is easy to imagine why a poet such as Rilke would feel
drawn to painters and sculptors. From the moment he entered
service as the great Rodin's secretary, almost all of Rilke's
poems cross the bridge to the visual arts. Cézanne and van
Gogh must be numbered among his inspirations, as well as
the artists of the Worpswede circle, his companions, with their
apple trees and chubby-cheeked nudes, their fruit still lifes
and roundelays of dancing maidens. And yet Rilke is a poet,
and as such he is interested at most in analogies and correspondences. In terms of plasticity and palette, a poem has
only limited resources at its disposal. A color is no more than
its name ("red, green, gray . . ."), an attribute ("a snow-white
elephant"), or if need be a combination of several color terms;
or (and this is the height of cunning) an equivalent, whereby a

thing, a natural phenomenon, some vivid accumulation of flo-
ral and faunal must serve as a precise representation of color
("Faded as a child's dress"). Similarly meager, in poetry, is the
sensation of colors. With most poets (Rilke is one of the
exceptions), color sensibility has simply remained undeveloped. Their repertoire is more impressive, however, when it
comes to portraying movement. And while poetry succeeds
less frequently at what prose has long mastered—the arts of
action and plot—when it does, it does so in the most condensed fashion and with utmost effect. Poets like Rilke have
shown how this is done. Typical of the verse structures of
his mature years is their basic tension, a sort of veritable
muscle tone, insofar as the word is wired to the nerve and
reacts as one; that is to say, it pushes incessantly toward discharge. With Rilke, the grammatical sentence is forever over-
reaching itself from line to line, such that the verbs appear as
it were in slow motion. There is the spiral staircase, its steps
built of verbs ascending on each other like rhymes, rising
until something falls. There is the pulse that drives the poem
from first line to last, as well as the run-up, crossed out and
interrupted again and again. And therein lies Rilke's greatest
discovery (the last chapter before every lyrical Cubism and
futurism): here, in the refinement of kinesthetic representation, he saw a potential for the plasticity of the imaginary. The
deliberate trajectory of the poetic line, the particular turning
point of a stanza, allows the poet to circle his object, to
observe it from multiple perspectives. Thus, his famous animals—sculptures that are both more evanescent and more
durable than their contemporary counterparts in plaster or
bronze—arise from merely verbal material. In this way, the
thing in his so-called thing poems reveals itself as dynamic
quantity. But what if the object around which the poem turns
is itself revolving?

Then we have something like "The Carousel," a poem
that gives the odd impression of having been composed while

asleep, as the direct transposition of a vinyl record from one's childhood, or of a barrel organ in the backyard. Often quoted, a sort of showpiece for every anthology, it makes one feel—even on the first reading—that one already knows it by heart. This catchy accessibility has everything to do with the poem's specific fusion of form and content, which makes it an exemplary instance of the very genre of the thing poem. The verse has seamlessly fitted itself to its object: the uniform, somewhat languorous torque of the carousel, its jerky stops and starts, this entire melancholy turning-in-place—all of this has become the lines' own singular dynamic. The rhymes, ringing with such quaint punctuality, merely underscore the apparently naïve subject; and even what is worn out and hackneyed serves to intensify the poem's expressiveness. The poem itself is a monument composed of melancholy and mechanics. It reminds us a little of one of those old-fashioned toy models made of tin. Listening closely, we catch the faint crackling of a record player, one of the primeval sounds that mark the beginning of modern German poetry. Here it is:

THE CAROUSEL
Jardin du Luxembourg

With roof and shade it turns
a little while, this motley band
of horses, each come from the land
that hesitates before it dies.
Though some of them are hitched to wagons
courage shows on every face;
a red and angry lion among them,
and now and then a snow-white elephant.

Even a stag is there, as in the wild,
though this one wears a saddle, and on top
a little blue girl sits buckled tight.

And a boy in white rides on the lion,
and holds on with his small hot hand,
while the lion bares its teeth and tongue.

And now and then a snow-white elephant.

And on their horses past they fly,
girls also, light, the horses' bound
almost outgrown; their eyes mid-round
look up, somewhere, and meet your eye—

And now and then a snow-white elephant.

And on it goes, hastening to end,
And spins and circles without goal.
A red, a green, a gray it sends,
a little, inchoate profile—.
And sometimes, too, a smile it throws you,
serene and blinding, gives itself away
amid such blind and breathless children's play . . .

Written in June of 1906, during the poet's second Paris resi-
dency, the poem belongs among the *New Poems* and is in close
proximity to *Malte Laurids Brigge* with its musical themes of
childhood, loss, the metropolis, and angst. Everything belong-
ing to a Rilke poem of this period is there. The ample foreign
territory—his Paris "full to the brim with sorrow"; a setting
whose very name sets off echoes—the Jardin du Luxembourg; a title of the kind one might see on a plaque adorning
a painting in a museum—"The Carousel"; an object, finally,
that in terms of motif and manner of presentation is in sync
with the latest trends in the visual arts at the time. One is
almost tempted to say that the poem belongs to Rilke's own
Blue or Rose Period. The poet here engenders an atmosphere

identical to that which at the same time and in the same city
Picasso was creating—albeit by different means—and yet
both didn't know of each other. Only years later will Rilke
recognize himself in the Spaniard. In 1915, by pure coincidence, at the Munich apartment of his friend the writer
Hertha König, he encounters Picasso's masterpiece *Les Saltim-
banques*. It contains a tonality that must have seemed familiar
to him. With astonishment he must have registered their
kinship of expression: here was that same unfathomable sorrow, the sorrow of form clinging to life. Even in the vertigi-
nous euphoria that seized Rilke while composing the *Duino
Elegies*, Picasso's motifs from this period were present to
him—how the painter froze tightrope walkers, clowns, and
jugglers in those delicate lines, thereby cutting a pattern for
lyric painting.

To say that the influence of the visual arts on poetry is
merely coincidental is not to say much. In the realm of words,
transitions are fluid, and it is often merely a line break that
separates Impressionism from Cubism. Abstraction in verse or
prose will never be the same as on canvas. Granted, a poem
like "The Carousel," with its emphatic naïveté, exhibits a certain proximity to the work of a particular lady friend from
Worpswede. And yet it could just as easily be the other way
around: knowing about Rilke's intense artistic friendship with
Paula Modersohn-Becker and about their parallel development as artists suffices to make one seek correspondences
between the poem and Modersohn-Becker's last paintings. To
be sure, Rilke's *New Poems*, with their strong, discrete color
accents, their solid contours, and their oddly suspended,
picture-book shapes, turn themselves, much more intentionally than their predecessors did, toward the eye—the inner
eye. Here, as in Modersohn-Becker's paintings, one might
with a little squinting speak of proto-Expressionistic harmonies; and this wouldn't be entirely off the mark. But some-

thing else is decisive here, and it is this *something else* that makes "The Carousel" so exemplary: the fact that here we have only materiality, only objectivity, only surface. Rilke's working principle, the new method of these years, demanded of the writer that he no longer merely describe or narrate the visible, but that he *make* it, as the carpenter makes a table, or the sculptor makes a horse or a ballerina. In precisely this sense, "The Carousel" is constructed—but constructed, mind you, as if a cabinetmaker and a choreographer had been melded into one, or rather, a poet and an illustrator of children's books. What astonishes us now is how early Rilke began something that in the coming years would assert itself throughout Europe and America with such avant-gardist noise. Here, under his own steam and with neither manifesto nor the moral support of a coterie, Rilke fulfilled the project of every subsequent imagism: poetry's exclusive concentration on the elements of seeing and visual content. What he was after, in his own testimony, were poems that would stand by themselves: sculptures made out of words.

Their distinguishing characteristic is a maximum economy of expressive means. And therein, despite all the emotional excess for which Rilke's verse has been faulted, lies an expressly reasonable moment—in both senses of the word: rational and thrifty. In other words: he who constructs his verse so efficiently as to achieve maximum expression with minimum signage is as much magician as concrete poet. Twenty-seven lines divided into six stanzas and broken by two free-standing lines: thus "The Carousel" appears in its written form. The poem's kinesthetic shape, however, arises from the aforementioned metrical pattern, a uniform if not to say monotonous rhythm, whose tempo is regulated by the distribution of vowel sounds. Accordingly, whenever the white elephant comes along, dragging with it the line's triple *a* sound (. . . d*a*nn . . . w*a*nn . . . Elef*a*nt), the rhythm turns "portly." The angry red lion, by contrast, drops the rhythm immediately into a slow, menacing creep. Only with the horses and their bounding does the carousel finally pick up speed, thereafter slowing down but once, namely, at the single caesura in the entire poem: the moment when the little horse lovers (these are girls, of course, and already somewhat older) gaze dreamily out, presumably toward their governesses, or perhaps also toward the silent, google-eyed gentleman with the goatee who sits at the periphery, writing. To be precise, he announces himself only in the final stanza. For the perception that this scene is fleeting, that it must soon come to an end, that it merely turns in place and never arrives, all of this is of course the point of view of maturity, or rather, of the pessimism that comes with experience, and as such it has something of the party pooper about it; much like the final line's depressing summation—that all the blessed laughter of children merely wastes itself in this "blind and breathless children's play." But what is all of this really about?

The question is trickier than it sounds. More easily than one would like, it leads to error and confusion, into the briar patch of biography, into the dark abysses of the author's psyche. An accredited Rilkean would presumably say that the poem is concerned with the fundamental solitude of the human being, even in the very moment of greatest self-forgetting. Hardly anything is so touching as the solitude of children, even if only because through empathy we recognize in the cosmos of childhood our own losses. In other words, we are in danger of falling into the trap of self-pity. Most people's memories reach no further back than the third or fourth year of life; only later do specific images begin to resolve themselves from the mirror. At the periphery of any sandbox, one can observe with what meditative rapture adults ogle their offspring. When an adult observes a child closely, when he looks in on the child's complete immersion in activity, he encounters without fail the child he himself once was at that early stage but of whom his memory retains nothing. Yet the sight makes him melancholy nonetheless, as does every awakening to something gone by and irrevocable.

This, then, would be the most general interpretation of the poem, though one that is not, as we have said, wholly free of narcissism. Apart from the uncanny machinery that turns children into passive puppets, what intensifies the feeling of solitude here is the lifeless world of objects—the wooden figures in the shapes of animals. A sense of foreboding already tells the children that they have let themselves be deceived— their bearing proves it. These stiff animal effigies have little in common with their real prototypes at the circus or the zoo. They are cold; one can bang against them and bruise oneself. The poet knows this, too, and sets the whole kit and caboodle in motion so that the figures may appear still more thinglike, which is why he sends the white elephant around again and again. He achieves thereby, and as it were en passant, a veritable modernist coup. Through pure repetition, the elephant is reduced to a mere word, a noun of the same species as that made famous by Gertrude Stein in her "a rose is a rose is a rose." (Here, too, we discover an affinity that seems to have been in the air of that peculiar Parisian atmosphere where literature provoked painting and vice versa.)

Things get perceptibly more uncanny if we call to mind how things really stand, *in natura*, with white elephants. Already the plural is totally inappropriate here. Rilke did the right thing by having it make its sad rounds as a loner. As zoologists well know, the exceedingly rare albino variety occurs with a statistical probability of one in ten thousand. By virtue of their rarity, these individuals have since ancient times been honored as sacred animals. In Thailand, for example, all white elephants belong by royal edict to the king, who refers to himself accordingly as "Lord of the White Elephants." Among

Hindus, the white elephant is regarded, along with the lotus blossom, as a symbol of enlightenment. Nor was Heinrich Heine ignorant of this when he dedicated a memorial to them in the first book of his *Romanzero*. In his history *The White Elephant*, which parodies a ballad, he relates the fantastical tale of the king of Siam, who has a private palace built for his favorite animal. Three hundred bodyguards—*Trabanten*—if only for the sake of rhyme, stand ready as the elephant's honorary sentries. And yet the chosen one is anything but happy, he is lovesick: "The white melancholic / stands moping in that abundance." Heine, rarely embarrassed by an absurd comparison, calls him a four-footed Werther, and prescribes a bit of travel for his sadness. Where? To the capital of the nineteenth century: Paris. There, the sight of the beloved—loved from afar until now—shall cure the noble animal. The beloved is a tall white woman named, not inappropriately, Baroness Bianca. Much is said of her white complexion and of the dazzling alabaster of her legs. Given the extraordinary attraction of the color white, the suspicion arises that we're dealing with a variation on the Narcissus myth. But the position of outsider can also have the most serious of consequences, as is shown by the oft-repeated cases of aggressive albinos, designated in professional circles as *rogues*. In a retrospective work that became popular as juvenile literature, John Hagenbeck, brother of the founder of the Hamburg Zoo and himself a tremendous circus entrepreneur and filmmaker (specializing in sensational carnivores during the silent era), tells the story of one such villain who spread universal horror. One of the main attractions in Hagenbeck's zoo was always the elephant ride. Imagine if it had fallen to one of the children's lot to take a seat on the back of such a dangerous animal—which outwardly approached you like a symbol of peace.

Does the white elephant then belong with those pitiable creatures who, absorbed in narcissism, circle endlessly around themselves? And with that we would seem to have arrived once again among the wooden figures of the carousel, with their aura of deep solitude. Their naïve design, looking as if they all had sprung from the world of some children's book, does little in terms of consolation. Far more than the echoes of circus and zoo, what forces its way into the foreground is a hopeless melancholy. These stags and lions, these horses and elephants, all of them are in fact no more than themselves: gloomy, lifeless objects concealing nothing, no mystery and no significance. The "rose is a rose is a rose," seen in this way, was nothing more than the chase after one's own reflection, a formula for the imprisonment-in-itself of both words and things. So much for the exterior of this New Poem.

As to the interior, it may very well prove a bit more complicated. At this point, the little blue girl of stanza two comes into play, of whom we read that she is "buckled" to a stag. It touches us to the quick to hear that Rilke himself, at the time he wrote this poem, had a daughter (his only child), a little girl of the age at which riding carousels is especially fun. But alas: she was not with him. It would have been unthinkable for him to make time to take her to the Jardin du Luxembourg. In fact, he hardly saw her at all, this Ruth, this accidental creature of a troubled artist relationship: his marriage to Klara Westhoff, a student of Rodin's. Rilke's notorious lonerhood, his chronic poverty (customary among Bohemians), and the mother's own, hardly less strong ambitions were the reasons they saw each other at most twice a year, during mutual holidays. Otherwise, the child grew up with Klara's grandparents. What's the point of these embarrassing details? Well, certainly not indiscretion. That would hardly be possible, since Rilke biographies now fill several meters of bookshelf space. If we have taken time to flip through the family album, it was only in the hopes of coming across a photograph that, as now seems obvious, cannot exist, among other reasons, because in 1906 there was no such thing as color photography: I mean the image of a little blue girl riding on a carousel.

Much has been written about Rilke's poetic conception of childhood. In terms of complexity and significance in his work, it ranks second only to angels and the motif of death, the latter of which, for Rilke, impinges ubiquitously upon life. "Be satisfied that childhood *was*, this nameless / troth of the celestial, not canceled by fate." Thus begins one of the great elegiac fragments of the late period, written by someone who didn't know where to begin with his own child. According to hearsay, Rilke could hardly stand children at all for extended periods of time. The nasty little word *buckled* allows us to guess at the distance separating father and daughter, even if we acknowledge that the forsakenness of the little girl in the poem is merely formal—read: symbolic—signifying much more the distance separating the child from the reified world. It's as if the poet had recognized childhood only and always from a distance, since for him it was reliably bound up with certain complexes: death, existential angst, and sexual confusion—"think how many spans alone from girl to man." And since we're on the subject already, we might as well mention another peculiarity, a biographical secret that must have been juicy indeed, considering how often and how eagerly Rilke revealed it—in *Malte Laurids Brigge* as well as in several of his love letters—namely, the story of the boy Rilke, whom, until he was six years old, his mother dressed in girls' clothes. She wanted to be reminded thereby of a daughter who had died in infancy; this, in any case, according to the storyteller, who had early on developed a penchant for authorial legends. Perhaps this has little bearing on the blue girl in the poem, but it makes reading it considerably more irritating. Nor do I contradict here in the least that doughty doctrine that would have the work of art free of all biographical contamination. Add but a pinch of depth psychology, and the work, with a poet like

Rilke at least, reacts like an acid bath, foaming up enormously.

Considering the numerous images in Rilke's work of the forsakenness of every human child, we can in good conscience add perhaps one more. It's a painting by Paula Modersohn-Becker that shows Rilke's daughter, Ruth, as a two-year-old—looking slightly goggle-eyed, and with the typical Rilke mouth easily recognizable with its wide, thick lips. Her sculptress-mother's hand rests heavily on the girl's shoulder. Her head is portrayed *en face*, but turn it ever so slightly and you have exactly the splotch of color flitting by in the spinning of a carousel: "a little, inchoate profile." But enough already, these few suggestions hardly count as circumstantial evidence. Better to break off the investigation here and turn our attention one last time to the poem itself.

Nothing but putty? Who dares say it? True: at bottom, every rhyme is, in its own fashion, limited—a quality, by the way, it shares with time, which we mortals experience only as tightly rationed, and not with space. Each rhyme is a segment of time rendered comprehensible, and therein lay for eons its necessity, until one day we changed our minds. It's still unclear whether this was done out of idleness or anarchy, for reasons aesthetic or sociological. In its regularity, rhyme may have a soporific effect; in the intentionality of its expected echo, it acts as the poem's basic tension, and it depends on the poet whether the surprise succeeds. A rhyme can alter the course of a poem; granted, for a carousel this is problematic, which is why the rhyme is here designed to increase the poem's torque. Rilke would have been silly indeed to have let this effect escape him. Throughout his life, and notwithstanding the very few exceptions (including the *Duino Elegies*), Rilke's conception of poetry was identical to that of Nietzsche. Poetry is a kind of rhythmical ticktock. The philosopher spoke of a magical serpent, thereby evoking the horrifying image of something that slowly constricts itself. Over and above this, we have the following rule of thumb: every poet possesses his own material and his own utterly idiosyncratic grammar and vocabulary of symbols. In Rilke's original poem, the word *and* appears more frequently than any other—almost like a verbal tic. It occurs a total of seventeen times: at the beginnings of lines as a kind of musical upbeat, and then as a copula binding the various elements of the carousel together, as if the poet were at the same time the machine's engineer. Toward the end of the poem, the word serves chiefly as a means of acceleration, until the whole thing grinds jerkily to a halt on the last word: *play*.

One final remark as to the occasion for this rather errant commentary. Some time ago, a group of friends invited me to the famous Marbach Literary Archive, the tomb of so many manuscripts dictated by some favorable moment or other to their creators. And then, without warning or preamble, and certainly without my having asked for it, my friends laid before me Rilke's poem "The Carousel," written in the poet's own hand: a real treasure. I must admit, I don't especially care for such surprise attacks. I always have the feeling of doing something illicit—and usually I pay for it immediately, it's like touching a hot stove. What I saw was a sheet of slightly yellowed paper, and scribbled in pencil on both sides, the all-too-familiar poem. Naturally, it was written in Sütterlin, an old-fashioned German script that reminded me of the letters of my high-principled grandmother from Thuringia. Astonishingly, it was the same shy, schoolboyish script that, twenty years later, guided the pen as it jotted down the *Sonnets to Orpheus*—unchanged down to the dotting of the *i*'s. Stefan Zweig, the collector of autographs and for years Rilke's interlocutor, spoke of Rilke's calligraphically round hand. He also emphasized its scrupulous accuracy, its moving sense of order—all of which sounds like a schoolboy's report card, certifying that he has maintained the correct distance, as mea-

sured with a ruler, between his lines. Yet, as the present manuscript shows, it wasn't all that extreme. Several peculiarities
do, however, stand out. We don't know whether we're dealing
here with the very first draft or with a so-called synthetic original; in any event, there is only a single correction. It is as if
the whole had been drafted in a single breath or, as suggested
above, dictated in its entirety during sleep. Naturally, that's
impossible, you tell yourself, especially with a poem of such
stanzaic complexity. On the other hand, we know of Rilke
that the breath of poetry often overcame him suddenly, in
spells, and that when this happened he could do nothing but
write along to the dictation of whatever his inner DJ spun for
him. It's understandable, then, that the stenographer of his
own creative transport could sometimes barely keep up and
would reach impatiently for abbreviations. The most notable
evidence of this creative haste is in the thrice-returning line
"And now and then . . . ," which ends with an ellipsis and
withholds the rest in the poet's original autograph. It appears
rather in the manner of a stage direction. The poet cranks
himself and his poem up, and at the same time wants to choke
down the speed. But perhaps the line also functions as a cursory musical notation, since in any case it was clear what must
come at this moment in the score. Be that as it may, the elephant is nowhere named—and should you be in the mood to
play, you might go on to say: . . . he was lost along the way . . .
And if you listen closely, you realize that the issue here is in
fact a superfluous rhyme—a kind of reverberation from previous rhymes. Somewhere between the lines, on the way from
"land" to "hitched" to "hand," the noble beast dropped out of
the race. And doesn't this also correspond precisely to the figure of speech itself? For what is a white elephant if not a
metaphorical illusion, a meaning-producing fata morgana
toward which all words are marching, and at the same time
the poem's blind spot? In this case, it has also, unremarked by

the reader, caused a little blue girl to disappear as well. Or
rather, it has conjured her away, and in her place it has left
behind, in the center of the colorful swirl, that which is most
fleeting and most luxurious: a serene smile.

I'm no graphologist, nor do I hold any high opinion of
script analysis as a crowbar for the study of character, because
I believe that one's manner of writing is above all dependent
on one's schooling, on certain youthful and stylistic fashions,
on historical forces, and only tangentially on personal idiosyncrasy. And thus only the reality of the text remains: in this
case a poem by Rainer Maria Rilke. The danger of weariness
emanating from it notwithstanding (a thing well wrought
bores and grows old so quickly), this poem is one of the few
masterpieces to which we can confidently entrust ourselves.
To be sure, it's not for tough guys, people like Benn or Brecht,
connoisseurs of crime novels, aficionados of boxing and literary gangster jargon.

THE THINKER'S VOICE

Will it never end, this prattle called Philosophy?
—Friedrich Klopstock

Allow me to begin with wingèd words. It is they that first hum
about the ears as soon as the conversation turns to the subject
of Friedrich Nietzsche. They are still on everybody's lips
even today, nor are they likely ever to be forgotten. If, as is
customary in this age of statistics, we were to take a survey—
something along the lines of "Name four Nietzsche catch-
phrases"—we would see them all trotted out, all the wild
formulae of this linguistic powerhouse from Saxony. Rare
indeed is the man or woman who will have failed to whisper
of the "will to power," of the "blond beast," or of the "super-
man" who threatens and provokes, alas, his miserable opposite, the "underman." That familiar turn of phrase "Thus
spake Zarathustra" is one I had occasion to hear more than
once on my grandfather's tongue as we played chess: a euphemism invented as if to offer a consoling distraction from the
brutal and heartless "checkmate." There's hardly a barstool in
the world where the proverb about dealing with women, in
which one is advised always to bring along a whip, hasn't been
repeated with relish. Oddly, the talk is still always of "broads"
while the original reads "women." But, as Heinrich Heine
writes in the *Harzreise*, "among common folk, such corruption

of texts is a matter of course." If someone wishes to appear rigorous and determined, he suggests that this or that question takes us "beyond Good and Evil." Certainly, most of it has gone out of fashion, as for example the adage "human, all too human," and without a doubt the verdict of so-called "herd morality." For to quote Nietzsche without having actually read him may still pass muster, but to take his malice upon oneself is out of the question. By contrast, it remains good taste to "interrogate" a claim, and even the college freshman takes himself more seriously when scratching "God is dead" into the plywood veneer of his library carrel. I know what I'm talking about—I scratched it there myself. And since I'm on the topic: years later, on the side of an apartment building, I read a kind of riposte that, compared to the original utterance, struck me as now truly brutal and heartless. Someone had sprayed, in screaming graffiti colors, the words "Nietzsche is dead. God." And that's how it goes in the fiefdom of Philosophy, I said to myself then: an eye for an eye, an argument for an argument. And then it happened that, for the first time, I perceived the rift that Nietzsche's sentence had left in our collective consciousness, mine included; and I noticed how much more potent his negative prayer was than every Lord's Prayer mumbled the world over. His calculated sarcasm could always and at any moment go off like an explosive device, while the daily credo amounted to no more than neutralization.

Even Friedrich Nietzsche himself has not been spared this fate. The trajectory of his wingèd words provides a case study in the wear and tear brought about by too frequent a misuse of quotation. In the end, it boils down to depletion of sense, and it happens with philosophical insights and with the most brilliant poems alike. No sooner was the masterful thinker dead and buried than every Tom, Dick, and Harry had his personal Nietzsche at his hip, ready for the quick draw.

The joke was that Nietzsche himself, to the very best of his ability, encouraged this. One might express it in Faustian terms: this man—and thus begins his tragedy—made a pact with his own mother tongue. God and the Devil, and who knows what ancient and modern Muses, granted him, the expressive genius, an ascent without parallel, only to plunge him thereafter into the abyss of absolute speechlessness. At the time of his greatest productivity as a writer, he was the unchallenged champion in the field of philosophical prose; he was *the* verbal-image-thinker in German, a master of every kind of idiom. This solitary Saxon knew all there was to know—since Goethe and Schopenhauer, Hölderlin, Kleist, and Heine—about the style, syntax, rhythm, and tempo of linguistic expression. This is true no less of his mastery of form and command of material than of his specific intonation, handwriting's counterpart—the spontaneous, lyrical agility in the medium of language.

•

It is his voice—one recognizes it from the first note—that word for word manifests itself as bundled semantic energy: voice, understood as the instrument of reason, instinct, musicality, judgment, personal strategy, and eros. This voice hits all registers, from the dovelike cooing of the tenderest soul to the most cutting tone of presumption. Everything is transferred into diction. Subtle changes in pitch and perspective ensure that from first line to last the basic tension never abates. Nietzsche's positions shift, sometimes within a single year, until the direct contrary becomes valid, but each of them commands the same urgency, the same explosive force. What is said of photography, which in his day was making its triumphal march and from which he himself immediately and consciously profited, applies equally well to Nietzsche's voice: by harnessing all available resources of linguistic expressivity,

just as photography harnessed the resources of visual repro-
ducibility, it became a function of expression as such. In
mathematical terms: a variable quantity, capable of registering
instantly each and every cognitive fluctuation. Now and again
it verged into totality, and from this followed the capacity to
annex everything, even the blind spots of signification itself.
And precisely here lies to this day its perennial power. Let's
not forget: among the Greeks, doing and creating were of
equal significance, poetry and action were considered one and
the same. Both were designated by a single word: *poiesis*. It
is the poetic voice that enforces what we feel and think, it
gives the root to which the reader will attune himself.

This much is certain: Friedrich Nietzsche knew a thing or
two about vocal technique. He understood better than most
of his philosopher colleagues the power of intonation to
enchant. His capacity for expression tests the boundaries
between literature and music. Thus, on his own testimony, his
prose is "a kind of music written, it so happened, not in notes,
but in words." Most telling, this "it so happened": it spills the
beans about the secret difference from which the artist-
philosopher suffered like no other. His ear was weaned on
daily improvisations at the piano. It is intriguing to imagine
how, at the same time in Paris, the poet Lautréamont—the
last of the black Romantics—composed, by night, his monstrous *Chants de Maldoror* while playing the piano. Next to
Baudelaire, whom Nietzsche mentions repeatedly and with
admiration, Lautréamont is considered the cofounder of the
modern prose poem. The same could be said of the author of
Zarathustra. Whenever he delves into the history of philosophy, he invariably begins with a critique of style. All parame-
ters of his prose point in the same direction. There is, for
example, the peculiar alliterative quality of his writing,
the frequent use of consonant rhyme: "*Wahn, Wille, Wehe*"—
"wacko," will, woe. And there is his punctuation, which is

everywhere full of meaning. As a test, one need only choose a page of Nietzsche at random and hold it far enough away from the eyes to perceive how commas, periods, and dashes are put to work there. Above all the dash: in this prose it serves as the musculature, while spaced letters serve as an optical stimulant.

Taken together, what is at work here is a language harnessed for maximum rhetorical effect. Even as a young man, Nietzsche is already collecting examples of felicitous writing in his notebooks, a practice he maintained throughout his life. Here we see his drive toward the creation of metaphors, which he himself calls a "fundamental drive of the human being." For him, as we know, truth itself was a mobile army of metaphors. This explains his enormous influence on European poetry that came after him. Nietzsche was well aware of what a Russian poet of our time once expressed thus: Poetry is language's highest form of existence. His sense of direction, as he soars through the various linguistic spheres, is infallible. He knows exactly how to beguile the reader, just as he knows that reading essentially amounts to self-implication, at least in the ideal case: that of a complex and soulful entanglement. This was the seducer in him, the orator with the tongue of an angel, the belletrist of the conscious mind. Yet he had other abilities as well, especially when he encountered resistance or had reason to fear being trapped. Then, all of a sudden the tone turns cold and imperious. Then the self-quotations pile up, and the familiar theses shower down on the reader's head until they take on the force of law. Nietzsche called this "philosophizing with a hammer," and in this he shows himself to be the inventor of a sales pitch that very soon made careers: as a weapon of propaganda in modern dictatorships, and as the principle of appeal for the entire advertising industry in free market economies. Persuasion, innuendo, repetition, authoritarian pointing and posturing: these are, next to the guaranteed terseness, the typical stylistic means by which Nietzsche turned philosophizing into an art form—so thoroughly, in fact, that it occasionally becomes difficult to say where the argument leaves off and the well-wrought aphorism begins. "Here comes Nietzsche," says Gottfried Benn, "and with him *the* language that intends (and is capable of) nothing but to phosphoresce, *luciferize*, enrapture, benumb."

What was that characteristic Nietzschean style? To be sure, more than just a movement within the boundaries of the sentence; an escape act à la Houdini would be more like it, a dynamism raised to the point of pathology, attacking the syntax from all sides and exploding it in order to overcome the dictates of time (in the guise of grammar and logic). His means are identical to those familiar from poetry: the leap of association, the use of enjambment, the deployment of echo and evocation, and, in the later texts, a strict staccato and da capo. What was new in his philosophical language was at the same time the oldest of all: an approximating return to the oracular speech of the pre-Socratics. What happened here was a revitalization of expressivity from the spirit of language—at the cost of the speaker himself, whom this exercise destroyed. The distinguishing mark of this style is its utmost brevity, its communication of inner states in the form of dramatic abbreviation. The genre is somewhat limited, or rather, highly concentrated; its constants are the thought monologue, the coloratura of the affects and passions, a variation on the very Cartesian theme of *"passions de l'âme,"* modeled on Richard Wagner's "endless melody." What from the outside often seems unintentionally comical, this entire heartrending orgy of narcissism, is in reality a paroxysm of self-consciousness. "Before me, one knew nothing of what could be done with the German language—what could be done with language as such." The familiar Nietzsche sound: Doesn't the philosopher's affinity with poetry, which continues to be attested to to this very day, originate here?

Philosophy and poetry, in essence the story of an unhappy

love affair. Nietzsche himself was completely in the know
about this. In his essay "Schopenhauer as Educator," he
relates with peculiar sympathy a portion of a letter by Heinrich von Kleist, in which the poet describes the first time he
read Immanuel Kant. This passage is worth quoting in its
entirety. "Not long ago," writes Kleist in his characteristically
bracing manner, "I became familiar with Kantian philosophy—and now I must relate to you a thought I found there, of
which I cannot permit myself to fear that it will shake you as
deeply, as painfully as it shook me. It is impossible for us to
decide whether what we call Truth is truly the Truth or
whether it merely appears so to us. If the latter, then the
Truth that we collect here is worthless after we die, and all
efforts to acquire property that will follow us into the grave
are utterly futile. Even if the point of this thought doesn't
strike your heart, do not belittle one who feels himself
wounded by it at the very core of his most sacred self. My
only, my highest goal is sunk into oblivion, and I have none
left." I know someone to whom a quite similar thing happened, except that Truth in his time, which was a politicized
time through and through, was called Utopia; and in the same
inescapable condition, this person wrote in an early poem,
". . . one / couldn't tell with us how / we felt as the destinies /
flickered out." That person was I, of course, but this is of
little relevance here, as little as a description of the circumstances in which I, an East German shade plant, first
stumbled upon Friedrich Nietzsche—there, in the GDR's
"valley of the clueless."* Or perhaps not? I grew up with the
blue-bound Nietzsche volumes published by the Alfred
Kröner Press, pirate's booty from my raids among the various

---

*A satirical designation during the time of the GDR (former East Germany) for the
Elbe River Valley region surrounding Dresden, one of the few areas of the country
where Western radio signals could not be received; hence the only sources of information for the residents were the official state media.

secondhand bookshops in Dresden. Today, it has long been forgotten that Nietzsche belonged to the most strictly forbidden authors in the GDR. Along with Sigmund Freud and Franz Kafka, he was consigned to the hazardous-materials departments of the national libraries. In this regard, my performance here fills me with a certain satisfaction. At the very least, it helps me get over a number of awkward memories, anecdotes like the one about the single Nietzsche publication that appeared during the GDR's existence. A year and a half before the collapse of the Wall, when the deluxe edition of *Ecce Homo*, of all things, lay in the display window of the Bertholt Brecht Book Store in Berlin, Wolfgang Harich—the Marxist and former student of that great despiser of Nietzsche, Georg Lukács—stood outside in the pouring rain and tried his hand at the disreputable art of agitation, admonishing every potential customer who sought to enter the store to stay away from this fascist abomination, the court jester of Adolf Hitler and secret accomplice to the murderous Himmler and Goebbels. At the time, I took this embarrassing scene as an omen. I can still remember how I rejoiced, thinking: *Now it's over.* Nietzsche in East Berlin, in direct proximity to Hegel's grave in the Dorotheenstadt cemetery, this was the downfall of the socialist world. Or the legend of how the critical edition of Nietzsche's works—the so-called Colli-Montinari edition—came about, according to which the scheming Kurt Hager, the GDR's minister of culture, had the doors of the Nietzsche archives in Weimar, of which he was chief custodian, barred to West German re-searchers, only to turn around with thievish glee and open them to two Italians. The story goes that Giorgio Colli and Mazzino Montinari, whom he entrusted personally with the publication of the texts, had allegedly earned their spurs in the Communist movement of their own country. Nietzsche as agent of Moscow's fifth column—such rumors made the rounds. Can you understand how I felt, as the "destinies flickered out"? But back to Kleist and his sad-unto-death confession. Nietzsche's commentary: "Yes, when will humanity once again feel things with such Kleistian naturalness, when will it learn to measure the meaning of a philosophy first by its *most sacred self*?"

Mind you, here a philosopher is speaking of a poet, and this in the tone of profoundest empathy, as a brother in spirit. Whoever writes so penetratingly about the despair of truth, about the dangers of creative solitude, which sometimes, with volcanic individuals, leads to an implosion of powers, that man is well acquainted with the nature of the artist. The metaphysician's solitude differs in this regard very little from that of the poet. To this extent, the case of Nietzsche may indeed render any kind of "budget balancing" inappropriate.

Philosophy and poetry—it was a euphemism to call it the story of an unhappy love. In reality, it was the story of a betrayal, a betrayal in love. Its long, muddled chronicle tells of the seizure and occupation of language for the purpose of privileging truth, and it coincides with the history of ideas. Let's not forget: philosophy is, at least in these parts, a Greek plant, and it grew—as a dark weed at the side of the road at first, in Plato's and Aristotle's greenhouses later—out of the soil of the incomparably more ancient epic poetry, that is to say, out of the fertile textual soil of Homer's heroic songs and the humus of Hesiod's didactic and cosmogonic poems. In other words, to be brief and blunt: philosophy is a by-product of the great narratives that existed long before it and that knew most of what there was to know already. In their shadow, philosophy prospered in the guise of arabesque and commentary until one day it rose up in the form of proverbial wisdom and blossomed into a wild sunflower in the mysterious and oracular speeches of the pre-Socratics.

Systematicity, wherever you looked: "Sing to me, O Muse,

of that man full of knowledge . . ." Thus Homer intones his *Odyssey*, clearly staking a claim to truth, except that here all ethics, all philosophy of life, all striving after knowledge dissolve entirely within an adventure story. And Hesiod's *Theogony* begins as factually and genealogically as you please, with an investigation of the Muses of Helicon as such. We're dealing here with a kind of primal scene. Before ontology, dialectic, and the doctrine of categories could spread out like they owned the place, the fundamental principles were established for the utterability of all phenomena, the roundelay of names and things was set in motion. Gathered here, albeit in mythological costume, was all that the world had to offer, visible and invisible. Long before higher mathematics existed, whatever possessed elemental potency was here sublated into constellations of words that were by no means trivial. There appeared here, like the dramatis personae of a play, and in metaphorical order according to the rules of intuition, everything that philosophy afterward, like a high-handed director, recast and drove out with abstract concepts. All was well, as long as logic and evidence held fast together. One can still tell the provenance of Parmenides' fragments: the hexameter form still testifies to the proximity of universal figurativeness and song. They begin with an apostrophe to the Muses, the inspirers of all knowledge; the "man full of knowledge," whose eyes were opened by Athena, makes an appearance there, too. By contrast, already from the prose tatters of Heraclitus there speaks a different language altogether: that of conscious polysemy, as well as obscurantism, the renunciation of all lexical constraints—the ideal precondition for every future semantic hegemony (*vulgo*: the will to power). What happened? Nothing less than a complete usurpation. In essence, all philosophizing began harmlessly enough as clever textual analysis and interpretation. Soon, however, such hermeneutics gave rise to the theft of the message by its own messenger—in this case, Hermes, the nimble courier god, who becomes the patron of philosophers by defrauding the poets of the fruits of their labor. It had to happen this way: "The Greater is namely knowledge," as Parmenides, with such traitorous iridescence, expresses it. And thus the history of a conflict takes its course, one that still has consequences today. It begins with the dispossession of poetry and ends with her complete disenfranchisement. After publicly questioning the ancestral authority of storytelling, it was but a stone's throw to Plato's perfidious suggestion that the poets themselves, this coterie of liars and illusionists, be banished from the city. The wordsmiths turned into washouts. A few thousand years of habit and discipline helped to repress the memory of this act of violence. And yet even now, from the individual conscience of this or that honest philosopher (from Empedocles through Vico, and Schelling to Benjamin and Deleuze) the memory of this betrayal will speak. Through the original sin of their rupture, the two have remained to this day chained together—to their mutual good fortune.

One can glean information about all this from Nietzsche. Assuming there really were such a thing, this line of demarcation between poetry and philosophy (or between poetry and truth, to put a fine point on it), then Nietzsche's life would have been a dance on the border, or better: in the no-man's-land separating the two realms. "I shall be the poet of my life . . ." goes his motto. He dreamed of being read the way philologists read their authors. And no one can say he did not succeed. He never forgot all that he had poetry (and, naturally, music as well) to thank for. Nor is this all: he knew, as few philosophers have known, what poetry itself actually is— a probe into the as-yet-unfamiliar zones of consciousness. "Thinking in visible and tactile processes, not in thoughts; therein consists what is truly poetic," he wrote in 1875 in a letter from Turin. But what is poetry? If one were to ask me:

the concentration on what is essential, perception according to rhythm and measure, the working out of vivid and in some cases drastic details, the word set upon the gold scale. However banal it may often appear, poetry is a variation on the invariables: life, love, time, space, and death. The verse turns back to the beginning, it maintains the connection to the universals of language and thought (and this alone suffices to explain its temporal resistance). Whether it is also useful—let that remain an open question; in felicitous instances, it is without a doubt sweet and comforting. The poets, says the soul expert, always know how to console themselves, whereby the envious accent falls entirely on *themselves*, the reflexive pronoun. As such it is the object of endless envy: he who can console himself is never lost.

And yet, the question is valid even today: If the poets were to give themselves airs as philosophers, where would we end up? Despite all the lofty flights of poetry, no one who considers himself of sound mind would dream of questioning the superiority of philosophy, nor its privileged access to the higher and highest principle. Philosophizing means following the god of brainpower, Apollo, the Bringer of Light. Whoever composes poems (*dichtet*), by contrast, places himself at the mercy of Dionysus, who leads us into the dense thicket (*Dickicht*) of our drives. The poet allies himself with the enchanting powers of song and music, with Orpheus, who experienced in his own body the dismemberment of all phenomena, torn into pieces by the Maenads. We know the grisly myths that tell of what happens to those who presume to compete with Apollo as the Muses' favorite. They land, every single one of them, in Hades on the losers' bench, or worse still, they're skinned alive and without anesthetic, as happened to poor Marsyas, who didn't stand a chance with his flute in competition with the lyre. As confusing as the origin myths may be with their jumble of stringed instruments and woodwinds, it's impossible to reduce it all to a common denominator; what's decisive is that the one playing the kithara always wins; that is, the god of thinkers, the head honcho of intellectuals—and his weapon, the lyre—is thoroughly symptomatic. His sovereign territory is the doctrine of wisdom, and whoever prides himself on being a philosopher will rely on him and on him alone. With that, he has taken sides against all that is phenomenologically imprecise, against all poetical doodling on the pan flute. He has placed himself, whether he realizes it or not, in the wrong, a hermeneutic chauvinist (see above).

Atonement, however, would mean writing a poetics of philosophy. And hasn't Nietzsche done precisely this, in his own way? Doesn't his greatest achievement consist precisely in making reparations to poetry? Not without reason do the Greek gods show up again here, as if pulled from a magic hat—and at a time when no serious philologist would have expected it. With the intensity to which Hölderlin, favorite poet from Nietzsche's early schooldays, encouraged him, he trots them out once again, and this time as physical forces in the midst of metaphysics. And this, the revivification of the myths for the sake of discourse, made him one of the most influential thinkers since the Romantics.

There are three characteristics that predestine a human being to become a poet. The author of *Beyond Good and Evil* knew all three intimately. First: an enormous capacity for wonder—for giving oneself completely over to the moment, to posing questions as otherwise only children pose them. In this regard, no significant difference separated Nietzsche from his favorites—and here, we are talking about the likes of Leopardi and Baudelaire, Byron, Poe, and Gogol. "For him, the world is a primeval forest that exists to be explored; only this makes it interesting," avows Nietzsche's publisher, Giorgio Colli. The quote is reminiscent of a remark by the Russian poet Marina Tsvetayeva, who was persuaded that "We are all wolves in the virgin forest of eternity." The second characteristic is somewhat more complicated; it has to do with the poet's interaction with his or her own native language. Here a rule of thumb might apply: in poetry, the word is translated into a higher state of oscillation. A poem becomes a poem—above and beyond the mere combination of words—because, within it, innumerable other poems vibrate in harmony. Because it makes the relationship of word to world, of thing to definition, start to hum. Because it electrifies the reader's sensitivity to language. The means are manifold in the extreme. The electric shocks are not limited to what has been called bound speech, nor yet to its opposite, free verse. By the way, one of the best justifications for the use of meter in verse comes from Nietzsche. He calls it "dancing in chains" and suggests that there might possibly be techniques to help one reach beyond oneself through a discipline of expression. The third required quality, and perhaps the most important of all, is: You shall be a primary author; you shall not concern yourself with how others before you have thought the same thoughts, you shall say it in your own way. Remain immune to the poisons of secondary literature. On this point, Nietzsche's gifted voice shows to advantage. In terms of originality of self-expression, he towered over the majority of his versifying contemporaries. One need but once read the chapter "Of Poets" in the second part of his *Zarathustra*: "But suppose someone said in all seriousness, The poets lie too much: he would be right, —*we* do lie too much." But not so fast! For here we also read, "I grew weary of the poets, of the old and of the new: they are superficial to me, and as shallow seas." Ah, Nietzsche . . .

The poet cannot claim membership in any guild, says Novalis. And the rejoicing—or let us rather say, schadenfreude—over this gave way long ago to discontent, ever since the word went around that no one in any profession can claim a firm status anymore. Everything on this globalized ball of dirt has begun to wobble, and most people buzz hither and thither like bumblebees between various short-term engagements that bring them less and less satisfaction. Only the poet walks where he has always walked, on the margin of society, a kind of wandering question mark. Only he does what his kind has done for the last two or three thousand years. Incidentally, what does it mean to finagle one's way through life as a poet? Even among those directly concerned, opinions on this vary greatly. Among the most plausible ones was that of the Russian poet Anna Akhmatova, who says, "A poet is someone to whom nothing can be given, and from whom nothing can be taken away." There it is again, right? They console themselves. These strange birds sublate all their longings, strivings, and thinking into these little verbal structures we call poems. And in these they are carried away, line for line, beyond all that has ever been thought or felt before. Insouciantly they sing, warbling away without responsibility—or rather, responsible only to themselves. The price of such obstinacy, such free singsong is occasionally rather steep. The expression "ivory tower" says it well: obstinacy can lead to solitary confinement, to cage and quarantine. Certainly the price is higher still for the one who, like Nietzsche, has seen through what the poets are really up to . . . seeking, in their flights, oblivion from an all-too-truthful memory, as he proclaims in *Beyond Good and Evil*. He himself was hardly free from such elevation. He was what many writers would imagine their ideal to be. We are dealing here with a human being who lived in a monstrous internal echo chamber. Correspondingly large was his resonator for everything between heaven and earth washed up by sound waves, for every imperious poetic timbre, every orphic oscillation. Nietzsche, the sounding board: the singular phenomenon of a philosophical system capable of vibration. The human being as amplifier, a wandering column of air wending its way through the growing desert. What a pitiful figure—hypernervously sensitivite to all oscillations, tides, halftones, physical and metaphysical dissonances. Like Hölderlin before him, he felt the stroke of Apollo deep in his bones; and yet his bloodstream roared with Dionysus, the god of transgression and inebriation. This, and his sensory attunement to all that spoke to him directly, engendered in him a multiplicity of voices that eventually detonated him from within.

In this human head, with its powerfully domed cranium, things must have carried on like an aviary full of parrots. Everything was fine as long as the animals in him maintained a balance. He celebrates the world, writes poems like those wonderful *Idylls from Messina*, where we read: "You a poet? You a poet? / Always with your head so bad?" At his peak, he mastered, like no other, the art of dramatizing the emergence of words at precisely the right moment. What happened then, we all know. Something shattered, and all that was left from now on was the solitary cry of the *Ara* macaw. And now, unfortunately, the awful word *schizophrenia* comes into play, and all further speculation must be ruled out. Yet this voice—even in the moment of psychic collapse, it could still be heard clearly. It's the same one that even in the last insane letters from Turin still struggles for words. One may dream along with that voice for a while, even though it's too late and all future history is long since out of reach. To Franz Overbeck, one of his oldest friends, Nietzsche writes: "I am just now having all Anti-Semites shot." Had one but paid attention to him, we might have been spared that other vocal giant. The phenomenon of voice is, as far as I can see, the only thing that binds the two together. How did Mazzino Montinari put it, the second of the pair of fortunate Italians and Nietzsche's eventual editor? "Through Hitler we know what Nietzsche was not;

through Stalin we know what Marx was not." And yet what prevails is sorrow—it outlives him: the flickering out of destinies.

Strange, in the midst of such fame, this grief. I look around among the library shelves of classical philology, and there they stand, upright and back-to-back, all the milestones of reawakened antiquity. Creuzer's *Symbolism* and the old Bachofen's *Matriarchy*, Jacob Burckhardt's *History of Greek Culture* and Erwin Rohde's *Psyche* (the magnum opus of Nietzsche's friend from his university days, who warned him early on: "You don't deduce enough . . . You pursue, it seems to me, not entirely happy, and often severely crippled, images.")—nothing but heroic exploits of German philology and genealogy. Only one is missing from the roundtable, one of the most talented of his guild, the solitary wanderer Friedrich Nietzsche. His work is shelved elsewhere in our libraries. Only he managed to break out of the philologists' circle—or better: to shoot like a rocket into the sky. He alone among all these competent scholars succeeded in giving himself an aura, an imperishable reputation. He, and he alone, was made by the Muses into something extraordinary: the first cult figure in the dawning age of the intellectual—the esoteric thinker as intellectual par excellence. *The Birth of Tragedy* announced his revenge on philology, in whose service he had become half-blind, collating indexes and excerpts. The revenge was fearsome; it forced him down the crooked paths of the anti-academic; it threw him out upon the ocean of intellectual solitude. It condemned him to his philosophy *for everyone and no one*. We think of Nietzsche whenever we read the aged Petrarch's bitter summation: "Books have led some into knowledge, and some into madness."

I look at the photograph of his death mask, located in the Marbach Literary Archive—this crooked face, ruined by psychosis—and I feel endlessly sorry for the man. That someone should have to run so far from humanity in order to arrive at himself: it seizes me with fear and horror. Yet there is no trace of catharsis when I tell myself: a philosopher, to be sure; very nearly a poet; so naked with all his wingèd words, so not-understood, so popular.

THE STROKE OF APOLLO

ON THE ACROPOLIS

> But are you nearer to me now, and am I to you?
> —Friedrich Schiller

He's never been here. Nor this, nor that, nor that one—
All small-town Germans with their hearts in Greece.
They came as far as Sicily, Bordeaux. One man alone
Was pondering all he'd known since school, in Jena,
Remaining distant still. Like servants whispering at the door,
The pundits in their cant confer.
Tourists, Kodak hunters, hold those stones today—
Still here, they're neatly numbered, their splendor long decayed,
They live in silence—the columns, steps are broken.
One man alone still felt it in his flesh, Apollo's stroke.
Forever seeking something else, on distant shores he languished.
A temple mount, from dawn to dusk by tourists ambushed.
The fathers, homeless, raved, the prodigal son,
Brought here by chance, arrives on top, one day.
A familiar sight, distraught, he sees:
Trash, a blue dress, and thyme abuzz with bees.

The Revolution is raging in Paris when a German youth writes a letter telling his friend about an audience he was granted: not long ago he had been received in Jena by Friedrich Schiller, the literary ringleader of an entire generation, whom the young people worship like an older brother.

The letter's author, however, has an unhappy hour to report. Something embarrassing, something hardly to be redeemed had happened to him. One scarcely believes it, reading about the budding young poet's encounter with a stranger at the Schiller house, whose identity was supposedly revealed to him only afterward. The stranger, as it turns out, was none other than Goethe. In the letter, he appears as someone who stays rather uncannily in the background, like a figure in some ghost story, or like the Stony Guest. And then we read, "Schiller introduced me to him, and him to me, but I didn't understand his name."

Among the famous anecdotes of literary history, this is truly one of the strangest, perhaps even a bit over the top. In a moment of extraordinary absentmindedness, Friedrich Hölderlin passes by the man whom all of Germany considered the greatest living poet. Should we believe this, or is it only a remarkably cunning legend, minted and brought into circulation by the youthful poet himself? The incident exemplifies what is known among psychoanalysts as a primal scene with all of its characteristics; it reveals the direction of the unconscious. "I greeted him coldly, almost without looking at him, and was concerned, both inwardly and outwardly, with Schiller alone; for a long time the stranger spoke not a word." The impression arises that a dream is being narrated here. The stranger remains nameless because his name is unpronounceable, like the name of a god. He must not be recognized, on pain of one's own destruction. "Had I only known what I know now, I would have turned white as a corpse." Twice the dreamer excuses himself with the words "But I suspected nothing." Should we really give credence to this?

Hölderlin is twenty-four as this apparent mishap befalls him. He has been a pupil at the Maulbronn Cloister, has studied theology in the Tübingen Seminary with fellows like Hegel and Schelling, the future philosophical elite of the country, and has been infected there with the enthusiasm for the French business; for ten years he has been regularly writing poems. Now he has his first job, as private tutor to a certain Charlotte von Kalb, who brings him into the vicinity of Schiller, himself the younger man's longtime role model and now his first editor as well. So much for cursory biography: it is quickly told, hardly exciting, and in fact rather typical for a pastor's son of his time and with his particular interests. And it tells us nothing of the soaring inner life of this young man, his daring projects and plans, his well-developed self-awareness. Here we have someone trembling with a sense of mission, to whom his homeland will soon become, on his own testimony, too narrow, a poet of the most radical extremity in both thinking and feeling and, by the way, the most modern poet of all. What Hölderlin offers is the highest standard for poetry. Does Goethe have any idea whom he has before him? An uncompromising spirit, who arrives with the accumulated power of an antiquity thoroughly understood. Schiller's protégé, the man whom Goethe years later negligently calls "Hölterlein," has already long stood on his own two feet at the point when both antipodes make his acquaintance, or rather, fail to make his acquaintance. It is, in truth, a period of incubation for all concerned. Goethe has shifted almost entirely over to prose, to novels and novellas; Schiller, for his part, is becalmed—it is the phase of his Kant studies and aesthetic reflections. In their correspondence, their classical positions get articulated. And this promising young man from Swabia, inspired by the most venerable ancestors—Homer, Hesiod, and Pindar—has completed within a few years the entire program of Idealism. Overnight, he is rhyming in the style of the new hymns of his time, a dedicated student of Schiller and Klopstock. What he creates is systematic and meant to be taken literally; the titles of his poems read like an agenda: "On the Spirit of Greece," "On Immortality," "On the Goddesses of Harmony." A few samples have recently appeared in Schiller's *Thalia* almanac, and in addition to these a first fragment of his epistolary novel, *Hyperion*. This was also the occasion for the meeting in Jena, where he is given his contributor's copy, which the stranger leafs through, glancing en passant at the youth's debut. It's his first large publication, and it sets the tone, that characteristic Hölderlin tone, at once arrogant and tender, suggestive and sententious: voice as script, script as a young man's voice—as he is depicted in a pastel drawing of that time, the most frequently reproduced of all his portraits. "I wish to return to my Ionia: I've left my fatherland for nothing, and sought the truth. / How could mere words have satisfied my thirsting soul? / I found words everywhere; clouds, and no Juno." It's this little piece of lyric prose that opens hearts to him in the epoch of epistolary novels and the dreamers of brotherhood. With this he makes his entrance into the world of one Suzette Gontard, a.k.a. Diotima, years before their great love begins. This, too, is so typical, the tendency toward self-fulfillment in his literary art, its existential, eventuating moment. With Hölderlin, all poetry is prophecy, and he is the first to use the German language in this sense. By the end of the year, the Frankfurt banker's wife will belong to him, and his word will have become flesh, the most beautiful fulfillment of a poet's dream. "Our essences recognized themselves, / before we'd ever seen each other, / as unfathomably kindred." Without a doubt, on that November day in Jena in 1794, a powerful destiny came into play in the life of Friedrich Hölderlin.

Why this old story? Because it sheds some light on certain patterns and on much that is to come in Hölderlin's life. His poetry lives, it virtually profits from the anecdotal, as contemporaries were already observing, voyeurs like Eduard Mörike, Gustav Schwab, and Bettina von Arnim, who early on sniffed out the stuff of legends in Hölderlin. It is this heartbreaking *vita* of the extreme loner that paved his poetry's way into maximum significance and polysemy, not the other way around. Before anything else there was the myth of the poet: Hölderlin the enlightened one, a German Orpheus, suddenly appearing among the living—a myth that soon dominated the market, and Hölderlin came as if right on cue to consolidate the monopoly. For it was the general will to the poet-myth that first created him as a collective bourgeois idol for a post-heroic age. As soon, however, as the role of the poet-priest and holy custodian of language had been cast, the towering truthfulness of his speech must necessarily follow. This single mortal was to stand closer than any other to the spirit of the mother tongue—and thus to become immortal. Or in the words of Bettina von Arnim: "So true! He must have kissed language itself." And: "He was in league with her, she made him a gift of her most intimate and soulful charms, not through the untouchable interiority of feeling, as with Goethe, but rather through her personal acquaintance." In Hölderlin's case, one can speak in good conscience of a poet-ics of the human record. Or one can make a test: What other poet is so easily associated with the idea of personal unhappi-ness, fatefulness, and tragic greatness? Hölderlin, prisoner of a triangle composed of love, religious faith, and—schizophrenia. What's paradoxical is that the speaker here is someone who, in his poems, utters the word *I* only in the most strictly con-trolled, purely strategic manner. "Alone I stood and gazed out across the barren / African plains . . ." The *I* plays the role in his verse of the *x* in a mathematical equation. In other words, however gripping and profoundly human his story may be, its connection to the actuality of his poems is only apparent. It has nothing to do with their visionary content, nor with the reverberation, the irresistible ringing of the melody that is unique to the German language. One need not say much about Goethe; he was the man whom Novalis considered a

thoroughly practical poet, and whose works he called remarkably simple, nice, comfortable, and durable—just like an En-
glishman's goods. Disregarding for the moment the question
of whether this unforgiving portrayal really hits the original
mark, it stems nevertheless from a contemporary of Hölderlin
and therefore belongs here: this is how the young saw Goethe
then. But the other man steps from the shadows for the first
time.

A primal scene from two hundred years ago, quoted here
because it touches on certain questions that still concern our
trade today. Two poets, each imagining himself closer to the
origin, and wanting to reach further into the future. Each in
his own way, they aspired to the greatness of Homer. And so
different were their temperaments, and the views on art
that followed from them, that it's worthwhile to take them
seriously. In musical terms, the differences separating the
two men are as grave as those between, say, Mozart and
Beethoven. Heroic passion, sensibility, and the power of the
imagination will soon part company, and there will appear
something far more explosive than mere lyric poetry—the
harsh realities of morality, religion, and the myth of the nation.
Goethe and Hölderlin embody the history of a split, the division of poetry into the confessional/private and the liturgical/
public, a duality that from this moment on and for all time will
remain tense. Hölderlin's lack of interest in folk songs and, in
general, in every short, intimate form of lyric, which Goethe
understood as the daily declaration of love to life itself, is well
known. On the one hand, a poetics of experience, or better,
poetry of occasion, as the elder poet himself defined his activity—and on the other, oracular speech in confederation with
the forces of nature. Or in the words of the vitriolic Bertolt
Brecht: "the beautiful contradictory unity fell to pieces immediately after Goethe, and HEINE took the completely profane, HÖLDERLIN the completely pontifical line."

No, what happened there in Jena was no mere faux pas. This misrecognition was methodical, it was a consciously executed evasive maneuver. As far as Goethe is concerned, one would like to give him the benefit of the doubt and chalk it up to his Olympian myopia, his affable mildness toward all phenomena. As far as Hölderlin is concerned, however, it was, clearly, an arrogant attempt to encounter the elder at eye level. Friedrich Hölderlin had early on discussed his relation to the great man of Weimar with clear-sighted bitterness. The only choice here would be between obstinacy and obsequiousness; and as it appears, *one* had decided long ago, and with the true instinct of an artist, on the former. It was reserve on both sides. Three years later, Hölderlin embodies the highest standard of poetry in his time. After reading the "Wanderer" hymns, Goethe advises the now fully matured Hölderlin to give the idylls another try. He urges him in all seriousness to switch genres, and to choose the human instead of the divine perspective. But too late; Hölderlin has already been writing lines like "Meanwhile I am grown old, the ice-pole blanched me, / And in the southern fire my curls fell out." In Paris, guillotine and terror hold sway, and thus speaks the hysteric. But Goethe's advice covers up something more fundamental: his disconcertment about the power of negation within the younger man, his revulsion before the other's oddly barbaric figurativeness. So unexpectedly does the wanderer in Hölderlin's poem walk out into the African plains, and so unexpectedly does he then stand all of a sudden at the North Pole that the listener is seized by a feeling of dizziness, as if time and space had been unhinged, the earth forevermore a raving globe. Here the world is truly out of joint, and it cannot be restored in any idyll; it quakes under the "giant strides of the Revolution," of which Hölderlin, helplessly fascinated, once writes, and we suspect he had in mind not only the Revolution in France. We are reminded here of Schlemihl's seven-league boots, and in general of all the high-flyers and eternal wanderers of incipient Romanticism; and from here it was only a short step to Rimbaud's self-imposed silence in Africa and to the surrealists of our day. What provoked Goethe's deepest mistrust, however, was something else. Behind the Hölderlinian longing for the return of the Greek gods lurks already, in an Apollonian light, the shadow of nihilism. *Nothing* and *no* and *bare* and *empty* are the most used ciphers in this spellbinding language. "Life sleeps in chains here, dead in the husk of snow, / And the iron sleep awaits the day in vain." We can hardly imagine with what uneasiness Goethe, in 1797, took note of such metaphorics. That he finally swallowed them is to his credit. Upon his recommendation, the deadly serious "Wanderer" was accepted in the journal *Horen*, in which his own frivolous "Roman Elegies" first appeared. And yet, what tragic diplomacy in the war of generations: Hölderlin's elegy appears without the author's name.

Yes, it is a lonely voice that resounds here, provocative and extreme, a voice that has worked itself up into the loftiest heights. Thus speaks one who will be unable to come to terms with the horrifying discrepancy between his talents and the position to which he has been appointed. A man who knows what lies before him in life because he has sounded the depths of his situation and its lack of opportunity as thoroughly as he has sounded himself. We need only peruse his letters; an utterly unsentimental voice speaks in them, an observer of his own impossible condition. He analyzes it, he sees it, he even affirms it; and what's even more important, he knowingly embraces it. But isn't it exactly this—embracing one's own destiny—that first makes the poet, even before all expressive gifts? Hölderlin was certainly not the first to be confined by miserable circumstances; what's so impressive is how he overcame them, how he took that splinter of life that is given to everyone, and steered it like a little boat into the safe harbor of world renown—he, above all, who is considered so pitiable, so hard up, such a failure. In his best hymns, this delicate soul had a linguistic force at its disposal that has commanded all German literature since, a density of thought that rewrote the history of philosophy. An extreme case, certainly, and utterly unique not only in German but in the entire literary history of modernity, with the one exception of Constantine Cavafy. He had to be born, it seems, in order once and for all to lay bare the wretchedness of bourgeois conditions in contrast to the wealth of every citizen's inner life. Hence, this inward-directed dialogue, this typically Hölderlinian inversion of speech, this conversation with those who are most distant, unattainable.

"But the sun of the spirit, the more beautiful world is gone down, / And only the storm winds squabble in the frosty night." It is by the specific tonality—the relation of tones, sounds, and harmonies—that one recognizes the poet; it is the only thing for which he himself is responsible and that identifies him, like his own fingerprint, unrepeatable in all evolution. Forget classicism or romantic irony, folksy humor or the pathos of distance: each follows his own particular daemon, and it guides him from the beginning, ideally into a new, expressive world. The one is dragged into the very abyss of the great chain of all meaning, the other is drawn around the corner into the amusement park of parody, where all literature is imitation and a roundelay of punning forms. Hölderlin knew that everything is at stake where poetry is concerned—and his advocates and critics knew this as well. What separated him from them was the severity of his vision, this stark impulse to postpone once more and perhaps for the last time the death of the gods and of the language that celebrated them. Here was a man who had felt the stroke of Apollo, who one day, as he wrote in a letter to his mother, had been "hardened and consecrated" by the southern sun on the streets of France. There the waves of memory—antiquity, present, future—crashed together over his head. Hölderlin was one who believed he had actually *seen* the gods, for him alone they were again expressive forms of all-encompassing nature; his poems, by virtue of conjuring them up, are epiphanous mirrors, they resemble the telescopes used by contemporary astronomers to eavesdrop on cosmic background radiation and the creation and destruction of stars. His verse aims at the universality of natural forces. Goethe's judgment to the effect that with Hölderlin objects were portrayed neither through sensuous nor through intellectual contemplation gives only half the truth. "But because they are so near, the present gods, / I must be as if they were far away, and shrouded in clouds / must their name be to me."

Whoever writes this has other categories in mind than merely those of naïve and sentimental, of idyll and pathos; he can't be reached with a friendly appeal to "portraying humanity," on which, as Goethe would have it, everything finally depends. Hölderlin, like his companions from the Tübingen Seminary, was concerned with nothing less than a new mythology. This was another version of Greece, a truth beyond the torsos and temple ruins, equally distant from classicism as from Romanticism. For this reason, though they were using the same words, they were never speaking about the same things. And every encounter with one of the Dioscuri could only deepen the Oedipal rift. They met on many occasions, in Jena, Weimar, and in Frankfurt, where, as a son of that city of commerce and industrial exhibitions, Goethe perhaps whispered into Hölderlin's ear what he himself knew all too well: "Poetry requires, yes, she demands composure, she isolates the human being against his will; she imposes herself again and again, and is, for an *homme du monde* (if not to say *grand monde*), as inconvenient as a faithful lover." One cannot but shudder at these words, thinking of Diotima, who at this exact time became Hölderlin's muse and his great happiness. "Poetry is an illness through which one must persevere," Goethe decreed later. But by then the other man had long ago ceased listening, a hermit now in his Tübingen tower. Thus in any case goes the legend. Or did he only wish to testify in his own way to the knowledge of the merely temporary grace of poetic inspiration? By way of farewell, shortly before he fell silent, he spelled out the new program to posterity: "The German poet is silent."

Before being buried alive by his contemporaries, Hölderlin was ever ready to oblige with his own observations. Everyone who holds sacrosanct the cliché of the mad poet ought to keep in mind that we're dealing here with the same person who in a conversation with his college friend Hegel consoled himself with the remark "I talked to Goethe, brother! It's the finest pleasure of our life to discover so much humanity coupled with so much greatness." The other, by contrast, very much the patriarch, completely submerged in his definitive poet's cosmos, has difficulty retaining the visitor's name correctly: ". . . around noon Hölterlein," he writes in his diary, and urges him once more to restrict himself to the small, fine poem. A nonencounter, as I have said, one of the greatest disappointments in the history of German literature. They stood face-to-face, and saw each other as if through inverted telescopes—and yet were connected, at however monstrous a distance, by a spiritual affinity. Why should Goethe, thoroughly interested as he was in all phenomena, have misrecognized this particular one? And Hölderlin? The last act seems to confirm that primal scene of which I spoke at the beginning. Strangely, Wilhelm Waiblinger, his first biographer and the one chiefly responsible for the fairy tale of the sick, misrecognized genius, attests to the Tübingen patient's extraordinary powers of memory. In company, he had everyone's name at his fingertips. There was only one person whom he couldn't, even with the best intentions, remember: Johann Wolfgang von Goethe.

VI

IN THE NAME OF EXTREMES
On the brevity of life

1

Wrists slashed, thighs and knee-backs streaming with blood, stomach pumped full of poison, choking to death in agony in a steam bath—this was the man who had once written, "We live only a small part of life. The rest of a lifetime is not life, only time." Upon my soul—or *by Jupiter*, as the saying was in those days—little remained to him of that precious life as it played out in the end. An existence free of worry, sanguine and tranquil—he could hardly have been further removed from his ideal than in the hour of death. Considering the core problem of his philosophy, one would have to say that he failed from start to finish. Shameful enough that it wasn't he himself, a free Roman citizen, a widely respected celebrity, who after careful consideration and under his own direction had determined the hour of his death, but rather, of all people, Nero, his own undisciplined disciple. There can be little doubt that as an educator he had failed quite miserably. And now this squalid impatience, this frenzy, with which one sought to get rid of him. In fear and trembling we register here the decadent prurience with which an insane student tests the intrepidity of his old teacher. It was as if he had explicitly sought to humiliate him, the deceived pedagogue, for all his ostentatious Stoicism. Shattered was the mirror he had held up to the future emperor in his treatise *On Clemency*, and in vain his appeal: ". . . to show you to yourself as a human being who shall become the greatest joy for all human beings."

Without question, he had thoroughly miscalculated. He had stuck his neck out a bit too far with his contempt for his industrious fellow humans and their antlike bustle. Had he not condemned the entire Roman society, lock, stock, and barrel? No trace of *otium*—the magic word he was pleased to hold up against the busy ones, the *occupati*. No sooner uttered than there it stood, as if chiseled in stone: the purest inner peace, free from politics and profit-hunting, a life of leisure in the country. And he had uttered it often and with relish. His letters to friends, numbering in the hundreds, are full of it— letters that in point of fact are really treatises: on equanimity, the good life, leisure, the steadfastness of the wise man. Hardly a speech in which it doesn't slide into place as the rhetorical keystone, as predictably as the "Amen" of these miserable Christians. *Otium*: how seductive its evocation of a restful retreat from civil service, far from Rome, the infernal city. A word that signaled the all clear for breathing deeply and closing one's eyes, that called forth the memory of those long, unperturbed afternoons in the shadow of one's private olive grove, those hours, viscous and golden as honey, in which one admitted to oneself, dozing over the pages of Theophrastus: Slowly, my friend, you're growing old. It was so marvelously easy to dream there of odes and epodes, of desultory leafing through poetry anthologies. It conjured up that mood, elegiac and excessive, in which one filed away contentedly at one's own epitaph and lost track of time. And yet, strange: *otium*, if listened to a while longer, didn't it begin to sound a bit like the creed of these same fanatics? Perhaps it was precisely here that compassion for their powerlessness caught up with him. Now, though he was himself wholly at the mercy of their chief persecutor, it can hardly have been more than an echo of that outlawed religion's creed. Yet there must have been a ringing in his ears as the idea came to him there on his estate outside Rome. It was the password he himself had one day forgotten. Everything that had moved him as a philosopher his whole life long was contained in its three rising and falling syllables. Now that the end was approaching, there appeared another triad of sound in its place, something like *vanitas*. The entire peregrination, then, boiled down to the simple theme of every third-rate poetic ditty. *Otium, vanitas* . . . back and forth in his humming skull the siren song's pendulum swung. There, in his consciousness, now slowly disappearing, sinking into all-encompassing night with the final breath, it mocked on and on: *vanitas, otium . . . otium, vanitas.*

2

But let's not forget: the dying man about whom we're speaking had a precise conception of the meaning of life. The central thought of his philosophy: human existence has been worthwhile only if as much of it as possible has been dedicated to reading books. Our lifetime, whether brief or long, can be quantitatively stretched and qualitatively intensified only if it serves the quest for knowledge. Only he who holds himself rigorously aloof from the rat race has lived in self-determination. No compromises: happiness was to be found only in the private sphere, far from the treadmill existence of the majority. What follows then, without ifs, ands, or buts, is the paradox of an ethics that sees the ultimate good in the greatest possible remove from other human beings. A standard of behavior that, first of all, was radically egoistic, and second, amounted to flight from the world. Its first commandment was distance from the public sphere, abstinence in the face of every society. The rule of thumb, after a motto of Epicurus, went: live in seclusion. Live so that your survival depends neither on nepotism nor on the secure belay of others. In all your dealings, remain within yourself. Ensconce yourself in your private garden, behind the grape arbor, among the beehives. It would be superfluous to point out that such a life presupposes certain means. Good intentions alone are of little use. Without property, such maxims remain little more than a pious wish. A proper education and a little liquid capital would be the bare minimum. A slave is required whose job it would be to make known to the pestering visitor outside the gate that the master is not available today. That Seneca spoke for his own kind can hardly surprise us. It's easy enough to hear the sermon; yet in the other ear, we hear Horace whisper, "Thus Alfius, the moneylender, / In his mind already half-farmer / Called in his capital on the Ides, / and on the Kalends loaned it out again." Here it is the usurer's pipe dream of country living that falls so precipitously into the filth of satire. Naturally the target of the poet's APB is the ridiculous upstart, not the philosophizing blue blood. But in all seriousness: the problem for which Seneca's philosophy offered answers was one of which most of his fellow Romans would never have heard tell. And even if they had, what the devil could plebeians have done with his ethics? Only for a very small, very-well-heeled elite could it have had any relevance at all. To them alone, the upper ten thousand or so in imperial Rome, was his moral advice valid. They are the ones meant when he whispers to his friend Paulinus, "Separate yourself at last from the masses and withdraw into a quieter haven!" He knew what he was talking about. They were both exposed to the dangers of life in the civil service. Both of them sat in the same trap, prisoners in the Augustan marble city of Rome.

3

Still, as far as life in the big city is concerned, a civilization-weary Roman was considerably more hard-boiled than his

Greek antecedent. Like a modern advice columnist, Seneca's point of view is essentially practical as he warns his friend against the various forms of dissipation, forms only he can know who has experienced them himself. He beseeches Paulinus to hold himself aloof from sporting events and other spectacles of entertainment. He advises him against circuses and gladiator contests, sumptuous feasting and sexual adventures. As compensation and as medicine against any and every ill he recommends books. Only a life devoted to studying the great poets and thinkers is worthy of being lived. Everything else ends, sooner or later, in frustration, a waterslide into the sheer existential void. He alone who speculates in the company of the great wordsmiths has invested the sum of his days securely, proof against every crisis. Avoid your contemporaries—day pilferers and parasites most of them, hell-bent on plundering your private time-treasure. Truly well-to-do is he alone who immerses himself, day in and day out, in the writings of great minds.

Admittedly, the thought was not entirely new. Viewed superficially, it was no more than the lowest common denominator of all ancient moral philosophy—a minimal ethical consensus, at least among Skeptics, Peripatetics, Epicureans, and Stoics, as well as their various imitators. On the reading of classics as a source of meaning in an existence that was otherwise quite meaningless, everyone could easily have agreed. With the exception of the Sophists, perhaps, to whom every principle was fodder for their silly word games—and the Cynics, of course, those hippies among philosophers, who preferred to throw themselves into the moment with compulsive insouciance and keep a distance from anything even remotely resembling a library. For all others, Seneca's teachings were required reading, familiar as an old tune. And who could object? In an age that consumed traditions no less eagerly than battle trophies, originality was by no means the highest literary priority. Written records were something with which one dealt rather casually. Despite the endless zeal for litigation in Seneca's time, plagiarism cases of the kind we see everywhere today would have been met with blank incomprehension. Philosophy meant collecting whatever wisdom was floating around in the air and passing it on. Whoever saw fit could advert to Plato, who understood thinking as anamnesis—as the calling up of mental contents whose simple givenness rendered all questions of copyright and correct attribution of sources superfluous. What counted was not the single stroke of genius but the batting average. Rhetoric meant wit. At a premium was the confident reach into the archive of general ideas. It was the golden age of rememorization—read: the breezy larceny of thought. Age-old certainties, polished up as bons mots and sold as fresh insights—that was the extent of belletristic ambition. How else, one asks oneself, could an adult Roman presume to appear before his friend in the role of a dispenser of advice? Apart from the chance to trot out a few aphorisms, why would someone sacrifice his precious leisure hours to write an essay on the theme "the brevity of life," for instance?

However promising the title, for the average Roman from a respectable house it evoked above all the memory of torturous hours at school, of exercises in Latin composition. Let us therefore assume that the author's immediate concern was really to pacify his own spirit. He simply anticipated what lay in store for him. How little time would remain to him, once things got started, for such paeans on the *vita contemplativa*. It's the younger man here who sits the elder down for a serious talk. As Prefect of the Granary, Paulinus was a very busy man and was certainly much more experienced than Seneca as far as self-sacrifice for the state was concerned. The other reason was doubtless Seneca's penchant for didacticism. In his day, and in literate circles, learning and teaching overlapped seamlessly. It was expected that one would keep one's chops up, long after the formal schooling had ended. For this purpose, the writing of didactic letters was considered the best exercise. Seneca was, to be sure, a pro in this genre. From the plethora of treatises and speeches, numerous tragedies and poems (the latter having been, unfortunately, lost—down to a few epigrams), the collection of letters, the so-called *Epistulae morales*, rises as a singular corpus. Their addressee was a certain Lucilius. In the same epistolary manner as these, only a decade earlier and addressed to Paulinus, he composed the treatise "On the Brevity of Life"—I say "manner" in the sense that the reader should take note that we are dealing here with a time-honored method. The strength of his argument stems from the ancestral line of all those who had made use of it before him.

4

The biographers like to portray Seneca as a man torn between his inclinations and his talents; a man who combined everything in one person: philosopher, politician, poet, and patron of a throng of slaves and clients. Be that as it may, all that remains accessible to the contemporary reader is Seneca the writer. But he did no more or less than what his colleagues have done as long as literature has existed. He swapped masks and metaphors. As a speaking subject, he deftly slipped into the most variegated roles and changed positions like sandals. In short, he developed his own style. And nothing furthers the development of obstinacy like the constraint of form. The stricter the rules, the more ardent the desire to become unmistakable. What the private citizen does is one thing. If he seems monosyllabic and reserved, all the better. The important thing is that the author snap open the peacock's fan with maximum élan. He lays emphasis where none expect it, he sharpens the effects, he remains constantly in motion between the extremes of his own discourse. Seneca loved exaggeration, the moment when the jaw drops in surprise. Rhetorical aces were a dime a dozen in his time, but expressionists such as he were hard to find. What elevates him above the masses of sweet-talkers was less his craftsmanly skill than his theatrical technique. The trick consisted in taking himself, this bundle of contradictions, and splitting it up into the ensemble of an imaginary drama with the title *Seneca*. The name stood for the repertoire. Midway through the tragedy he changes the register, and the chorus segues into the beat of philosophical meditation. Without warning, the uniform murmur of expository prose is interrupted by a line of verse. And a satire shows how closely neighbored noblesse is to malice, and punning to being dead serious. Everything has its place in one and the same person. Or a letter, the most intimate of the forms of literary expression: after a few lines, it pops from the cocoon as a piece of belletristic moralizing. In a chatty tone, one friend lectures another on commonplaces any half-educated Roman would know from Latin class. The only thing that counts is the choreography. The text is staged according to a late-Greek recipe for success: as diatribe. The fictive objection, the obscure quotation, the historical example: the cunning interplay guarantees its entertainment value. The author merely reports, he offers for our consideration and keeps himself concealed. That it is a poet who speaks here is suggested by the author's gift of farsightedness, which makes up for any deficiency of experience. He offers his fatherly warning to the pen pal: "Separate yourself then from the masses, dearest Paulinus. The greatest part of your life and certainly the better was devoted to politics. Take some part for yourself, too!"

Seneca was one to talk. For in the same year in which these lines appeared, he took up a post at court as private tutor. It seems he didn't have to be asked twice. He agreed

out of gratitude for Empress Agrippina, who had stuck with
him through his exile from Rome, a time when no one gave a
hoot about him anymore. Her wish was his command. And
loyalty was a virtue that ranked fairly high up with him,
notwithstanding the letter's making no mention of it. The
writer in any event now did exactly what he had warned his
friend so earnestly against. He dispensed with his own peace
of mind, his dear *otium*. He, who a moment ago had been
preaching withdrawal from the world, now sat himself down
among the lions in that very hell. Of course, it all began casually enough, with private chambers, cultivated audiences, sab-
baticals, and copious leisure hours for study. Let privacy come
and go; the strength of Stoicism lay in its adaptability. Evil
tongues alleged: the elasticity of its concepts. Whatever suited
one's nature was allowed. But on one condition: that *ratio* sit
in the judgment seat. And if translated as plain old human
understanding, *ratio* leaves you considerable wiggle room.
Both, according to Stoic doctrine, were sensible: retreat into
the ivory tower and service for the common good, both were
legitimate. Seneca had opted for the latter. And why not?
After all, it amounted at first to little more than teaching the
future emperor his ABCs and some good manners along the
way. One can easily picture him reading the latest discourse
out loud to his young charge. A man like Paulinus, grown old
in the civil service, was certainly a more grateful listener. But
of course this didn't compare with a twelve-year-old boy! And
a crown prince and son of the Muses to boot! And one, moreover, who worshipped him and who would soon enough rule
the world?

5

Jesus Christ hadn't been dead fifty years when the essay "On
the Brevity of Life" was written. A waxing horde of fanatics
called him "savior." What would the man whose mouth had

uttered the Sermon on the Mount have to say about the theses hammered out here? "On the Brevity of Life"—it sounds like a warning to everyone and no one. And nothing short of apodictic, this: "We live only a small part of life. The rest of a lifetime is not life, only time." In a bid for our confidence, the writer evokes the most intimate fear in everyone, the fear of loss: "Not one man can be found, who would willingly part with his money; and yet life itself—to how many does nearly everyone give it away!" And adds with a sarcastic sneer, "Thus you have no reason to say of someone, on account of gray hairs or wrinkles, that he has lived long. He hasn't lived long; he's only been around a long time." And yet no sooner have the evils been tallied up than the solution beckons to the insightful reader: "Those and only those possess leisure who devote their time to philosophy. Those alone truly live."

Oddly enough, these sentences must have been pure music to Christian ears. The melody sounded intimate. Wasn't it reminiscent of certain passages in the Gospel of Matthew? "Enter ye in at the strait gate:"—so goes the text there. "For wide is the gate, and broad is the way, that leadeth to destruction, and many there be which go in thereat: Because strait is the gate, and narrow is the way, which leadeth unto life, and few there be that find it." However fundamentally different, the respective solutions to the problem harmonized beautifully in their intonation. Or rather, since both conformed to the rules of classical rhetoric, no wonder then that the structures of their argumentation were so unmistakably similar.

Let's say someone seeks refuge from all human hustle and bustle. He raises his head, gazes about him, and asks himself: "How do I become my own master?" Through solitude, says the one, through self-reflection in leisure. Through humility, maintains the other, through charity and compassion. The first, ensconced in power and weary of the majority, seeks the still point in his own soul. The other, eternal Jew, yet, being a minority, highly motivated, has long since found it outside himself, out there in humanity. Trusting God, he builds upon his neighbors. The other, misanthropic from bald pate to sandals, counts on no one but himself. God or Mammon: thus the watchword of the one who from birth possesses nothing. I or they—the incorrigible masses: thus the other who would soon be Rome's second-richest man. As tempting as it is to draw parallels, this is where they part company. Any further comparison would be pure cynicism. Even if two thousand years, taken in at a glance, seem to resemble that eternity in which parallel lines supposedly intersect. The embarrassment is simply this: that Seneca's logic is immediately and without further ado comprehensible to us, moderns. The optimism of the Sermon on the Mount, by contrast, sounds rather otherworldly in our ears. Surely the vision of the Messiah can wait, can it not? But a sermon like "On the Brevity of Life" is always relevant. Christian or pagan, whoever lives in a mass society knows what the deal is here. Beyond a certain population density, it's simply easier to identify with the concerns of a metropolitan than with the strange exhortations of a pitiable dropout. The error lies in the direction of the gaze. To the parallel lines themselves it is a matter of indifference whether they intersect or not, in the distant future or some long-gone biblical distance. One thing is certain: they cut through every individual human heart and have done so not just since the classical period. Don't the Psalms say as much, long before both Seneca *and* Jesus Christ: "So teach us to number our days, that we may apply our heart unto wisdom."

6

Who was he, then, this peculiar Seneca? Dozens of biographers have toiled away on the portrait of his character. Hardly another life from the classical period has been illuminated in such multifaceted richness and sketched with such anecdotal surfeit. But the crux is that, under closer scrutiny, all these portraits collapse into a heap of shards. Tragic poet? To be sure: the writing of tragedies was a party game, even Nero succumbed to the temptation. Philosopher? Of course: with the acumen of the autodidact who knew his way around his library. Educator of the noble class? Admittedly: in a flight of monomania, he believed the empire could be reformed through learning. Influential politician? But how strange: a man with his ambitions, a man of letters through and through, a man who couldn't do without the solitude and silence in which to work—what possible aptitude could he have for such power games, dependent as they are on unrelenting watchfulness? So many roles, too many for a single human being. One would require a second Lucian, the classical Cubist, to unify in a single picture puzzle the many contradictions of this man's life. Contradictions on every side, the entire person a question mark. All that remains to the interpreter, after reading and rereading, are texts that glimmer with possible meanings. Even the layman stares in amazement. Rarely has a human being been so Janus-faced.

No wonder, then, that even the sculptors who have attempted to convey to us his appearance have delivered multiple variations of our many-sided Roman. We have for instance the corpulent aristocrat, a well-fed Roman intellectual, as shown by one double herm. In accordance with an iconographic fashion of the times, the back of his bald head morphs into that of Socrates, like him both glutton and brainiac. And then we have the perfect complement, the marble bust in Florence that portrays a starveling, an emaciated geezer with matted beard and hair unruly and dangling in his face. Where to begin? In editions of Seneca's work, sometimes this image, sometimes that one shows up; the work itself offers evidence for both interpretations. No less confusing is the multiplicity of genres in which he offers himself to the reader even today: drama, satire, court report, didactic epistle, philosophical commentary; of each of these many examples survive. The imagination finds places to linger everywhere, but nowhere a conclusive answer for this embodied human riddle. In recent times, psychiatrists would have preferred to speak of a multiple personality, according to a theory that quickly came to seem dubious and that occupied the science sections of newspapers until its refutation. Thus here, too, little in the way of enlightenment is to be expected. Nothing's to be done: for good or ill, the reader must decide for himself how to assemble the puzzle into a portrait.

Who, then, was this multifaceted, multilayered, multitalented man, Rome's own incarnation of the mythical Proteus? He was—and here the chroniclers are unanimous—one of those who tower above their contemporaries. He anticipated that type which historians, in referring to certain harbingers arising centuries later from the darkest gloom of the Middle Ages, have dubbed the Renaissance Man. Shakespeare, Montaigne, and Rubens were cast in the same mold. Seneca's phenomenal rebirth in their tumultuous time proves nothing if not an elective affinity. To them, the pioneers of Old Europe, he was a Mentor—understood, of course, in the full mythical sense of the name. Not the private tutor of Nero: what was meant was the overlord of the great Odysseus. To the intellectual and artistic giants of the Renaissance, Seneca appeared as one of their own. Rubens, to take one example, had a niche reserved for the philosopher in the private Pantheon of his house in Antwerp. It was no accident that he stood watch there at the gate beside Plato and Aristotle, with the inscription *artes liberales*. What predestined him to become patron saint of the seven liberal arts was nothing other than the multifariousness of his interests. The educated classes re-

membered him as the preacher of self-discipline, and until
recently—and thanks to rote learning and the cane that
enforced it—every schoolkid knew his name.

He considered himself, above all, a follower of the Stoa.
Which was not without contention: Stoicism enjoyed a rather
poor reputation at court. During civic crises, the teachings of
the Stoics tended to be viewed as a threat to state security.
Understandably, since an ideology that glorified a lofty equanimity could easily plunge its adherents into conflicts of alle-
giance. The duty of the civil servant lay not with his own
spiritual welfare, but with patriotic self-sacrifice. Anyone who
mastered his own emotions and remained arrogantly poised
within himself was not to be trusted. Nero in his persecution
mania knew exactly what he was doing when he put his
teacher to the test. Tacitus recounts the scene in which
Seneca, now an old man, seeks an audience with the emperor
and requests leave to give up his wealth and withdraw into
retirement, a request that Nero promptly denies. Not without
cunning, as Tacitus maliciously observes. For the treacherous
pupil, spawn of Seneca's own failed pedagogy, answers him
quite coolly: "Neither thy moderation, in surrendering thy
wealth, nor thy desire for rest, in leaving thy post as Princeps,
will be on every tongue, but rather my avarice, and thy fear of
my cruelty. Therefore, while thy renunciation would certainly
earn praise, it is not honorable for a wise man to seek fame
for himself by a deed that will bring disapprobation on his
friend."

His friend? That stings, to be sure; but this, too, our
chameleon must sooner or later have had to sit and take. A
friend of the powerful he was indeed, and all posterity knows
of it. *Ataraxia* be what it may, the fact remains that Seneca was
a willing member of that club of demigods that determined
the destinies of Rome's masses. His career, despite certain
impediments and ruptures, speaks volumes about his over-

developed instinct for politics. He started off, as was the common practice at that time, with a stint as orator, gathered experience then as a lawyer, soon thereafter became quaestor and, finally, senator. With the enthronement of Claudius, a court intrigue interrupts his safe ascent. He spends seven years in exile on Corsica. Then comes his second chance, in the form of the strong-willed Agrippina, Nero's mother and spouse of Emperor Claudius (who, unnerved by the strain of rule and weary of that scum known as the *populus romanus*, fakes insanity). She becomes Seneca's patroness. As empress, to whom the future belongs, she summons the hermit against his will back to Rome. From now on the road leads steeply upward for our bookworm, who allegedly wants one thing only: his inner peace, an existence free of all office and honor. In Agrippina's game plan, however, there is only one position for him to play: that of role model for Nero, her one and only, the prince who, as heir to the throne, will avenge her ruined life. Seneca's job is to get the pudgy kid in shape for his historic mission. And he was the ideal means to this end: pedagogue, trainer, guru, Praeceptor Romae—all in one person. He would polish the Augustus of the future into a brilliant diamond. To be sure, after his hours of service there remains sufficient free time, which he devotes to versifying his spiteful satires, by virtue of which he writes himself into the hearts of the future rulers. Naturally, and merely as an aside, he also pulls off the jump to praetor, a status that at the very least would have predestined him, first, to the command of an imperial army division, then to the office of procurator, as was a certain Pontius Pilate. He belonged henceforth to that most exclusive circle of twelve to eighteen men who were permitted to sashay around in the *toga praetexta*. Their omnipotence would more or less correspond to that of a Supreme Court justice today. Had he so desired, he might have played governor in one of the imperial provinces or high magistrate in the city government. That he preferred instead to work behind the scenes, hidden from public view, in the secrecy-enshrouded chambers of the imperial palace, bespeaks little in the way of a renunciation of power. To all appearances, he was snug as a bug in a rug right in the middle of the whirlwind. All that have survived of his complaints at the center of Roman imperial power are his philosophical headaches. As for Stoic reserve and social asceticism, there is little evidence. One would do well to read "On the Brevity of Life" as a sort of confession, a literary unburdening for the writer himself and his fractured persona.

7

It is high time, I think, for a few clarifications about the slovenly commentator. It's bad form, especially from safe cover, and without so much as a by-your-leave, to presume to review a life long departed. Two thousand years of history are a spacious hideout for loose tongues, and not every one of them belongs to a Plutarch. Besides, hacking around at a marble bust is not art. More difficult by far is tracing the grain of its surfaces, which can be so full of meaning: the temple branched with blood vessels, the bruise beneath the angular chin. Given that the text we're talking about here is in fact equivalent to marble, that hard limestone which the vast majority of architects and sculptors in Seneca's day had at their disposal: Can one do anything but break one's teeth on it? With Latin prose you fare about as well as with the sculptures in a museum. Surreptitiously, insofar as they're not mere headless torsos, you seek eye contact with these colorless orbs, and imagine pupils and irises into the bargain. All that has ever become flesh seems to be swallowed up in this pale, neutral, expressionless material. Its state of aggregation repels the museum visitor, even before he has furtively brushed the cool surfaces. And like the material, so too the language, Latin, with its rock-hard grammar, leaves little wiggle room. You hear, in every turn of syntax, the discipline, the final meaning. Everything seems to have been formulated for eternity, in taut diction, conceived for the ear of the soldier habituated to orders. Unlike Greek, a language that is communicative, supple, and dialectical in the extreme, the effect of Latin is strangely rigid. It is difficult to believe that poets such as Catullus or Propertius managed to chirp like siskins in Latin, hypernervous in their erotic unrest—a state they managed to capture to perfection (without in the least petrifying it) both syntactically and prosodically. From today's perspective, it is a language that seems ideally suited to epitaphs: the essence of what we mean by the phrase "dead language." The power of definition, not the capacity for dialogue, is its linguistic trademark; and the Romance languages that descend from it bear this mark like a deep imprint. Theology, medicine, physics, and chemistry: here, in the eternal hunting grounds of nomenclature and abstraction, Latin has posthumously set itself up as the daily bread of communicability. Its jurisdiction begins far from all that has ever lived, stuttered, and quivered with desire, in a logical beyond, in which language itself struggles for conceptuality, for freedom from contradiction, for identity, dominance, or simple semantic duration. For centuries now, languages by the thousands have fought for their own survival; and since the world became round, many have died out to the last song and syllable. Yet there is one that has outlasted every migration, every education reform, every religious war, and even the latest computer crash of the graduate student who despairs over the lost footnotes to his dissertation. Regardless of what the individual larynx may feel of it, Latin sticks deep in the bones of almost every modern European language, while Greek has been more like a second skin on top of it. What connects us, however loosely, with the authors of antiquity is not only a web of quotation but, above all, the spine at the center of our languages, the etymological joints. What links us—Lucius Annaeus Seneca and a belated visitor to his writings such as myself—is a common skeletal structure, one that still guarantees an upright gait.

In other words, we're both stuck in the same trap. Nor is it the same simply because the concepts in which his head was once entangled have long since snagged my own as well. No, it's much worse than that: since, along with the ideals drummed into me by his Latin, I must also swallow the inconsistency resulting from the impossibility of their fulfillment. Well do I know what certain lexical vertebrae and shoulder bones enjoin upon us, and yet I must learn to see clearly how little we, as weak-limbed, all too easily bent beings, are capable of doing justice to their meaning. In the end, none of us is a match for marble. Nonorganic, brainless, and time-resistant—the attributes of this building material do not apply to us. The same is true of the language that was better suited to marble than any other since. A language bristling with postulates, nothing if not airtight. A language that from the very start was superior to its speakers; for which nothing and no one can suffice—certainly not Seneca, this prototype of the conflicted philosopher, a brittle sculpture fused of politics and passion, to say nothing of me, his late-born reader, mollycoddled on artificial ingredients and synthetic fibers.

8

It begins with the fact that I stumbled upon Seneca like the browsing youth upon Winnetou and Old Shatterhand in the novels of Karl May. When I consider it closely, the reason I write of Seneca here at all is a simple boyhood error. Not an especially solid foundation—though typical of my genera-

tion—of which it can be said, among other things, that it consists of a mixture of half-baked education, an enthusiasm for
the naïve association of ideas, and all kinds of neo-Romantic
fantasies. Much has drifted to us by way of error, brushing our
spoiled temples and briefly taken up like an exotic thrift-store
find. Thus did the metaphor end up on the T-shirt, the erro-
neous Nietzsche quote in the notebook, the Chinese poem in
a blue tattoo on the upper arm. And just so did the name, any
name, arrive in our memory, a junk drawer otherwise reserved
for advertising jingles, automobile brands, the guitar solos and
lyrics of our favorite rock bands. This is the sad footing, I
regret to say, these the idiotic, absurd, epoch-determined, and
arbitrary tracks that led me at age fourteen to Seneca. *Tracks*,
at the very least, is the right word. Why? To make a long story
short: the name was not whispered to me by that tidbit of
Latin class—a mere year and a half of it, now long since forgotten—but rather, long before cramming for vocabulary tests
began, by a book that to me then was everything. It was about
Indians, this much I remember. As to the remainder of its contents, although filtered down deep inside me and hardly
accessible any longer, they are subject less to a repression à la
Freud than to childish discretion. It was the work of an eth-
nologist, and it dealt with the diverse Indian tribes of North
America that had, like the languages mentioned above, completely died out. Richly illustrated, it told of the most romantic life one could possibly imagine. At least for someone like
me, born in Dresden, and thus in the neighborhood adjacent
to the wigwam of a certain Karl May.

The subject was the proud tribe of the Iroquois, those
warriors with the flamelike, bristling hairdos of London
punks. It was in connection with them that the name Seneca
first popped up. I have long wondered, was it the designation
of an entire clan, or only the appellation of one of the chiefs? I
could make it easy for myself and blame the confusion on a

certain portrait that was reproduced in the book. It showed a
man wearing a turban and holding a small pipe in his hand,
a sight that rather disappointed me at the time. This was how
a Turk looked, or maybe some kind of Oriental, but certainly
not an Indian. Something arid and civilized, something un-
warrior-like hung about him. He looked to me like a scholar,
perhaps the chronicler of his tribe. It was my grandfather who
cleared this exotic matter up for me. This was a man who, during the short retirement granted him by lung cancer, designed
crossword puzzles for the largest daily paper in Thuringia, one
that he himself, as someone who walked the line rather casually, called "The Party Rag." His answer came like a pistol
shot. Roman philosopher with six letters?—Seneca. The years
4 B.C.E. to 65 C.E. Stoic, tragedian, teacher of Emperor Nero,
by whom coerced to suicide. So much for the official report.
And yet, for years I remained skeptical. The real track, impossible to erase, was this trace in Native American culture.
The name Seneca lead me, redskin fan that I was then,
straight into the mysterious world of Karl May's novels and
the Leatherstocking Tales of James Fenimore Cooper. To
renounce these, just because some *Brockhaus Encyclopedia* presented me with this marble dude, was unthinkable. Roman
Empire? No dice. At best it made me think of a movie poster.
In the same breath, I associated it with the word *decline* and
with Sophia Loren. And apropos Nero: wasn't he the nut job
who set Rome on fire and afterward blamed it on the poor
Christians? And give me a break: Philosophy? Who cared,
when we had the heroic deeds of the *red man*? For half of my
childhood, nothing held more importance for me and my
playmates than the mythical world of those Indians, familiar
to us in its finest details from books and movies. Only the little pipe continued to irritate me. I would have preferred a
talisman. Or, for my money, wampum, like the ones the Algon-
quin wore. At the same time, I knew that most Indians had a

weakness for glass pearls and trinkets of every kind. Was the name Seneca perhaps yet another treacherous gift from the *white man*? Now I know it was the name of the tribe itself, not the chief who had looked so much like an Arab to me, like Karl May's Kara Ben Nemsi or Hadshi Halef Omar. He should at least have had a tomahawk on his arm.

9

Some mental associations are like the sins of youth. They lead nowhere and are best forgotten. Or if need be, they proclaim the wayward paths on which you nearly got lost as a child or during puberty. The more abstruse they appear, the more violent the reflex to shake them off for good, if only you knew how. For the awful thing about them is the persistence of their regular return, often at the most ridiculous moments. No sooner have you made it through school, majored in this or that, lived a while overseas, married, started a family, than— *boing!*—up they pop again. What really bugs you is their fast motion effect, the blithe audacity with which they simply skip entire phases of life. Horrifying, isn't it? For when considered closely, it demonstrates—well, what if not the brevity of life? Goethe spoke not amiss when he said, "It is the mind that ages Youth and rejuvenates Age." Do what you will, there are certain ineluctable representations you will never in your entire life be rid of. You are forever monkeying around at the bars of some dim cognitive cage. For this as for various other private embarrassments, psychology has furnished us with a concept. It speaks of *perseveration*. What this means is a pathological insistence upon one and the same thought. In other words, a hiccup of the brain.

Despite appearances, this author has by no means lost the thread of his argument. The topic here is still Seneca. Or rather, it is the errant echoes and confused illustrations that the name sets off in his cranium. Embarrassing, but true: ad hoc, I still first see the chief in war paint, and only then the Roman aristocrat in his toga. The picture puzzle out of which the two, Roman and "redskin," take their turns appearing is, alas, unretouchable. The irritation is complete when I call to mind the little boy as well. Knees all scratched, feather stuck in his headband, he squats there in the cherry tree murmuring reverently to himself: *Seneca, Seneca.*

10

And then this ignominious ending. Tacitus describes the disaster in minute detail, as if he'd been there himself, so precise is his report. On the other hand, he need have done nothing more than quote; there were eyewitnesses galore. Slaves and scribes, the entire household of servants was in attendance, including the faithful spouse, Paulina. Socrates had shown how to do it. To be a philosopher was one thing; to become a legend as a philosopher was something different entirely. In the memory of humankind, he alone survived who departed before an assembled audience. The only thing he had to worry about was to ensure that he retained the gift of speech to the last breath, and, of course, that the others, all of them, the truest of the true, hung upon his lips. As far as the eloquence of last words, Seneca was never in danger of embarrassment. The genre was called *meditatio mortis*, preparation for death, and in this stock role he was unbeatable. In this respect, all of his writings, with the possible exception of the dramas, were early études for the one final monologue. If, taken together, they give the impression of monotony, this is because their message seldom varied. The soporific effect stems from a lesson that is everywhere the same: *bethink thou, mortal, how little time remains.* It's quite possible that Seneca even quoted himself in these last minutes. "No one can give

you back your years, no one can return you to yourself. Your
life hastens away, just as it began." But what if, instead of that,
he thought of some unpaid bill, or a manuscript still uncor-
rected, or a compromising letter of which posterity must know
nothing? Perhaps what came to mind was some triviality,
paired with the wildest associations. "Observe how, even
among the Romans, the foolish craving to memorize triviali-
ties has taken root." Information trash like the fact "that Pom-
pey was the first to organize a battle with eighteen elephants
as part of the circus; that Sulla was the last to move the holy
city-limits." Without a doubt, he too was caught up in his own
neural net. Nevertheless, as a philosopher, he attempted to
bring some sense of order into the private tissue. A few of the
knots, certainly the thicker ones, are well known to us. As far
as anyone can tell, there was nothing among them to resemble
the infamous Gordian one. Or perhaps Seneca was just not
the kind of guy to hack through it with a single blow. What's
worse, as his biography amply attests, he was often pleased
instead to cinch them even tighter. Lust for fame and
equipoise; retreat from the world and public office; politics
and bucolics; a single, hopelessly tangled mass. When, as an
old man, he finally wanted out, it was much too late. Smiling,
Nero gave him a kiss, laid the noose gently around his neck,
and pulled tight.

11

To get an impression of the brevity of life, it suffices to imagine the distance between a cause and its deadly effect. The
problem is this: What to do, when there are simply too many
causes and all of them end up producing the same effect?
What if the human being, this incarnation of a multiplicity of
interests, one day loses the overview of their inner squabbles?
Personal union functions well only as long as the different

role-players maintain control. As soon as one goes weak, the entire ensemble collapses. The armor cracks open, the body displays its nakedness. And nakedness meant: now you were just this one entity, for whom every false move turned deadly, and fast. Rome's second-richest man, suddenly there he stood like a run-of-the-mill conspirator. The most impressive personality far and wide, once stripped naked, there remained only the ham actor. And he knew quite well: as an actor, Nero was far superior. Assuming Seneca had in fact no connection whatsoever to Piso's conspiracy, he deserved the death sentence nonetheless—as Nero's accessory. He was what the jealous press today calls an insider; he was in the know. Like no other, he was intimately familiar with the explosive concoction of hubris and paranoia that was Nero. No one else was so thoroughly privy to the destructive fantasies of the emperor. The perfect informant, thinks the reader. And yet what is he offered? Not the slightest indiscretion, not the minutest dirty detail. Instead we have allegories en masse, allusions that were already quaint even at the time. Oh yes, and these apocalyptic alarms in the tragedies. The last of which hardly count, since he allegedly spun them as didactic material for Nero alone. And they did fulfill their curricular purpose in contrast to the importuning formulas of his treatises "On Clemency" and "On Leisure," which rustled past the ear of his pupil without leaving a trace. Nero could do as he pleased, being able for a long time to rely on Seneca's own clemency and leisurely reserve toward him. Even after the first couple of murders, approval seemed the most appropriate pedagogical measure.

If anything, Seneca's contribution to the conspiracy was this: his Stoical opportunism. His instinct for adaptation, guided by his tireless intelligence. In retrospect, the greatest evil was nothing other than the decades-long conspiracy against himself. This colossal ambition to be a cause in one's own right, rather than remain forever the mere plaything of various inscrutable effects. He knew the punishment one could expect for this, having formulated it word for word himself. Still, in the end, he was man enough to accept it with composure.

How was it again? Every happiness eventually ruins itself, even without disruptions from the outside. If that holds true, then Seneca was far more consistent than most who came after him. From the plethora of causes that make life brief, he extracted the single dead-ringer. From the standpoint of drama, it was also the most fertile one. *Amor fati*, love thy fate, would have well suited him as a motto. If he made little fuss about it, chalk it up to courtesy. As a Stoic he knew, despite all the propaganda for a fulfilling life on earth, that the best comes at the end. And this he withheld from Paulinus at the time: in the moment of death, eternity celebrates a birthday with each of us. What's the point of haggling when everything is but an episode? A few years more or less—cause here, effect there—makes no big difference. In a few seconds, every gap shrinks to nothing with a sigh.

A TEAR FOR PETRONIUS
On the Satyricon

There are certain books, let's call them novels, that lead their readers out into the wide world, into all kinds of adventures—and their heroes into the heart of some darkness or other, or along the path of *Bildung* to themselves. Petronius' *Satyricon* leads nowhere at all, unless (and this rather incidentally) it be into the submerged world of classical antiquity: to the Roman Empire at the time of Nero and to various points of interest in southern Italy, which for the most part still bore Greek names at the time.

For this reason, one can consider it without much exaggeration the first modern novel in world literature, and without doubt one of the craziest books ever written. Its title has long been a matter of controversy. What we know today under the title *Satyricon*, this artful botchery from the quill of a certain Petronius, is at best a shard heap, a pile of textual fragments, a puzzle put together by philologists into the semirecognizable semblance of a narrative that is presumed to have been of epic proportions. All that survives are sections of books 14, 15, and 16. Written in approximately 65 C.E., they are the fragments of a picaresque novel, an accumulation of brazen erotica and ghost stories, set in the milieu of Rome's nouveaux riches, slaves, and manumitted. Or else it's the remains of a great pornographic epic, depending on one's point of view. As far as the plot itself is concerned, I fear the less said, the better. That this novel is in fact the parody of a novel, the mockery of all conceivable epics, is recognizable in the protagonist himself, one Encolpius. It also doesn't take a particularly fine philological nose to recognize the first-person narrator as an embarrassing avatar of Odysseus, nor the portrayal of his still more embarrassing misadventures as a remarkably shameless homage to Odysseus' biographer, the great ur-narrator, Homer.

The trick here is killing several birds with one stone. And they are some truly gargantuan fowl. Among them one finds, for example, the rules of classical Greek prosody; the auras of the Homeric heroes; any state authority whatsoever; good manners; the brilliance of Roman rhetoric (for example, Cato's and Cicero's); as well as any sort of class distinction or idea of good breeding, hierarchy, or nobility, no less than the belief in the goodness of the individual, in manly dignity (*virtus*) and character. Nor is this all: a few bona fide pterodactyls lie among the fallen as well, including the entire Greek pantheon, along with the full phalanx of Rome's own stylites— the solitary exception being Priapus, around whom everything revolves, but more on that later. Again: all of this with a single stone. The specific techniques that Petronius deploys here and that he refines at the same time beyond all preceding measure are called satire and realism. Granted, the latter, if not the former, too, is a thoroughly malleable aesthetic category, and one that will keep people busy in the arts for two-thousand-plus years to come. Certainly, it has proven itself no less hardy, no less adaptable, than satire, its incestuous sibling. Such an affinity may at first appear implausible. What do caricature, hyperbole, and ridicule have to do with the representation of objectivity and a portrayal that is, to the highest degree possible, true to nature? Are they not in fact contrary principles? And yet, strange to say, one need only go far enough back in the history of literature to ascertain, with some surprise, that both crawl forth from the same filthy corner. Whether by fate or accident, their hotbed is of all places this same Roman Empire at the time of Petronius. And without a doubt, under both of them gapes one and the same abyss—or better yet, that new cloaca maxima: a world without gods, a civilization in which all human relationships have been relativized. Here, realism means first and foremost nothing more than the opposition to myth, or rather its infiltration by the mundane realities of everyday life. If myth is the species-appropriate, the XL size in the form of divine fables and family legends from the early dawn of one's own tribe, then realism is the collective movement that, by virtue of fitting everything to reality, shrinks it down to normal size. The result was, as the Romans themselves knew, profanation or worse, decadence—read: degeneration. In this sense, every realism amounts to sawing at the bough of tradition, the daily demolition work performed on one's own mythology, which had once been drummed into the head of every schoolkid. In all probability, this impulse is as old as humanity itself; at least there is much among the Greeks of the fifth century B.C.E. that points in this direction. The comedies of Aristophanes are a case in point, as are the uncouth farces in the popular theater of the Hellenistic period, the mime with his phallic gags—and no tragedy in ancient Athens was without the follow-up of a satyr play. Realistic interludes as a holiday from myth certainly date way back; realism as fundamental attitude, however, as dominant style and taste, henceforth considered modern, is a distinguishing feature of the frivolities of imperial Rome, and from here, it has asserted itself worldwide and across all epochs. And yet, after so many centuries, can realism still mean anything at all?

As far as satire is concerned, there is by and large consensus as to its origin. Though the form may be traceable to a Greek of the third century—the cynic Menippos—the expression itself is a thoroughly Roman invention. A certain

Ennius (239–169 B.C.E.), who used it for his collection of miscellaneous poems, was likely the one who coined the term, by way of reference to a bowl filled with all manner of offerings, but chiefly with fruit (the *lanx satura*). In other words, the designation of an entire literary genre is bound up first with the practice of sacrifice, and second with sensual pleasure. And as a colorful salad bowl of prose and verse, it finally became an eminently Roman concern. Its compost was the collapse of republican values, the attrition of moral boundaries at every level of society, and the whorish free-for-all of patricians and plebeians. Its incubators were the alleyways and squares of Rome, the gladiator schools and thermal baths in the city center, and the swanky villas of the nouveaux riches perched out in the country. How else but in the style of satire was one to reach a society whose nonmilitary sector was dominated less by the civilian, that is, by the good citizen and taxpayer, than by the parasite? (The latter appearing in so many forms—con man, inheritance poacher, rent boy, procuress, ass-kissing client—that he seemed ubiquitous.) Where a slave could, within a generation's time, go from being bedpan washer to millionaire, much was possible. Where a foundling could rise from the gutter to being sole heir, silver-plate everything he owns, make a killing in wholesale, and thereupon withdraw to his own private Tusculum—there, now the perfect aristocrat, to lounge about in idleness—it would be difficult not to write satires. Juvenal got it right: as the last and most cunning of the Roman satirists, he simply struck the balance on his everyday experience. What other literary form would have been better suited to circumstances such as these? Where everything that once appeared as distinct milieu or subculture flows together into a single, great, metropolitan swamp, that's where Satire crawls forth into the light of day. Regardless of the connotations that may come to mind—from the raunchy satyr to saturation to the obscene yearly Saturnalia: satire belonged to a world that had literally been turned on its head. Why? Because economics played a role in its destiny as never before in antiquity. Satire was the lowest common denominator, a code word as universally applicable as the word *pop* is today. It reached its full bloom, however, between the Domus Aurea, Nero's imperial palace, and the taverns and iniquitous dens of the Subura quarter. In the face of such surrealism, realism must have protected satire's nerves. Out of this racial hodge-podge, thrown together from all corners of the empire, satire brought forth its knowledge of human nature. The most gifted poets of the time placed their expressive genius at the service of this new discipline—people such as Lucilius, Martial, Persius, Juvenal. Even Seneca, the honorable philosopher, wrote a spoof on Emperor Claudius, and instead of the appropriate apotheosis, produced his *apocolocyntosis* of the dearly departed, his most impertinent lampoon, all for the amusement of the late emperor's adopted son and successor, the spiteful Nero. Not even Horace, the aesthete, was too squeamish to dedicate a few satires to his patron Maecenas, albeit with a wink. Everyone who knew a thing about poetry was eager to do his best in matters of targeted malice, jargon, verbal punching power, in order to turn that hottest contemporary form of tabloid gossip into an artistic genre. Petronius, scratching out his prose on papyrus, was surrounded by experts. This was the situation, as this entertainer from Nero's court got down to work. And apropos the *Satyricon*: if it's true that the title is the author's own, then it was his first bull's-eye. To this day it has remained proverbial, as catchy as *Decameron* and *Pitaval*. Let the Roman reader hear the familiar satire latent in the foreign Greek word and his appetite was immediately steered to mythological hanky-panky. A "satyricon" was a book that promised a collection of satyrlike stories, as for example that of the soldier who morphs into a werewolf, or the donkey on the roof tiles. The point being:

the characters lead lives as gloriously harum-scarum as those
merry satyrs themselves. Unfortunately, what the contemporary reader gets is only
a small piece of the original novel—it's as if only the eighth
chapter of Joyce's *Ulysses* survived, in which Leopold Bloom
visits the Dublin Laestrygonians in their pubs and cheap
restaurants. However, upon surveying the patchwork of the
novel's extant and partially reconstructed fragments, it's safe
to say that even its contemporary Roman readers would have
in good conscience considered it a true *pars pro toto*: a part
that stands in for the whole. The "Cena Trimalchionis" ("Trimalchio's Banquet"), as it is commonly referred to in all separate book editions, is the longest extant continuous scene—an
expression, by the way, that invites punning. *Scaena* and *cena*
lie much too close together in Latin not to fire the imagination. Where the one gestures toward stagecraft and the theater, the other stands for one of the most important pastimes
of cultivated individuals, namely, lounging around at a dinner
party with food and drink. In both cases, the point is convivi-
ality. In this sense, the core of the *Satyricon*, "Trimalchio's
Banquet," deals with a fundamental human situation, in light
of which the distinction between antiquity and modernity
ceases to be valid. The only thing old-fashioned about it is
that the contemporaries at Trimalchio's feast felt reminded of
a much more famous banquet, in fact one of the pinnacles
of Greek philosophy: Plato's Symposium. The allusions are
numerous and impossible to overlook. Just as the great minds
of Athens once gathered for a solemn dinner, here truly
massive wights like Hermeros, Habinnas, and Agamemnon
stretch out on their dining couches and shoot the bull about
Homer and astrology. Modern readers may be reminded,
albeit furtively, of the Christian eucharist by this, an irony that
in all likelihood escaped Petronius. What could hardly have
escaped him, however, was the ambiguity of a Latin expres-

290 THE BARS OF ATLANTIS

sion like *parasite*. This is what is so magnificently staged here. The guests at Trimalchio's table are one and all moochers and freeloaders, and as such, as we have said, typical of Roman society at that time.

But who exactly is this Roman Croesus, this Trimalchio, around whom everything revolves? The best character description in our time was provided by a French scholar of ancient history. If one is to believe Paul Veyne, Trimalchio is by no means the typical parvenu he is generally considered to be by literary historians. As such, he would of course have had to have been an arrivé. But this manumitted and economically emancipated former slave has never escaped his caste. In terms of civil rights, he is completely impoverished, a being without a future, a ghostly apparition, neither parvenu, nor capitalist, nor bourgeois citizen. Tragicomically, because so utterly without effect, he attempts to pass off his wealth as nobility and social distinction, egged on all the while by the applause of a few have-nots. Though no one disabuses him of this fairy tale, still his phenomenal rise can hardly cause his low origins to be forgotten. Deported from Asia Minor, he is sold with a placard around his neck at the slave market in Rome. His master treats him as a member of the family: his first small winnings in the lottery of happiness. Already at a tender age he is allowed to serve domestically, and is thus spared the hard work in the fields; his studiousness and loyalty soon make him his master's favorite. With this, he has already risen above the masses of free plebeians outside the gated communities, those teeming hordes of men without property, who must scramble for a living without a safety net. Being a slave turns out to be an advantage. Then, one day— he had long ago learned to read and count—he is appointed private treasurer. The structure of Roman society is more complicated, writes Veyne, than your typical class pyramid: every rank in the hierarchy of free men had its correlative in the parallel stepladder of slaves and *emancipés*. Trimalchio at least has reached the top. For the benefit of his table mates he brags about how he finally made the leap into independence: "And then, as heaven willed it, I ended up chief of the household staff and, get a load of this, I caught my master's eye. What's the point of going on? Basically, he put me in his will next to the emperor, and I got a fortune like a senator." From now on, one must address him as C. Pompeius Trimalchio. And yet, as he manages to give away, it was his submissiveness to his master (and more important, to his mistress), not least of all in sexual terms, that won him this status. His master, dying, set Trimalchio free; that the man was also childless constituted the second major winning in Trimalchio's life. He received quite a sum through this bequest, and yet his legal status stands in no relation whatsoever to his economic potency. As sole heir, endowed with plentiful capital, he plunges at once into commerce, which, given the risks of maritime trade at the time, presented at first tremendous losses, then unbelievable gains. And the long and short of it is: no sooner has he "hamstered together" a few millions than he buys back the lands of his former master, converts these possessions into new capital investment, a phenomenon Karl Marx originally called "accumulation," and henceforth acts the country aristocrat with slaves and livestock and a staff of overseers. This is the man who curses his wife as a "jackboot Cassandra," and who at the table will mention in passing, "Now, I'm thinking I want to round off my little holdings with Sicily, so that, whenever I feel like going to Africa, I can sail through my own territory."

Paul Veyne called this breed the "yeast of Italy." They are transport entrepreneurs, craftspeople, merchants, ship owners, people who would not scruple to turn a profit from the slave trade themselves—in short, Rome's new middle class. And yet something is missing that would secure them perfect happiness: that decisive iota of certainty about their legal position. This is exactly what irritates one of the guests at table, the quarrelsome Hermeros, to such a degree that he lays into his mocker, Askyltos, with "What does he think's so funny? You're a Roman knight? Well, then I'm a prince!" Such a one as he represents the average social climber, uneducated and without legal rights, whom nothing but his personal Mammon can lend an identity. "I never learned all that bullshit like geometry or literary criticism or that nonsense à la 'Sing the Wrath,' but I can read the letters on billboards, and I can give percents in pennies, nickels, dimes, and quarters." Trimalchio surrounds himself with such people; it is for them he serves up all that kitchen and cellar have to offer, and we have the feeling he is himself not only one of them, but has never been anything else. They are all among their own kind, as centuries later the heroes of Balzac will be, and the railroad kings and captains of industry in the dawning era of America. Like them, they are recognizable by their bad manners, their affected speech, and their pompous names. It's hardly accidental that most of these sound a little Greek, as if freshly drawn from the mythical trust fund of Father Homer. The story's setting is everything here: the episodes of the *Satyricon* take place mostly in southern Italy, an area that once belonged to Greater Greece, around Crotone and along the coast of Campania. The absurd banquet, where Trimalchio's band gathers, takes place here as well, although the exact location is impossible to determine. Banquet? Rather, we have to do here with a tremendous gorging, one that finally, with the increasing drunkenness of all participants, goes bottoms-up in the sentimentality of the host, who indulges himself at great length in reflections upon his own mausoleum and is moved to tears.

Whether a portrait of manners, a Roman parody, a poetic *amuse-gueule* for the titillation of Nero—in the end it matters little; what is alone decisive is the skill with which the story is told. Take note: this Petronius was much more than a dilettante. Here was a man at work, a man with complete mastery of his materials, a satirist and realist with a gift for sharp observation and a feel for the perfect word. One should also be able to tell a writer's greatness by the number of devils (or in this case, demons) in the details; and here the reader of the *Satyricon* can easily lose track of things. Choosing at random from the plethora of possibilities, one might take a second look, for example, at the dishes on display. Not just the pot roast, but everything that makes its appearance on the table is larded with innuendos. Hardly a palate pleaser but shows up as allegory, as mythologem. Or the countless figures of speech, the picture puzzles and spoofed quotations. The whole "Cena Trimalchionis" is nothing but a great big babble session. No accident, then, that the one to welcome the guests across the threshold is the proverbially garrulous magpie. In his use of the vulgate, the Latin of the common people, Petronius far outstrips his literary colleagues. Most of us can only dream of such a fireworks display of idioms. As for textures of sound, the author inclines toward coarsely realistic colloquial language, with its childlike pleasure in sonorous vowels and brash, loud-popping consonants. By the way, it was allegedly by virtue of just these stylistic idiosyncrasies that Petronius was first identified. If one is to believe the philologists, no other Roman author gathered so rich a word hoard from the gutter. One sees him there in the flesh, as it were, the eternal collagist, as soon as one imagines how a certain James Joyce soaked up the jargon of his countrymen in the pubs of Dublin. Like *Ulysses*, Petronius' novel turns the vast, multifaceted wealth of his mother tongue completely inside out. And in terms of narrative technique, he need fear comparison neither with the author of the *Odyssey* nor of the *Aeneid*.

One need only consider the indirect way in which he

introduces the main character, through the description of a fresco, before the man himself appears at table—a sleight of hand that increases the dramatic tension almost imperceptibly. A few strokes, and a figure is bodied forth and set in motion. Trimalchio appears as a bald-headed old man who plays ball in a red tunic with a group of long-haired boys. Or the lightning-quick transitions from prose to verse, which serve for change of pace and thus break up the text into so many aphorisms. To say nothing of the cunning deployment of what much later Marcel Proust will call pastiche: the implanting of flawlessly ventriloquized foreign writing styles. Here several birds are indeed dispatched with one stone. And if there are losses, the reader is royally compensated. Buried among the trash of the gutter lie the Homeric heroes, although it is the likes of Giton and Eumolpus who are resurrected in their place. Instead of the sublime monotony of hexameter, we get the joyride of the most hyperactive prosimetry, that is, the interweaving of metrical and nonmetrical speech, a technique that belonged in the basic toolbox of every satirist but that few handled as masterfully as Petronius. And even for the classical gods, who get brushed aside like the crumbs from the table, one receives generous reimbursement in this novel. Isn't there, standing at the center, that very god who appears to set off all others, Priapus? In him, we have the tutelary god of satire, easily recognizable by his erect phallus, a primitive symbol that incites to the coarser pleasures, those of the loins. When everything man once knew as mystery has lost its magic—this remains. A fertility god is the last thing a culture will toss overboard. In him, the hope of procreation and the fear of death stand in covetous equilibrium; to convince oneself of this, a stroll through the ruins of Pompeii would suffice. In the rudimentary scenes of the house of pleasure at the beginning of the *Satyricon*, and in the madcap pornography of the Circe scene at the end, Petronius has erected a monument to this tumescent god. Presumably the entire anti-*Odyssey* of the book presents nothing other than the pilgrimage of a few strange birds to the shrine of Priapus.

Lucky for us. What we have in these few pages of unsurpassed Latin is upon closer inspection a wide-open window, a window into another time, through which we voyeurs, two-thousand-plus years later, might have a furtive look at a part of humanity that moldered away long ago, and see it engaged in activities that are all too familiar. Granted, it may be that in terms of excess, decadence, and dramaturgy we have long been used to more hard-core material; yet the spectacle of these wriggling little creatures, their lust for life, their delusions of grandeur, their boundless appetite, all this remains enchanting. The fact that in the case of the *Satyricon* we are dealing with the prototype of all European novels is beyond question. At least, nothing else that has been passed down to us from the satirical writing of the ancients comes anywhere close. The scholar of comparative literature Erich Auerbach devoted an entire chapter of his great study *Mimesis: The Representation of Reality in Western Literature* to this earliest predecessor of realistic narrative art. He sees in the binge-eating that takes place in Trimalchio's house the oldest evidence for that new, flickering perspectivism of narration that arises from a radical subjectivity of speech, from the imbrication of the observer in the action itself. Never before had a social milieu been articulated with such multifaceted richness—in the jargon of its most shameless representatives, as the most authentic gossip of all. What the neighboring guests whisper to each other at table about their host, Trimalchio, and his fearsome spouse, Fortuna, gives rise to a general picture, in which each of those caricatured, including the trash-talkers who comment on the feast, is put in his precise place. "Modern writers, say, Proust, work no differently, albeit much more coherently even within the tragic and the problematic." Thus Auerbach. "The procedure of Petronius is therefore to the highest degree artistic and, assuming he had no predecessors, ingenious . . ."

It would be impolite to stop here without a word in honor of the man who discovered this technique and who created this illustrious horde of characters. Who, then, was this Petronius? Let's assume it really was that T. Petronius Niger mentioned by the historian Tacitus. "*C. Petronius proconsul Bithyniae et mox consul vigentem se ac parem negotiis ostendit. etc. etc. . . . elegantiae arbiter . . . ,*" it says in the *Annals.* In English and complete: "As proconsul of Bithynia, however, and later as consul, he showed himself to be energetic and equal to his tasks. Then, having returned to a life of depravity, or because he gave the appearance of such a life, he was drawn into the small circle of Nero's intimate friends as umpire in matters of taste, since he [Nero] considered nothing charming or pleasant, regardless of how luxurious, unless Petronius had recommended it to him." This is the only picture we have of him, a thoroughly self-contradictory portrait, a faint picture puzzle made of Latin letters. Sword-and-sandal-epic lovers will be reminded of *Quo Vadis*, the famous Hollywood flick in which Peter Ustinov—in the role of Emperor Nero—upon receiving the news of Petronius' death, asks for a "weeping vase," a minuscule glass vial, which he holds up under his eyelid, exclaiming with mournful face, unforgettably: "I weep for you, Petronius! One tear for you . . . and one for me . . ."

Taste consultant: the man at court responsible for everything that passed there as chic. We can only guess at how all-encompassing the jurisdiction must have been for such an *arbiter elegantiae.* From the dress code for every occasion to questions of etiquette to the seasoning of food to the appropriate knickknacks for decorating the palace halls—nothing could be left to chance. It is to be assumed that he would have had a word or two to say even about the construction of

Nero's Golden House, the Domus Aurea. An entirely new
dimension of luxury makes its appearance, if we can trust
Suetonius: "The dining halls had coffered ceilings, the panels
of which were movable, such that one could strew flowers
from above; the panels themselves were also fitted out with
fine tubes, so that one could be sprinkled from above with
oils. The main dining hall was circular; the domed roof was
rotated day and night without ceasing, exactly in the manner
of the cosmos." It is alleged that Nero, as he looked upon this
fresh splendor for the first time, remarked that now he could
finally begin to live like a human being.

There's no accounting for taste, says a Roman proverb. So
much the worse for the man, then, for whom everything
depends on infallibility. When Tacitus sneeringly calls Petronius one of the amphibians in Nero's entourage, a shady character, sleeping all day and active at night, the thing that's
surprising is that, with so many responsibilities, he managed
to sleep at all. He was, and this the historian confirms, anything but a bon vivant and spendthrift; and how could he have
been? He was the one responsible, day and night, for the
feasting and excessive spending of others—when he wasn't
actually working on a novel, which, one might add, gradually
threatened to leap its banks. Of blind excess and endless par-
tying, not a trace. One can more easily imagine him as a contemplative observer. A scoundrel, to be sure, but one with a
good eye and a nose for the intrigues of others, and for their
aversions, as for example those of Seneca, who saw in him
nothing but the night owl. Among the scanty bits of evidence
we have about him, one should probably count a scene from
the *Satyricon* itself. The historian Ludwig Friedländer, author
of a four-volume history of Roman customs, refers to a place
where the thick weave of the narrative suddenly rips open,
granting us a glimpse of the author. The narrator Encolpius
describes how a couple of slaves scamper by to perfume the

guests and rub them down with oil. This, says Friedländer, was a custom that originated with Otho, one of Nero's childhood playmates, who later became emperor himself for a time (after Galba and before Vitellius and Vespasian), in the so-called Year of Four Emperors, 69 C.E. It is said of him that he taught Nero a number of bad habits, until the latter, in an attack of envy, posted him off as governor of Lusitania.

Otherwise, all that remains is a tablet unearthed in 1946 during excavations in Herculaneum, with an inscription in which, surprisingly, the name Petronius appears. If nothing else, a sign of life. The fact that so little of his life on earth has survived bespeaks only the discretion of the perfect courtier, who saw things more realistically and according to nature. For professional self-promoters such as your "writers" of today, huffing and puffing may be part of the business; it behooved the satirist bearding the lion in his den, however, to proceed with caution. Only once, in the year 66 C.E., does Petronius appear to have given up his reserve. A certain Tigellinus, a pretty boy who apparently would have sold his own grandmother if he thought he could benefit by it, had bad-mouthed Petronius to Nero. We can imagine the self-discipline it had cost Petronius to keep quiet his entire life: only in the hour of death did he drop the mask. What grandeur, if Tacitus speaks true, in the way this Roman Oscar Wilde, sentenced to suicide, takes leave with perfect equanimity of spirit, an aesthete to the last breath. "Yet he did not cast life off precipitously, but rather had his arteries opened, then, as he bethought him, bound up again, and again opened; all the while conversing with his friends, not on serious matters or in words that would win him the fame of unshakable composure. And he listened when they presented not discourses on the immortality of the soul or the teachings of the sages, but frivolous songs and pleasant verses." This is how someone dies who is a poet through and through, and as such averse to all hypocrisy. Even the exit is staged like the final act of a slapstick comedy in which he gives the death of Socrates a pull on the leg. It is the same procedure, as he well knows, that will make his *Satyricon* immortal. Still, two years before him, Seneca made his quietus, the man who was his complete opposite as a character— the better Stoic, as hedonist a loser. The departure of Petronius is to Seneca's worthy philosopher's death what the satyr play is to the great tragedy. Whether Nero, who in terms of the annihilation of literary masters was surpassed by Stalin alone, really wept, can no longer be verified.

BROTHER JUVENAL

1

It was Nietzsche who, as so often, blazed the trail. In the flashes of insight and stray paragraphs that he bundled together under the title "The Gay Science"—thus giving away the secret of their making, namely, on loose reflections and wool-gathering philologizing—in that collection of loosely concatenated essayistic writings, there is one thought that casts new light on the problem of satire:

> *Translations.* We can gauge the degree of the historical sense of an age by the way it makes *translations* and endeavors to absorb past ages and books. The French in the age of Corneille as well as those in the age of the Revolution took hold of Roman antiquity in a way we would no longer have the courage to—owing to our heightened historical sense. And take Roman antiquity itself: how violently and naïvely it laid hand on everything that was good and valuable in classical Greece! How the Romans translated into the Roman present! How they deliberately and carelessly smudged the dust of that butterfly called "blink of an eye"! This is how Horace would translate Alcaeus and Archilochus, this is how Propertius would translate Callimachus and Philetas (two poets of Theocritus' rank, if we *may be allowed* to judge): What did they

care that the original poet had experienced this or that and inscribed the signs of it into his poems! As poets they were averse to the antiquarian sleuth's spirit that precedes the historical sense, as poets they didn't acknowledge anything that smacked of the personal—things, names, and everything that gave a city, a coast, a century appearance and personality—but immediately replaced it with their own, Roman present . . . They did not know the pleasures of the historical sense; the past and the foreign were an embarrassment to them, it demanded to be conquered—Roman-style. Indeed, in those days translating meant conquering—and not only by dropping the historical, but also by adding allusions to the translator's present, and, above all, by striking the original poet's name and replacing it with one's own—and this, without any sense of theft, but, on the contrary, with the consummate good conscience of the *imperium romanum*.

Mention is made of an epochal shift in literature. But also of historical meaning translated into the present, whatever was exemplary and successful in the past. It is the Romans in the early post-Christian empire to whom the German philosopher refers, Horace and Propertius and their ilk, subjects according to Mommsen of a reactionary form of government. Their work is evidence of the way the new and conquest-mad Rome dealt with the cultural trophies of Greece, how it laid roads through the old jungle of mythology, and in good old barbarian fashion, grabbed everything that was precious and finely wrought. Note how this is not said critically, but with that typically Nietzschean sympathy that sees forceful acquisition as a sign of vital strength.

Because the thing was that here for the first time—certainly on such a world-historical scale—a later epoch doesn't merely annihilate its predecessor, but with cool purpose assimilates and digests the best of it. And not shamefacedly with fearful philological shilly-shallying, but with a frank grab—with the best nouveau riche swagger. Because with their feeling for great stories and deathless scenes, the Romans weren't just the inventors and forerunners of an age of classicism in the arts—which, following their example, keeps repeating itself—in the way they laid claim to something and reused it, they were the first postmoderns as well. Their hunger for all things Greek shows their good taste, but even more their healthy appetite. Because this was no light snack, and for all their love of superficial representation and decoration, it was more than a sort of land grab. Nero put his own prestige on the line when, during his tour of Greece, he entered the singing contest with his kithara. His showy Versace aesthetic didn't get in the way of his gratitude to the province, to which he generously gave freedom. Traces of Hadrian's philhellenic policy with regard to buildings and monuments are still visible today. Marcus Aurelius' reversion to the Greek alphabet was long accounted the most noble and classic instance of spiritual asceticism and self-knowledge on the basis of *sola scriptura* ("by writing alone").

However diverse the modes employed, each manifests the same sense of history. The Romans immersed themselves in the unimprovable Greek laws of form: they took on a literary canon, a library of exemplary works, while architecture, sculpture, and painting all acquired standards and expectations that could not be underbid. The old temples were reclad in shiny new marble and decorated with fresh images, instead of—as was normal in history to this point, and afterward—just being sacked and plundered. One may well speak of Roman sculpture in terms of an assembly line, but the wholesale copying of Polycletus and Praxiteles bore some strange fruit as well: the bearded, scowling imperial busts and the nudes of

Adonis, overloaded ornamentation in private villas, outsize bronzes of breathtaking ugliness, colossal statuary that was transported—how else—by elephant. All this monumentalism and a realism that did not stop short of the repulsive was based on classical rules of proportion.

It was naïve and violent, this conquest, Nietzsche says, and it's impossible here to be unaware of the sexual overtones. They just took what they needed, acquisition was self-gratification, without regard to whatever the taken items had of history. What in art history seminars comes under the bland heading of reception is a bizarre form of kleptomania, sometimes called theft of intellectual rights. But this blithe acquisition, with a shot of Roman reality, is acclaimed as a new degree of civilization—which it no doubt was. The archaic and the Greek were a stimulus to the Romans, who simply helped themselves, governed by their artistic impulses. The consequence was immediate fertilization: an intensification of the sense of their own present.

One has to picture the poets of imperial Rome sucking their lines out of the—at that point still imaginary—Greek Anthology through long straws. But for all one's admiration of the canny adaptor and rearranger Horace, and all astonishment at Ovid, the most modern and inventive of them all—a precursor of the numbered epics and special effects of Hollywood with his truly encyclopedic retrospective of myth—the authors to whom we feel greatest affinity, the ones we understand even without Latin or Greek, are the satirists like Martial and Juvenal. When the latter intones the ironic lament, just after the opening of his First Satire, "I know my way around your mythic groves better than my own house," he hits a nerve. Just like today's reader, the satirists automatically teed off on anything high-sounding. They punctured the bombast of would-be tragedians and quaking togaed authors of amateur epics with their scathing streetwise filth. The wispy lyrics of the Callimachan disciples and neo-bucolics in the Nietzsche passage don't do much for most people today, but in the crudities of the Roman satirists we feel right at home.

It's truer in fact to say it of *them* than of the disciples of Alcaeus and Theocritus that the past and the exotic were an embarrassment. Translation was a booty raid—back to the present. They needed to catch their distant object in sharp focus, so that it could be properly subjected to their withering gaze. Nowhere is this process clearer than in satire, which works always with contrast. It is, as Quintilian noted, the only truly Roman form, and at the same time the best model of a translation of the lofty past into a crazy and unpredictable present. Today we are pretty much agreed that the point of satire is not so much the attribution of moral blame, much less cultural critique (the Romans were far too keen on the seamy side of their civilization to bother about anything like that), but simply entertainment, entertainment, entertainment.

But it would be going too far to compare them, as sometimes happens, to the smug mockery of today's comedy clubs. Satire has greater linguistic and stylistic sophistication. The word is everywhere, there is little that doesn't fly its flag. We have satirical magazines, satirical programs, even the perplexing expression "real satire," which causes aficionados to nod knowledgeably. But satire like Juvenal's has as much in common with the tag lines of TV jokemeisters, or the annual speeches at carnivals and fairs, as pâté and soup. And to take it for a sort of precursor to the Lutheran sermon, as some Protestant philologists claim to do, is simply deluded. No question, Juvenal enjoyed great popularity among Christian commentators during the Middle Ages and the Renaissance. The reason is obvious: Horace's poems were hardly useful for propaganda purposes, but here was a master of self-accusation, who wrote off the entire heathen world with his tales of the metropolitan sink called Rome. It was Juvenal's deepest conviction that he was alive at a time of so much vice, so much accumulated social squalor that no future age could ever compete with it. But if you think about it, wasn't his sense of the rottenness of everything just a form of heightened awareness of the present moment?

2

There were eight of them who it seems in no time brought the new genre to flower. Take away three of these (Ennius, whose satire was a by-product; Varro, who left only scraps that are barely enough to judge him on; and Petronius, whose *Satyricon* so far overshot the mark that his prose fragment is among the foundational texts of the modern novel), we are left with a pentangle, composed of Lucilius, Horace, Persius, Martial, and Juvenal. The contagion was passed on from one to the other, becoming in time such a powerful antitradition that the classic lyric poem never quite got over it. In the space of just two centuries, these master caricaturists of their society accomplished something like a revolution in popular literary tastes.

Satire is a flow of speech on demand, something that will wash away everything in its path, all the garbage that accrues in the daily life of a decently corrupt, averagely squalid, that is, modern society. At the end of its development, it stood in the monstrous guise of a stream of sewage bubbling merrily down the concrete bed of its hexametric rhythm. Because proper satire can be detected by the meter alone. Martial the epigrammatist was an exception.

This new verse form rose like dough; and its yeast was something that in many lines assaulted the eye, the contemptuously spat-out syllable—*faex* (with or without the *populi*): the human scum, the lees, froth that was left after every murderous social conflict. Superfluous to remark that *faex* (not at all identical to *plebs*) was used quite un-Marxistically in both directions as invective. It's the common masses on either side of the money divide: it can be applied to the nouveaux riches, with their nasty fantasies and their repulsive orgies, or just as well to the have-nots willingly submitting to all forms of humiliation in the hope of one day getting there. One leitmotif of Juvenal's Third Satire, for instance, is the *ambitiosa paupertas* (l. 182), the well-accoutered poverty, the widespread sickness of all those who live beyond their means and are therefore desperate to do anything to curry favor. It's been a symptom of the lower classes over two thousand years: the falling into debt, the comical prostrations, the rage to consume among the poorest of the Romans, driving them first into total dependence and finally into an unavoidable ruination. This, in its many variations, is the principal theme of most of the Satires—their unconscious, as Freudians would say. It's as though social criticism can only be expressed in a form of delirium, that's how desperate and insoluble the human situation has become. And it's in just this delirium that the realism in every satire is to be found.

3

The earliest was Lucilius. Everything needed for good satire is already present in him and fully formed, the big city, the daily grind, the timbre of speech, the indiscretions, the autobiographical note. As the *inventor generis*, Lucilius determined the direction, he was a freestyle critic of his time, still a little indiscriminate in his selection of means—repeated targeting of political small fry betrays the provincial journalist in him—stylistically often a little clumsy, but of an outspokenness of which his successors in more closely regulated times could only dream. No censorship hindered the well-born poet (he was a knight by birth) from naming the names of villains and opponents. He left thirty books of satires, sometimes preferred to those of Horace, while no less an authority than Quintilian liked them better than all other poetry. Alas, only fragments survive.

Then we have Horace, the wholesale importer of Greek meters and for hundreds of years the great arbiter of poetic taste: Princeps Aeolium Carmen, as he modestly has it in one of the Odes. He is the pleasing salon poet, perfect in his entertainer role, protégé of the wealthy Maecenas and therefore arbiter of all things poetry-related in the court of Augustus. He always does everything correctly, takes up the higher ground, shows balance, is respectably patriotic, gently ironic, a Roman Thomas Mann, if you will. In his hands, satire becomes a fashion catalogue of gilded phrases and harmonious tropes.

Then up comes Persius, a hot young nihilist. He's the toughest of the lot, though personally gentle and of poor health, the introverted young man, so close to the cliché of the Romantic poet he seems irresistibly familiar. He dies at twenty-eight—a digestive problem. Some of his bold and youthfully exuberant verses anticipate the technique of film cuts. In his tumbling succession of images he recalls another meteor, who won't fall to earth for another eighteen centuries: Arthur Rimbaud. The same visceral mockery of the language, the same satanic pleasure in nonsense and infantile synesthesia. "Who taught the parrot to say *'Bonjour'*?" Persius asks in surreal astonishment, in a swift little prologue that opens the suite of his satires. He openly admits to never having imbibed from the Castalian spring, nor yet to have dreamed on Mount Parnassus, but still he demands full poetic license: *"Corvos poetas et poetridas picas / cantare credas Pegaseium nectae"* ("that from poet-raven and poetess-magpie / Pegasian nectar may stream from the throat"). Such word games and inspired sillinesses won't return for another two thousand years, not until the time of the modernists, with the poetic dodecaphonists like Apollinaire and E. E. Cummings. In him language is hexed into something fearfully ambiguous, comments one of his editors. But everything is terribly simple really. The only reason his sarcasm is so dark and his verse so oracular is because here someone is speaking who saw the grim monotony and predictability of life terribly early. Persius was the born anarchist poet. Beings like him, hard to classify, are often described as enfants terribles. Sound effects in him are not so much indications of exuberance as expressions of despair at the boredom of existence, as it showed itself early to his sensitive ears in the form of cliché. Listen to the beginning of his Fifth Satire, where he settles the hash of those same salon poets with whom Juvenal will deal summarily at the beginning of his career. You can tell this is someone in his element by the onomatopoetic roots of his Latin—each line is a stinging slap—when he says:

> But you, you don't squeeze air till the iron mash boils
>   on the stove,
> Air from the panting bellows, or hum close-mouthed,
> Creak like the crow, pick greedily at higher nonsense
> or smack your full cheeks till it echoes.

And then there was Martial, far and away the sharpest-tongued and the subtlest as well. His preferred form was the epigram, the short form, twisted into a barb of a few lines. He wasn't just the loosest, most slanderous tongue, but also evidently the most popular in the entire Roman Empire in his lifetime. Sign of their popularity, his epigrams were often memorized and passed on. The fact that, for all their radicalness, these were the comprehensively weighed witticisms of a privileged person, who wasted his best years as a lickspittle to

Domitian, did nothing to diminish his fame. In him it may be observed how sweet posthumous fame can be, and how in the long run humankind will forgive even the most transparent cynicism. Some of his tropes he really rode to death, among them his most celebrated: that of the rabbit in the arena, who emerges unscathed from the lion's jaws. His bons mots are often just a pretext for sadistic ill intentions—and a guarantee of filth to his secret readers. To quote Martial—why, over hundreds of years that meant breaking the ultimate erotic taboos. In times of free-to-air pornography that thrill is gone, and after being outed, one last time, as an archchauvinist and sexist by feminists and the likes of the sexologist Ernst Bornemann, he looks rather woebegone. He composed several thumbnail sketches of his unlucky friend Juvenal. They affirm the fellow feeling among the satirists, who saw themselves as a sort of avant-garde. In the twelfth book of epigrams, there is praise for rural life (Martial went to live in Bilbilis in his native Spain) that anticipates Juvenal. The latter's epic theme of sleeplessness is briefly sounded:

> Even now, dear Juvenal, as you restlessly
> wander around the noisy Suburan streets
>
> After many Decembers have been and gone,
> My Bilbilis, proud of its gold, its iron,
> Has me back again, and a peasant.
>
> Here I enjoy a deep and dreamless sleep,
> No din at 3 a.m. regularly disrupts.

Juvenal was the great mystery at that time. His poetic career didn't begin until the following century, long after Domitian's death. He was in his early fifties when the First Satire was published. Once, Martial defends him—a nobody, who hadn't published a line yet—against a well-known calumniator. He stylizes their friendship as that of the Greek pair of Orestes and Pylades. Elsewhere he praises him as *fecundus*—eloquent, flowingly original, stimulating: the born rhetorician, which at that time was a high compliment. To the word-besotted, word-mastering Romans, offering such a flattering attribute was code for: I've marked your card, this is the guy to watch, you read it here first!

> O Juvenal, genius with words, from my country estate
> I send you a small gift of nuts for the coming
>   Saturnalia.

4

Juvenal marks the culmination of this movement, this form, this new manifestation. A black crow in the white marble city of Augustus . . . That he became the harshest of the satirists, the most vividly figurative in his language, unequaled in his sarcasm is probably partly due to the fact that he came to it late. The blackest and most quoted lines are almost all of them his. Pessimism was his prompter. He was the one who had seen the world, who had fought, he was the least unworldly one. You have to picture him as a commander in the Egyptian desert, as paying his respects to hundred-gated Thebes, listening to the wind whistle through the wrecked colossus of Memnon. He was in command of the garrison at Syene on the western shore of the Nile, where he saw with his own eyes the pendulous bottle-shaped breasts of the Nubian women. He saw the huts of the inhabitants of Mauritania and in the wooded mountains of Thabraca the mother ape scratching her wrinkled arse. It is certain that he passed through the Strait of Gibraltar, that he visited Crete and came into the teeming ports along the Mediterranean shore. Far out in the

Atlantic, beyond the Pillars of Hercules, he sensed the monsters of the deep and the mermen, strange mixtures of fish and human that sailors mentioned in their tales. In Britain, he participated in Agricola's campaigns, at the head of a cohort of Dalmatians, he tasted the oysters of Rutupiae, and observed the whales beyond the Orkney Isles, so much more impressive than the dolphins of his native waters.

Juvenal is the new type, the poet—literally—of autopsy. He takes great pride in having seen everything with his own eyes. As an ex-army man, he is in a grotesque way the embodiment of an ideal going back to Cato, and that persisted even in the worst days of political decline—the *vir bonus dicendi peritus*. His Pegasus wasn't some mythological beast, but an honest-to-goodness cavalry horse that had borne him to the far limits of the Roman Empire. The occasionally clumsy and galumphing quality of his hexameters is just what you'd expect from an old soldier who has knocked around a bit. Juvenal is the anti-aesthete who somehow blundered into the preserves of poetry, a nightmare for literary theorists, stubborn, equally homo- and gynophobic, and of course xenophobic. Few things disgust the adventurer so much as the salon versings of stay-at-homes. He is in every respect the opposite of the golden-tongued poets of the Augustan Age, whose work he has nevertheless thoroughly studied, Horace, Ovid, Virgil. He knew every one of their poetic tricks. His much-praised eloquence was all sorts of things—except for one, bel canto. We know little about the way satires were performed, but there is evidence to suggest that he may have had more in common with the chanting drone of contemporary hip-hop artists than with the feminine modulations of the troubadours of Aquitania.

His audience is a matter for conjecture. Is it possible that Juvenal set off his little poem-squibs in the tavernas and bars of Subura? Maybe not. His tendency to lay it on thick says much about his possible hearers. Who is satire for?—it's the perennial question. It's the direct antithesis to all court tradition. Doesn't it contain or subsume within itself the collision between transmitter and receiver, between addressee and subject? When you think about what Ovid was exiled for . . . But Juvenal too seems to have had more than one run-in with the authorities. The report is as uncertain as everything else in his biography, but it hasn't been completely ruled out either. Whether it makes the uncommon combination of officer and society poet any easier to take is another matter, but at any rate he was to have been punished for his loose words with a garrison posting to somewhere at the edge of the empire. Ludwig Friedländer's comment is succinct: "Evidently he didn't like to talk about himself." There remains the fact of a long absence from Rome in the later years of Domitian, whom he hated just as much as "baldy Nero."

To read his Satires is to find an index of the laxities of Roman life. Many things the encyclopedias tell us about everyday Roman culture are based entirely on him. The most shining examples, the most drastic illustrations to individual terms, are derived from Juvenal. If there were need for one more defense of poetry, here it is. We get to know the jumpiness of a typical Roman tenement (*insula*), what coiffures were fashionable among Roman ladies, and that women had to pay a slightly higher price to go to the public baths. Or the universally known thumbs-up, thumbs-down: as every schoolkid knows, or every PlayStation owner, every cinemagoer who's seen *Gladiator*, it was the custom for a bored public to decide the fate of a defeated gladiator. The thumb held pointing up against the chest was the sign for the death blow, held downward it was clemency (that way around, by the way). It was Juvenal (and only Juvenal) who gave us that nasty little gesture (in line 36 in the Third Satire). He has immortalized one of the many revolting aspects of the culture of the fun-loving Romans.

BROTHER JUVENAL   313

•

Someone like him would have gaped with disbelief if he'd
been explained some institution like our modern-day swinger
clubs. Ever since Augustus' edict, adultery was heavily punished, certainly among the higher social ranks. A public part-
ner swap was about the last thing those allegedly so corrupt
Romans would have countenanced. That needed the input
of two thousand years of Christianity. Of course the great
panoply of pornography of today's mass culture puts in the
shade everything that Hadrian's and Domitian's had to offer
in the way of erotica. It's difficult to suppress a melancholy
half-smile when you read in the commentaries to Juvenal's—
unfortunately, all too mysogynistic—Sixth Satire (its subject:
what those wild society ladies liked to get up to) about the
mistress's gay servants and their oh-so-suggestive names. I
mean: "probably expression for one who performs *cunnilingus*
and/or *fellator*," as the footnotes report with a slight frisson.
The last person, presumably, to go gaga over this was the
teacher at the Wilhelmine Gymnasium who coughed his
charges past the tricky place. The really exciting bit—apropos
school education—remains the celebrated passage in the Sev-
enth Satire, on the subject of overworked teachers. The subject of that satire—the low esteem of intellectual professions
in ancient Rome—is strikingly relevant to our time. It concerns the miserable hand-to-mouth existence of poets, who
might have the admiration of stingy moneybags but were
rarely commensurately rewarded for their labors. The golden
days of Maecenas are gone. An old fellow-struggler and lucky
so-and-so like Horace gets a little poke in the ribs in the line
"and Horace is well-fed for calling *evoe*." The reference is to
the boisterous drinking party in the second book of Horace's
Odes that set standards in matters of luxury and lust for life.
"Hurrah! Hurrah! Bacchus, there's enough," the favorite of
the emperor and the observer of living standards among the

new oligarchs had written at the time. Those were times when Horatius Flaccus saw "wine flow in rivers, milk in streams." Even the lot of the historian is pitied by Juvenal, barely a century afterward. "Who pays the chronicler what he pays the man who reads the newspaper aloud?" Remarkable lines—we're in the age of the mass media. There's talk of authors who try their luck at running baths and bakeries, poor knights with their bare ankles poking through their torn soldier's buskins, and the wretchedly paid job of the *grammaticus*, or Latin teacher. And then comes that unforgettable place, a classic in the history of sexual culture, when Juvenal raises his cultural pessimistic lament to the height of great poetry: "And you would like / him to be father to the class, to prevent immoral games, / and that they do it for each other: difficult with so many boys / to keep your eyes on their hands, the eyes glazing over when they come."

Of course much of this already existed, the themes, the self-same dramaturgy followed since Lucilius: only Juvenal gives it the necessary dose of resentment, and the barrel overflows. In his satires, he tried to outdo all those that had gone before. Juvenal is where you can discern the evolution of this poetic form: winding the spiral of indignation ever tighter, releasing the maximum of shock. Can anything get worse? He doesn't flirt with his readership like Martial, there are neither dedication nor introduction. There are none of the standard literary decencies. Here is someone speaking for himself and himself alone, a surprise opponent, someone who with military discipline emerges from cover only at the last moment, as an old man. With the pride of the outsider, he comes out fighting. If he should lack talent, he writes somewhere, then his rage can fill his lines; and this poet's rage was enormous. Nietzsche calls him "that poisonous lizard with the eyes of Venus"—in one of the few moments, by the way, when he gives Christianity an even break and sees it as ointment and cure after the collapse of all values, as Juvenal describes.

BETWEEN ANTIQUITY AND *X*

1

Going back to the roots or in medias res: Yes, I too have Roman literature to thank for the most important writing lessons. All critique of the verbal craft came to me from there. It awakened in me a consciousness of the subjective (beauty) and the objective (comprehension) aspects of certain combinations of words. In whatever epoch, language, or poetic tradition, the traces always led back to the hard kernel of the Roman art of expression. It was the taut and relentless quality of Latin verse that captivated me, its aesthetic style, manifested from the tightly fitted grammar, from the interplay of these syntactic units, locked as it were into one another like toothy gears. *Perpetuum mobile*—no other language was so much like a machine; a machine that transformed everything mental and fleeting into something precise and transitive, into a product with durable meaning. The thrust power of syntax, the play of expressive musculature in the grip of syntactic units had the effect that the poetic word in Latin approached me like something quasi-objective, as a sculpture made of syllables, a vocal artifact. And so strong was the impression, that even the afternoon drowsiness during adult education class at the *Volkshochschule* could not obscure it. The real, nature, and society, so difficult to domesticate, took shape in this language, leaving its stamp on subsequent ages. Latin was the perfect container in which the affects could blow off steam, a kind of thought armor, poured tight around the ideas themselves, unshakable from the outside but with room enough inside for variable emphases, a medium that seemed made for jurisprudence and the art of poetry. Where else were lines like this one by Horace possible: *"nos numerus sumus et fruges consumere nati"*—"We are but numbers, born to consume the fruits of the earth"?

Language as codex: a supply of signifiers for the stranger on earth, the surveyor who seeks his utopia and who carries within himself the desert. It was the rhetoric of anthropology that called me again and again back into antiquity. For the one addressed in this way, the poetry of the ancients became a means of interpreting his own existence. From Ovid's song of lamentation among the barbarians at Pontos Euxeinos to the satirical poets' big-city squabbling before the gates of the Coliseum in Rome—in all of it stood recorded how bodies ran to ruin as long as the affects drove them. The censorship of sensuality came later, as a symptom of modernity, a result of the habituation to a single god. Ancient poetry can be thought only in multiple voices, as a physical polytheism. Nothing was excluded, not one of the drives was left without speech. From the idiosyncrasies of the individual to the infamies of the political animal en masse, from the melancholy of eros to the coldest cruelty, measure was always taken in ode and epigram, epos and elegy. The magic of form—*ultima ratio* in the verbal flurry, the longest-lasting phantasmagoria for the like-minded. This would explain why Latin fascinates lovers of language to this very day. It appears as if we had here a *lingua universalis*, in which the lyrical meters were so inherent that they came to light through mere self-contemplation. The metrical patterns comprised the mobile scale armor that held together the eloquent bodies, the bodies clad in speech with their antagonistic affects. In the Latin language lies the command to walk upright, the alphabet for the shaping of character: the letter is the *character*. A language that gathered up reality, more compact and forceful in its concepts than almost any other since. This is how gravity itself would speak if it were given vocal cords. Everything in this language was proportion, compelling flow, a maximum of meaning in the narrowest space. Here the *physis* and *psyche* of *homo mortalis*, his remembrance of the ancestors and gods, the inexhaustible mythic cosmos and his own brief life, were apprehended simultaneously and unified as declined and conjugated time. In the verses of its poets, the language became a requiem for the *disjecta membra* of all the millions for whom Latin was once the mother tongue, a virtuosic and strict accompaniment to their advent on earth. Today it is entirely literature, the object of philological envy, at most still useful as the instrument of pathologists and scholars of antiquity, a dead language for dead objects. Oddly and by contrast, one can still imagine Greek as a parlando among contemporaries. The murmur of Sappho sounds so near and intimate, as if one had just concluded a long-distance call with Lesbos, the receiver still warm from the ear. "When one day you die / you will vanish forever. / No one will think of you. / . . . / And you will soon lose your way / fleeing without direction / among the pale dead."

2

In order to account for the far-reaching impact of antiquity, we must first of all, like the companions of Odysseus, stop up our ears. We don't get very far by listening to the Christian siren song, which for centuries has distracted from the classical texts. Nor is this all: we would first have to learn to suppress the voices of our own egos, for all the reassurances come from within, out of our own echo chambers.

To speak of ancient poetry means, as Nietzsche has shown, to speak of the repressed. Everything having wasted away to a handful of coins, we remain in bondage to the

Gospels with their subtle censorship, or to the orations of the Enlightenment, in which the thicket of riddles is cleared away for the Apollonian legend. "The poets tell many lies," goes the pre-Socratic aphorism. Yet this lying was full of anthropological insights, on which the improvers of the world and of the conscience of man have been breaking their teeth since Plato. Reading the Greeks and the Romans helps us rediscover the physical human being, this mortal creature who accepted mortality with the equanimity of the Stoics. From Simonides to, let's say, Boethius, unanimity reigned on this point. The memory of the dramas of our species is no invention of the Bible. It began when the human being became conscious of himself, when he understood himself as one among many, and it begins under the sign of crisis. Boethius' *Consolation of Philosophy*, however late it was written, contains as much on this as the fragments of Heraclitus. A politician sits in solitary confinement, having been condemned to death, and writes his philosophical testament. His last interlocutor is a woman, a being like Diotima, the priestess of *philosophia*. She asks him: "But don't you remember that you are a human being?" And Boethius rejoins: "How could I forget?" To which she: "Are you able to define what that is, then: a human being?" "I know it, and I confess myself one," responds the condemned man. "And what else you are besides, do you not know that?" "How should I?" From which she concludes: "Thus do I now recognize the other, greater cause of your sickness: you no longer know what you yourself are." For an entire millennium, through questions and answers like these, the human being of antiquity sought to find himself out. The dialogue was the preferred tool of such research. Within it, the stratagem of thinking—*techné* as well as *mechané*—finds expression. It is the unsurpassed art form of the ancients, and next to tragedy, epistle, and ode, the high point among literary techniques. Having outgrown himself, every certainty escaped the human being. He had become uncanny to himself, only language still lent him support. Who could still say what he himself was, who could cease from asking himself in the quiet that followed? Full of horror and curiosity, he observed himself in the mirror. What he saw were the terrors of disintegration, the travesty of his own features. Henceforth, philosophizing meant stoking one's own mistrust, raising skepticism to unbearable levels. Antiquity rummaged around and around in this nervous heap of cells called man, even as far as the hereditary factors, in search of a single spark of self-certainty after the gods had left him. Here and there, it showed him, and then only fleetingly, *humanitas*, that mirage made out of kindness, intellectual and emotional education, and civilization. No sooner glimpsed than it disappeared from view every time. All that remained were the consciousness of mortality and the courage of reason, a fragile foundation upon which the ages that followed could build.

3

To whom could it matter to separate Greek thought from Roman praxis? What does it mean to say, "one doesn't learn from the Greeks," as the ill-mannered Nietzsche decrees? The imperative may lie precisely in what is fluid, in what is alien to the soul. Besides: What use have we for imperatives, when we have been given thoughts? It's true, German, too, has evolved around the Latin hardness of expression and according to the Roman style. It crystallized beneath the frosty patina of its grammar, exactly as did the Romance languages, Racine's fragile joints, or Anglo-Saxon, Shakespeare's instrumental idiom. Of all European languages, only Russian is still flesh of Greek flesh, with well-known consequences in history and poetry. To Russian alone was granted the gift of the flexible psyche.

The artistic element in modern literature, however, is composed of a combination of both elements, and it has the Greeks to thank no less than the Romans. In other words, the literature of antiquity taken together stands for the nontrivial, the nonbanal in linguistic reflection. Only in this way does the enormous aftereffect on everything that came later become comprehensible. It is the compendium of all insoluble questions, the wellspring of all aporias that have kept us in suspense to the present day. It is the nourishing etymological soil of our languages, the originary gathering of categories, the founding act behind all cultural routines. On the bottom of Menippo's bowl, with its salad of styles and motifs, we see the delicate lines of the ground plan. Mind you, it is not that of some individual house or other, but of an entire city, in which we are still at home today, of a societal form that still defines us as social creatures. The Greek language was the prelude to logical thinking, the beginning of all human dialogue (with oneself and with others), while the Roman language compelled our thinking into an alphanumerical system of coordinates. They both domesticated us, in "antagonistic fashion," as Heraclitus has it: Latin as school of discipline, ancient Greek as inspiration's coming into its own. In Greek lay the Alpha, which brings with it the longing for the Omega, the desire of *physis* for beauty and metaphysics.

ACKNOWLEDGMENTS

"Preface" (excerpt from Durs Grünbein's "Berlin Lecture," delivered at the Renaissance Theater in Berlin, Germany, in January 2008), translated by Michael Hofmann

"Brief Report to an Academy" (speech delivered on the occasion of being elected into the *Deutsche Akademie für Sprache und Dichtung* [German Academy for Language and Poetry] on October 20, 1995), translated by Michael Hofmann, in *Warum schriftlos leben: Aufsätze* (2003)

"Volcano and Poem," translated by Michael Hofmann, in *Galilei vermißt Dantes Hölle und bleibt an den Maßen hängen: Aufsätze* (1996)

"Breaking the Body," translated by Andrew Shields, in *Galilei vermißt Dantes Hölle und bleibt an den Maßen hängen: Aufsätze* (1996)

"Childhood in the Diorama," translated by Michael Hofmann, in *Galilei vermißt Dantes Hölle und bleibt an den Maßen hängen: Aufsätze* (1996)

"Three Miniatures," translated by Michael Hofmann, in *Das erste Jahr: Berliner Aufzeichnungen* (2001)

"The Age of Deep-Sea Fish," translated by Andrew Shields, in *Galilei vermißt Dantes Hölle und bleibt an den Maßen hängen: Aufsätze* (1996)

"Darwin's Eyes," translated by Andrew Shields, in *Das erste Jahr: Berliner Aufzeichnungen* (2001)

"My Babylonish Brain," translated by Michael Hofmann, in *Galilei vermißt Dantes Hölle und bleibt an den Maßen hängen: Aufsätze* (1996)

"To Lord Chandos: A Fax from the Future," translated by Andrew Shields, in *Gedicht und Geheimnis: Aufsätze* (2007)

"*Q* as in Quotation" (article commissioned for the *Dizionario della Libertà*, published by the Academia della Crusca Firenze in 2002), translated by Andrew Shields, in *Warum schriftlos leben: Aufsätze* (2003)

"On the Question of Style" (commentary on T. W. Adorno's essay "Behind the Mirror," in: *Minima Moralia* [#51]), translated by Andrew Shields, in *Warum schriftlos leben: Aufsätze* (2003)

"The Poem and Its Secret," translated by Andrew Shields, in *Gedicht und Geheimnis: Aufsätze* (2007)

"Why Live Without Writing" (lecture delivered at the Hamburger Bahnhof in Berlin on May 27, 1999, as part of the lecture series "The Twentieth Century"), translated by Michael Hofmann, in *Warum schriftlos leben: Aufsätze* (2003)

"Accented Time" (lecture delivered at the Tokyo Summer Festival "Music and Literature" on June 29, 2002), translated by Andrew Shields, in *Warum schriftlos leben: Aufsätze* (2003)

"The Bars of Atlantis: On the abyss of the imagination—A descant in fourteen descents," translated by Michael Hofmann (first published in this volume)

"Madonna and Venus," translated by Andrew Shields, in *Gedicht und Geheimnis: Aufsätze* (2007)

"One Sunday of Life," translated by Michael Hofmann, in *Frankfurter Allgemeine Zeitung* (December 29, 2007)

"The Vanished Square" (lecture delivered at the Literaturhaus Berlin on September 26, 2000), translated by John Crutchfield, in *Warum schriftlos leben: Aufsätze* (2003)

"A Little Blue Girl," translated by John Crutchfield, in *Gedicht und Geheimnis: Aufsätze* (2007)

"The Thinker's Voice" (speech delivered in Naumburg on August 27, 2004, on the occasion of being awarded the Friedrich Nietzsche Prize), translated by John Crutchfield, in *Gedicht und Geheimnis: Aufsätze* (2007)

"The Stroke of Apollo" (speech delivered on the occasion of being awarded the Friedrich Hölderlin Prize 2005), translated by John Crutchfield, in *Gedicht und Geheimnis: Aufsätze* (2007)

"In the Name of Extremes: On the brevity of life," translated by John Crutchfield, in *An Seneca. Postscriptum* (2003)

"A Tear for Petronius: On the *Satyricon*," translated by John Crutchfield, in *Petronius Arbiter: Das Gasmahl des Trimalchio* (2006)

"Brother Juvenal," translated by Michael Hofmann, in *Neue Rundschau* 119 (2008)

"Between Antiquity and *X*," translated by John Crutchfield, in *Warum schriftlos leben: Aufsätze* (2003)

The poem "Childhood in the Diorama" by Durs Grünbein, translated by Michael Eskin

The poem "The Carousel" by R. M. Rilke, in "A Little Blue Girl," translated by Michael Eskin

The long quotation from F. Nietzsche in "Brother Juvenal," titled "Translations," translated by Michael Eskin